May God bless you.

Binu

THE ACCENT

Exploring the Path to a Rejuvenating Life

BINU EDATHUMPARAMBIL

WESTBOW®
PRESS
A DIVISION OF THOMAS NELSON
& ZONDERVAN

All Scripture quotations are from the New Revised Standard Version Bible: Catholic Edition, copyright © 1989, 1993 the Division of Christian Education of the National Council of the Churches of Christ in the United States of America. Used by permission. All rights reserved.

WestBow Press books may be ordered through booksellers or by contacting:

WestBow Press
A Division of Thomas Nelson & Zondervan
1663 Liberty Drive
Bloomington, IN 47403
www.westbowpress.com
1 (866) 928-1240

ISBN: 978-1-4908-7921-5 (sc)
ISBN: 978-1-4908-7920-8 (hc)
ISBN: 978-1-4908-7919-2 (e)

Library of Congress Control Number: 2015908059

Print information available on the last page.

WestBow Press rev. date: 05/12/2015

Dedicated to all those who work to reduce conflicts
and promote peace and love in our world.

Contents

Introduction

Life is beautiful and yet immensely hard. As individuals and communities, we passionately follow our goals and dreams, and take ourselves to frontiers that we have not traversed before. We are amazed at what we have accomplished, and we surge on with an indomitable spirit. However, we also experience enormous difficulties in our personal and communal living. We long for a happy and fulfilling life, but more often than not, we fall far short of that ideal. We are constantly fighting the evils in us and in our world. We come across roadblock after roadblock and get stuck in our personal growth and interpersonal relationships.

For this state of affairs we find ourselves in, many of us may have asked that perennial question: why? Why are things the way they are? Why are we getting stuck in our growth and development? Why are we not able to get along with each other? Why are conversations so painfully difficult in some of our families and communities? I suggest an answer. It is called *The Accent*.

The word "accent" means "the way in which people in a particular area, country or social group pronounce words" (Cambridge Advanced Learner's Dictionary, 2005). Certain languages are known for varieties of accents. English, for example, has acquired innumerable accents all over the world, depending on where it is spoken. American English is much different from British, Indian, or Australian English. Sometimes the difference in the accent is so severe that it makes us wonder whether we are speaking the same language. The accentual differences make our communications with one another difficult.

Accentual differences are present not only in our languages but also in our lives. As individuals and communities, we have our own accents. We differ in myriad ways: in the way we are made up; in our personalities and preferences; in our meanings and vocabulary; in our genetics and environment; in our contexts and experiences; in our physical, psychological, and spiritual characteristics; in our thoughts and feelings; in our imaginations and fantasies; in our beliefs, values, and judgments; in our structures and systems; in our races and ethnicities; in our interests and interpretations; in our likes and dislikes; in our reactions and responses; and in our struggles and troubles. We differ in the way we understand things. We don't see, hear, and perceive things in the same way. And above all else, we differ in the way we see our differences.

Because we differ so much, it is no surprise that we find it difficult to understand and relate to each other. These differences make our personal and communal living difficult. But sometimes these differences are coupled with other undesirable and unhelpful characteristics as well. Negativity and destructiveness characterize certain people's personalities and environments. Perpetual physical, emotional, and psychological issues paralyze some people's lives. And some people's daily lives are a chain of deprivations, troubles, and misfortunes. Personal development and communal living become enormously difficult when such undesirable elements plague our lives. "Accent" is a metaphor that I use to refer to these differences and difficulties that we face in our life.

When faced with problems and difficulties, whether they are personal or communal, we look for solutions. We want answers for our questions, and we want our problems fixed. But often our search for solutions stays on the surface level. We look for quick fixes, and the changes that we make are cosmetic and superficial. We often don't get to the bottom of things. Consequently, our problems don't go away. They reappear in different shapes and forms. To understand why certain people behave in certain ways or why we get into conflicts and problems, we have to get to the bottom of things. We have to understand how we develop our accents or individual differences. We have to understand who we are and how we become what we become. We have to understand why our lives are plagued by suffering of all kinds. We have to understand what makes it hard for some of us to get along with others. We need to understand why some of us take the path of violence and hatred. We need to know why some of us become a problem wherever we go. And we need to know why some of us bring the best out of ourselves and others bring the worst out of themselves. As individuals and communities, we might passionately pursue our goals and dreams, but unless we get to the bottom of things and address some of these fundamental facts about our lives, many of our problems will reappear over and over again.

One of the routes that people in every age and culture have taken to get to the bottom of things and find answers for the fundamental questions about their lives is religion and spirituality. They look to a higher power who is believed to have a better view of things and who can answer all their questions and solve all their problems. This path has been tried and tested over and over again, and on this path people have found comfort and solace beyond description. In the last couple of centuries, psychology has been added to the list of choices that people can use to find answers for their questions and problems. It either works alongside religion and spirituality or does its business on its own. But the focus of each is pretty much the same. People have questions, and they need answers. Some turn to religion and spirituality, and others turn to psychology. Some seek the help of both.

To move past our issues and problems and live a healthy and happy life, I see the need for an integration of both religion and psychology. This book, *The Accent*, achieves just that. It explores what God tells us about who we are and what we are meant to be, and what psychology tells us about why we do things the way we do. It explores how we develop our accents, or differences, and how we can transcend those accents to move toward a rejuvenating and healthy life.

With reference to religion and spirituality, my primary focus in this book is on Jesus and his message. If we really want to transcend our accents and defeat the powers of evil and darkness in us and in our world, we have to allow Jesus and his message to come alive again. He is our way to salvation and fullness of life. Jesus says, "I am the way, and the truth, and the life. No one comes to the Father except through me" (Jn 14:6). To those who believe in him, Jesus says, "If you continue in my word, you are truly my disciples; and you will know the truth, and the truth will make you free" (Jn 8:31–32). A world that is caught up in a great amount of mismatched accents, intolerance, vengeance, and hatred needs to hear the message of Jesus that only love can save us. The culture of negative living and uncontrolled passions has to make way for a God-centered life and relationships. The principle of "an eye for an eye and a tooth for a tooth" (Mt 5:38) needs to give way to forgiveness, mercy, and compassion. The path of bigotry and bloodshed has to give way to mutual respect and peaceful coexistence.

We fight like cats and dogs and kill or hurt each other. We act like venomous snakes, spilling and spewing hatred and anger onto each other. The dark sides of our personalities shut out the lighter sides of ourselves. We are ignorant of or forget who we are and what we are meant to be. We need redemption from such ways of life. And that is what Jesus offers. He came to right the wrong and put our lives back on track. Individuals and families do better if they heed the voice of Jesus. Communities and nations get along with each other better if they listen to the message of Jesus. Jesus keeps reminding all of us, "For what will it profit them if they gain the whole world but forfeit their life?" (Mt 16:26). If we want to keep our world going, we have to keep Jesus alive in our hearts. If we want to stop the culture of death and darkness, we have to become a counterculture with Jesus as our center.

Jesus says to each one of us, "You are the light of the world. A city built on a hill cannot be hid. No one after lighting a lamp puts it under the bushel basket, but on the lamp stand, and it gives light to all in the house. In the same way, let your light shine before others, so that they may see your good works and give glory to your Father in heaven" (Mt 5:14–16). If we are the light of the world, we have a great responsibility to keep our world free from the powers of darkness. But we know that it is not easy to keep that light shining. The powers of evil and sin lurk at our door constantly. We get tested and tempted. We struggle with our imperfections and illnesses, and our lives become burdensome and heavy. Jesus is not unaware of these struggles that we face. He knows that transcending our accents and moving forward with our eyes set on our goal is not easy. He knows what it means to fight the powers of evil and sin. He knows what it means to be hated, mistreated, and crucified. He has been there, and he knows what it is all like.

We read in the Letter to the Hebrews, "For we do not have a high priest who is unable to sympathize with our weaknesses, but we have one who in every respect has been tested as we are, yet without sin" (Heb 4:15). Knowing full well how we struggle with our problems and difficulties in life, he comes to us with his peace and strength. He says, "Come to me, all you that are weary and are carrying heavy burdens, and I will give you rest" (Mt 11:28). He has been victorious over the powers of evil, sin, and death, and in him we will find refuge and strength. Recognizing the strength of this power that comes from on high, Saint Paul says, "If God is for us, who is against us?" (Rom 8:31). Jesus is not just showing us the way, but rather, he is the way. He walks with us on our life journey. Those who live in him will find the strength for the journey and experience the fullness of life.

The path to salvation and fullness of life that Jesus offers is not just for Christians or Catholics, but rather for all people. Saint Paul, in his letter to the Galatians, says, "There is no longer Jew or Greek, there is no longer slave or free, there is no longer male and female; for all of you are one in Christ Jesus" (Gal 3:28). Jesus makes no difference between people. For him, we are all important, and he is a savior to all. Although there have been attempts by many people to monopolize, misinterpret, and misrepresent Jesus, he is beyond all borders and barriers. He was born for all, and he died for all. We are all his children, and he wants all of us to be united with him and one another. To transcend our accents and move toward a healthy and happy life, we need to allow Jesus and his message to come alive again. He is our way to a joyful and fulfilling life.

Although Jesus and his message are the primary focus of my discussions in this book, I also use thoughts and insights from other cultures and traditions. God speaks to us in many ways, and we never stop learning from each other.

With reference to the value of psychology, my focus in this book is on its usefulness in understanding ourselves better. Human sciences have helped us tremendously to understand ourselves better. Psychology helps us to understand why we do what we do. It tells us what contributes to our progress or growth and development. It helps us to understand why we see, hear, and perceive things differently. And it helps us to understand why we regress or why we get stuck in our personal growth and development and interpersonal relationships. To move past our accents and problems and live a healthy and happy life, we need a better understanding of ourselves. Thus, we need to understand the psychology and spirituality of our being. Transcending our accents is hard work, but it is not impossible. With a better understanding of ourselves, and with the grace and wisdom of God, we can move toward health and happiness.

In part I of this book, I discuss how we, the human beings, are an amazing species. We surprise ourselves in many ways. We set certain goals and ideals for ourselves, which are often encapsulated in our legends and stories, and we are in a relentless pursuit of materializing them. However, we experience insurmountable problems in getting closer to those ideals and dreams because we differ in many ways or we differ in our accents. We don't seem to be speaking the same language. We can't understand each other, let alone pursue common goals and dreams. I cite instances from our everyday life where our mismatched accents cause problems and difficulties. I also propose and discuss two phenomena, the drive to survive (DTS) and the drive to thrive (DTT), that are key to understanding our accents, or differences.

In part II, I discuss the unfolding of the two phenomena in the various developmental stages of our life. I talk about our drive to survive and drive to thrive being helpful as well as detrimental to our personal and interpersonal growth and development.

In part III, I talk about the wrong direction that the two phenomena could take and how they could create mismatches in our accents. I discuss how the two phenomena sometimes become painfully negative and destructive in some people's lives and how they sabotage or compromise their growth and relationships.

In part IV, I look at what causes mismatched accents and wrong direction in the manifestation of the two phenomena. I discuss our distorted sense of self and vision of life. I also discuss how elements such as our genetics and environment, past experiences, debilitating character structures, inequality in our thriving avenues and survival possibilities, and unhealthy elements of our present-day culture play into the development of mismatched accents in our lives.

In the final section, part V, I discuss what we need to do to transcend our accents and move toward a healthy and rejuvenating life. I talk about the need to find the union between the self, God, and community.

I also suggest several practical ways to go beyond our differences and difficulties.

This book is essentially about our personal journeys and relationships, our ideals and dreams, and our common destiny. It is about who we are, why we do what we do, and where we are destined to be. It is also about things that threaten a healthy and happy life. It offers us a new way of looking at our life and suggests some unique ways to get to our ideals and goals. With a fine balance of Eastern and Western thought, the chapters in this book take us through the different contours and corners of our lives and tell us some truths that we need to hear.

PART I

What We Know
about Ourselves

1

An Extraordinary Species

Curiosity, the six-wheeled rover developed by NASA, landed on Mars in August 2012 after a 352-million-mile journey. The new endeavor was to explore whether Mars was ever habitable for some form of life. India sent an orbiter mission spacecraft named *Mangalyaan* to Mars in November 2013 to study the planet and see whether there is any indication or possibility of life on it. The rocket traveled 485 million miles over three hundred days before it reached its destination on September 24, 2014.

Great efforts and amazing achievements! The possibility of man-made equipment being able to travel that far through outer space is mind-boggling. Aren't our scientists and researchers incredible? Isn't the human mind, which has conceived all these maneuvers into the unfathomable universe, amazing? Who knows what is awaiting us a few centuries from now, when brainy men and women can use more of their potential. To date, we have fathomed only a tiny part of the vast universe. Even the latest discoveries are still inconsequential in comparison with the larger part that is yet to be explored and discovered. However, we have made great strides in our research, discoveries, and explorations.

The universe has mesmerized human minds with its vastness and profundity. But much more mesmerizing are the human beings themselves. Who can understand human beings? Who can comprehend the inner being and movements of the human person? Who can discern what is on a person's mind? Who can understand the longings and desires, the thoughts and emotions, and the judgments and dispositions of a human person?

To the extent we know it, everything in the universe moves and functions according to certain patterns. There may be a few that act out of the way every now and then, but otherwise, the planets, the solar systems, the galaxies, the Milky Way, and whatever other things we can think of in this vast universe have their particular way of being, and they move and function according to that pattern. The same rule applies to many other beings and phenomena in nature. Consider animals, birds, plants, and seas. Everything has its particular way of being and functioning. However, this universe is not without exceptions. Among all the creatures, forces, and realities in the universe, as far as we know it, there is one that stands out: human beings. We are different. We do things out of the ordinary. And our ways are often unpredictable. The sun and the moon are grand beyond description, and the seas and the skies have depths that are difficult to fathom, but there is nothing so grand and yet unfathomable as human beings themselves. We are extraordinary and exceptional.

Our extraordinariness is mightily visible in every aspect of our lives. Be it in reference to the physical, psychological, social, or spiritual dimensions of our lives, we know we have no comparison in the whole known universe. We are conscious and conscientious beings that are capable of making decisions that take us to frontiers we wish to explore. We have the faculties to think, feel, reflect, and decide. We have the intellect and reason to figure out things differently. We are insightful and intuitive. We act consciously, and if we have pushed something down to the unconscious or preconscious realms of our mind, we are able to bring it up to the conscious level again.

Physically we can be in one place, but mentally we can be on another continent. Our thoughts take us back to another country in a moment, traveling faster than light or sound. We can be driving on a highway but be lost in our thoughts about somebody on another continent, dwell on the dream that we had the previous night, or listen to some tapes or music, and we still reach our destination without causing an accident. We can be the subject and object of our thoughts and observations.

We engage in self-talk and laugh at ourselves. We cry and laugh, altering our emotions in a split second. We cry when we are sad, and we cry when we are happy. We stir up passions and emotions with our speech and voice. We bring tears to people's eyes with our words and melodies. We write poems and stories. We compose music and songs. We create movies and plays.

We carpet our rooms and air-condition our buildings. We pave our roads and light our streets. We build cars, planes, and ships. We construct tunnels, roads, and runways on top of each other. We fly like birds and swim like fish. We conquer mountains and hills, and explore oceans and skies.

We surprise ourselves in many ways. We are an amazing species. We are different, and we have the ability to be different. Psalm 8 in the Bible talks of the grandiosity of human beings: "When I look at your heavens, the work of your fingers, the moon and the stars that you have established; what are human beings that you are mindful of them, mortals that you care for them? Yet you have made them a little lower than God, and crowned them with glory and honor" (Ps 8:3–5). If there are grander and more intelligent beings or creatures in this creation, we have not found them yet, or they have not found us yet. No one has rivaled us so far.

But we have our imperfections and contradictions too. In one moment we are the best human beings, but in the next, we are the worst. Today we fight, but tomorrow we reconcile. Today we decide something, but tomorrow we change our decision. Today we spend lavishly, but tomorrow we live in poverty. We build and destroy, and gather and scatter. We connect with people, and we distance ourselves from others. We marry and divorce; we love and hate. We occupy lands and overthrow governments. We enslave people and terrorize communities. We enthrone kings and dethrone dictators. We stockpile arms and ammunitions on the one side and sign peace treaties on the other. We kill to save and die to resurrect. We kill for freedom and die for freedom. We die for the love of God, and we kill for the love of God. We believe that God created us, but we also create our own gods. We say we cannot understand God, but we act like we know everything about God. We call some uncivilized, but we ourselves behave like barbarians.

Our hearts break when we see someone suffering, but our hearts also take pleasure in inflicting pain and suffering on others. We say we are powerless, and yet we claim mastery over everything.

The little we know about ourselves is already overwhelming. We still remain a mystery to a great extent. Mystery is not something that is totally unknown. We know something about it, but we don't know everything about it. Many people who believe in God consider him a mystery because they know something about him, but at the same time they don't know everything about him. Likewise, we know something about ourselves, but we don't know everything. And mystery is something that we always want to know more about. So we keep searching and learning, and remain open to new discoveries and revelations.

The attempts we make to understand ourselves better may be baby steps, but they are still significant steps. Look at the number of disciplines and theories that have come up in the mental health field. Theorists have strived to understand human beings and the working of our psyche. Think of all the discoveries we have made about the functioning of the human body and mind. How about all the philosophical and theological concepts and theories that have been developed? Philosophers and theologians have been relentlessly trying to answer some of the fundamental questions about our life. We have made much progress in our understanding of our social and communal relationships. We keep learning about the internal and external forces that impact our thoughts, feelings, and actions. We know a lot about ourselves, but we are not done yet. Many of our perennial questions about our life still remain unanswered. So we keep searching and learning.

2

A Legend

We are not only an extraordinary species that has accomplished great achievements and discoveries but also a people with amazing stories to tell. In Kerala, my home state in India, we have an amazing story that we treasure, titled "Ōnam." "Ōnam" is the story of a mythical emperor called Mahābali (also called Bali and Māveli), who is believed to have ruled the universe once upon a time. Kerala was the capital of his empire, and his people experienced the best of times during his reign.

The story of Mahābali is deeply rooted in *the Vedic and post-Vedic traditions* and literature. The Vedic Age in India began in around 1500 BCE with the arrival of Aryans, a people from Central Asia who spoke an Indo-European language. They conquered or settled alongside the native Dravidians and other inhabitants in India, and established a new culture and social system. They also brought with them their religion, which was based on the worship of many gods and goddesses. It is believed that many religious traditions existed in India before the arrival of the Aryans, but it seems that after their arrival, they established supremacy over others.

However, the Aryans were not completely free from the influence of the religious beliefs and practices of the natives. The association between the Aryans and the native Dravidians and other inhabitants gave rise to new religious beliefs and practices, and it gradually developed into a distinctive religion called Hinduism, although the terms, "Hindu" and "Hinduism" themselves are of later origin. In the new creed, three gods—Brahma, Vishnu, and Shiva—gained prominence. Brahma was the creator; Shiva, the destroyer; and Vishnu, the preserver. There were also other celestial beings, gods and goddesses, and avatars (incarnations) that people worshipped and revered. The celestial beings were generally grouped into two categories known as *Asuras* and *Devas,* and they are mentioned in the Vedic and post-Vedic literature.

Although the Aryans first settled along the Gangetic Plain in northern India, their influence and religious beliefs seem to have gradually spread across the whole subcontinent. The story of Mahābali and the history of the people of Kerala speak to this broader influence of the Aryans in the South. The original inhabitants of the state of Kerala and most of South India were believed to have been Dravidians by race. Of course, when we use the term "original inhabitants," we have to always wonder how original those inhabitants are. We have to assume or admit that there were people in Kerala before even the Dravidians inhabited the land.

Anyhow, after the Aryans moved into India, it appears a marriage between the Aryan and Dravidian cultures in Kerala took place. Along with other cultural changes, the Keralites (natives of Kerala) seem to have accommodated the religious beliefs and practices of the newcomers, or rather the existing religions seem to have gradually given way to the new beliefs and practices introduced by the newcomers. Given this background, there is no wonder why the story of Mahābali, which has its roots in Hinduism and Vedic literature, becomes the most cherished story of most Keralites. Several other cultures and traditions, both religious and secular, were also absorbed into the Kerala culture in later times. However, the story of Mahābali continues to be a common story shared by most communities in the state. People of different faith traditions embrace this story. As time passed, it became more a cultural story than a religious one. It is now the common story of the Keralites rather than the story of a particular group or faith tradition, and Ōnam is more a cultural and harvest festival than a religious festival.

However, in its religious background, the story of Mahābali is associated with the rivalry between Asuras and Devas, the celestial beings whom the people of Vedic and post-Vedic times revered and worshipped. Both groups, according to the beliefs, had designated roles: the Devas presided over the natural phenomena, and the Asuras presided over the moral and social phenomena. Over time Asuras fell out of favor with most of their worshippers because they were thought to have changed in their nature by becoming wicked, power hungry, and evil. Devas, on the other hand, continued to remain benevolent and holy.

Being archrivals, the Asuras and Devas engaged in constant battles with each other. They often fought to obtain supremacy over the three worlds: heaven, the earth, and the underworld. At one time, Mahābali was the leader of the Asuras and Indra was the leader of the Devas. In his battle with Mahābali, Indra lost authority over the heavens, and the former established his supremacy over the three worlds. Unlike his predecessors and other Asuras, Mahābali was a good ruler. His reign was characterized by righteousness, prosperity, and peace. He even shocked the Devas with his righteous rule and benevolence. He did nothing wrong or sinful. The story of Ōnam is all about this righteous emperor, Mahābali. According to the legend, Kerala was the capital of Mahābali's empire. Kerala witnessed its golden era during his reign, and everybody was happy and content. There was no discrimination on the basis of caste or class. Crime and corruption were unknown in the land. There was no poverty, sorrow, or disease. Kerala was even better than the heavens.

The Devas, however, were not happy with the situation. They were not only angry that they lost their control over the heavens but also grew envious and jealous of their rival, the able ruler Mahābali. To put an end to his growing popularity and restore Indra, their leader, to the lordship over the three worlds, they approached Vishnu, one of the supreme gods, to intervene on their behalf. They also coaxed Vishnu to test the sincerity of Mahābali, who claimed to be magnanimous and kind.

Vishnu, according to the beliefs, had appeared incarnate on the earth in different forms in the past in service of his role as the maintainer and preserver of the cosmos. Heeding the demands of the Devas, Vishnu once again incarnated himself (for the fifth time), this time as Vamana, who is sometimes depicted as a dwarf and other times as a boy. He trapped Mahābali in a well-plotted scheme. Having disguised himself as a boy, he presented himself before Mahābali as if to ask for some favors. Mahābali was known for his kindness to those who came to visit him.

Being unaware of the plot, Mahābali received the boy with gifts and other traditional honors, and asked him what he could give him for blessing him with his gracious presence.

The boy, Vishnu, pretended that he did not need anything except a portion of land equal to three paces. Mahābali's guru, Sukracharya, was meanwhile watching the drama that was unfolding. He felt something was not right about the sudden appearance of the boy and his request for three paces of land. He concluded that the boy was no ordinary boy and saw a well-planned plot behind his request. He warned Mahābali not to grant the boy his wish. However, Mahābali, who had vowed not to refuse anyone anything, and who prided himself as a benevolent ruler, promptly granted the boy's wish. In his guileless thinking, three paces of land did not amount to anything big. But for Vishnu three paces were not ordinary paces. He was the supreme god, and the entire universe appeared tiny to him.

Once Mahābali granted his wish, the little boy, Vishnu, revealed his real identity and grew into an immense size. With two paces he measured the heaven, the earth, and the underworld. He still needed one more pace, and he turned to Mahābali. Unable to fulfill his promise, Mahābali offered himself for the third pace. Vishnu took his third pace on Mahābali's head and banished him from the face of the earth. Mahābali was thus banished from his capital, Kerala. Vishnu, however, was moved by Mahābali's unselfish devotion, magnanimity, and unwavering humility. He raised Mahābali to a greater position than the Devas. Knowing that Mahābali dearly loved his people in Kerala, Vishnu also granted him the permission to visit his subjects, the people of Kerala, once every year. Ōnam thus marks the imaginary annual visit of Mahābali to his people in Kerala.

It is a legend, and there are several versions of it. But the way the people of Kerala believe in this story and celebrate Ōnam would make anyone think that this is a true story. Celebrated as a state festival with pomp and gaiety, it lasts for ten days. A sumptuous meal, folk songs and dances, martial arts performances, the creation of beautiful floral designs, purchases of new dresses or clothes, and boat races in the backwaters of Kerala are some of the prominent features of the celebration.

Although it is deeply rooted in the Vedic and Hindu tradition, Ōnam is widely celebrated as a cultural festival by most Keralites. Growing up, I always looked forward to the celebration of this imaginary visit of Mahābali to us, his subjects in Kerala, every year. It is something akin to kids in the West waiting for Santa Claus every year.

Malayalam is the native language of Kerala, and the month of Karkkidakam, the last month of the Malayalam calendar, falls between the months of July and August in the Roman calendar. Karkkidakam used to be known as the month of famine and extreme scarcity. During this month, the monsoon season is at its peak, and agricultural products and food used to be scarce during this time. Ōnam is celebrated immediately after the end of this season. Chingam, the first month of the Malayalam calendar (August–September), marks the beginning of the new year and a period of prosperity and plenitude. The rain subsides, vegetables and fruits are plentiful, and the harvest season is around the corner. There is no better time to celebrate Ōnam than this time of abundance.

The beauty of Kerala combined with such celebrations and legends would make anyone think that once upon a time Kerala was a land better than even the heavens. Kerala is popularly known as "God's own country." Bordered by the Arabian Sea on the one side and a range of mountains known as the Western Ghats on the other, the state is famous for its sprawling backwaters and lush green vegetation. It is a tropical paradise of waving palms and wide sandy beaches.

Although the main theme of the narrative is the righteous rule of Mahābali, there are several subplots incorporated into this one unifying story of Ōnam. The subplots are the jealousy and envy of Devas toward Mahābali, the constant fighting between Devas and Asuras for supremacy over the cosmos, and the pride and grandiosity of Mahābali regarding his own magnanimity and righteousness. However, above all these subplots stands the core story of Ōnam, the story of the victory of righteousness over malice, benevolence over greed, humility over pride, and goodwill over resentment. The land of Mahābali was not just a land of festivities and material prosperity alone. It was also a land of peace, brotherhood, and love. I shall cite here the English translation of one of the most popular songs in Malayalam that all of us used to memorize and sing often, especially during the season of Ōnam. The song echoes the core beliefs behind the celebration:

> When Māveli ruled the land,
> All were equal.
> Everyone was living happy;
> And all were free from harm.
> There was neither lie nor deceit;
> And no one engaged in false speech.
> Measures and weights were right;
> And there was no cheating or wrongdoing.
> There were no anxieties or sicknesses;
> And deaths of children were unheard of.

The core message of the song is not so much about material prosperity but rather righteousness, peace, honesty, and the overall goodness of all people. Cheating, deceit, and false speech were unheard of. There was no discrimination; no distinction. All were equal. Although the absence of diseases and worries is specially noted, the mention of zero occurrences of children's deaths denotes the priority given to the protection and safety of the weak and the less privileged.

Although it is a legend, the story of Mahābali is powerful, and it united the Keralites for centuries. The story speaks of the harmonious coexistence of different communities. Irrespective of caste, color, or creed, everyone takes pride in identifying with that common story of the community. Everyone looks forward to the celebration of that story. And everyone hands over that story to the subsequent generations. That story is kept alive in and out of season, generation after generation.

It is amazing that the story of Mahābali's rule is kept alive generation after generation even though none of these people ever saw the actual unfolding of that story or lived long enough to see its reenactment. Whether it is real or not, achievable or not, everyone takes pride in being connected to that age-old story.

Reading between the lines, Mahābali's story can be seen on two levels: physical and spiritual, and actual and symbolic. It can tell us what actually may have happened as well as what it symbolizes. In psychology, these two levels of story are often referred to as the manifest content and the latent content, respectively. When a patient comes for psychotherapy, for example, there is the surface level story that he or she presents, and then there is a deeper story behind that story that the psychotherapist and the patient need to unravel. To understand the full story, we have to understand both the manifest and latent content, the surface meaning and the deeper meaning. Mahābali's story needs to be understood on both these levels. If we get stuck with the manifest content or the surface-level meaning of the story, we might become too literal and miss the real message.

First of all, the story of Mahābali tells us that it is not simply a fairy tale. It contains the faith and hope of a community. It contains the community's deep faith in humanity's goodness. It contains the community's unquenchable longing for a peaceful, happy, and prosperous life. It contains the dreams and ideals of the community. If not every day, at least for a few days during the year, the community wants to make it look like a reality and a possibility.

Secondly, the story of Mahābali points to the desire of the community for a new culture and society. The story speaks of the merger of different races and communities. The largely Dravidian Keralites blended with the Aryans and others who moved into their territory from time to time. The visitors were integrated into the social, cultural, and religious life of the natives. Refining whatever was to be refined, and blending the old and the new, they developed—or hoped to develop—a new story.

The Aryan culture, for example, needed some refinement. In the Aryan society in Vedic and post-Vedic times, people were classified into four different castes: Brahmins, Kshatriyas, Vaishyas, and Shudras. And then there were the untouchables, who did not belong to any of these castes. The caste affiliations dictated the behavior and life chances of individuals in the society. Some castes had supremacy over others. The Brahmins, who belonged to the highest caste, for example, enjoyed economic prosperity, while the low-caste people, such as Shudras, were socially disadvantaged. The untouchables did not have any recognition or rights in the society. They did the most despicable jobs, such as carrying the night soil. The caste system institutionalized inequality and discrimination. The story of Mahābali is a rejection of this unequal and discriminatory culture and social system.

There is no reason to believe that everyone was forced into accepting one faith or religion, but there is a clear indication that the Keralites developed or desired to develop a new culture in which everyone was equal and respected. In the popular song connected with Ōnam that I cited above, it is clear that the people of Kerala desired a society based on equality and brotherhood, respect and honor. It was a society in which everyone coexisted peacefully. They went beyond races and religions, and castes and classes. It was a society in which everyone was united with God and others. There was no discrimination, no cheating, and no ill feelings. There was a desire for a new culture and society free from debilitating elements. Mahābali, the protagonist, becomes the champion of this changed culture and society. Even if it never existed, the story of Mahābali encapsulates this desire of the community for a refined and renewed life and culture.

Thirdly, the story of Mahābali points to the birth of a new race and community. Out of the miscegenation of Dravidians, Aryans and others arose a new community in Kerala. The present-day Keralites are a result of the marriage between different races and ethnicities. No one knows for sure how many races and ethnicities have been blended in Kerala in the last ten thousand years. The story of Mahābali tells us that races and ethnicities are always in the making not only in Kerala but also all over the world. We move from one land to the other, mixing with others and establishing new identities. When we interact with others or get immersed in their life and culture, we never come out the same. As individuals and communities, we are always changing.

When it comes to our life as a separate species, the only "race" that is constant is the "human race." All other races that we identify with are in a process of change. If not in our lifetime, those changes are bound to happen somewhere in later generations. And it happened over and over before we ever appeared on the face of this earth. We could wonder what our ancestors' race or ethnicity was a million years ago. And we could wonder what our future generations' race will be a million years from now. Mahābali's Kerala is a representation of people's willingness and need to go beyond their races and ethnicities to build a new community.

Fourthly, the story of Mahābali is also a reminder to us that we are all pilgrims on this earth. We are not permanent residents here, although some might like to think that they are. Even Mahābali's reign was not permanent. Pride and arrogance gave way to humility. And Mahābali was raised above the Devas for his humility and righteousness. The story is a reminder that the earth belongs to no one but God alone. We are pilgrims, and we need to make way for other pilgrims who land on our doorsteps. The Aryans and others came to Kerala, the Dravidian land, and made their home there. There was space for all. They coexisted well. Even the Dravidians might have had a similar history. They have to wonder where they came from and how they became a race by themselves. Going back to our ancestors of different ages, we have to wonder how many lands and seas they might have traversed and crossed to find a suitable place to settle down and live. And how much do we desire that we feel welcome in the new places and territories that we explore!

But how sad it is to see people in many societies today claiming sole ownership over the lands and not letting anyone else enter their territories. Many people often forget that they or their ancestors were also conquerors or pilgrims once upon a time, looking for a place to settle down and make a living. How easy it is to forget our past and shut others out of our territories. There is no permanent ownership or residence on this earth. We are all pilgrims. This is very well captured by Saint Paul, one of the greatest authors in the Bible. In his letter to the Corinthians, he says, "For we know that if the earthly tent we live in is destroyed, we have a building from God, a house not made with hands, eternal in the heavens" (2Co 5:1). Our life on this earth is like putting up a temporary tent. A time will come when we will have to fold it up and leave. The story of Mahābali reiterates this truth. We are pilgrims, and we put up a tent here for a while. How wonderful would it be if we could allow others to find some space in our tents or pitch their tents next to ours!

It appears that every community needs a story like that of Mahābali to keep the people moving forward and yet stay grounded. The story is something that the community can fall back on and learn from. It reminds us about the need for constant renewal in our personal and communal lives. The story reminds us about what it takes to form a just, righteous, and prosperous community. The story tells us how we can go beyond our cultural and community boundaries and construct a common story. Our stories are always in the making, but we always have some ideals and dreams that we follow. Our stories generate a sense of pride in the glory and goodness of our past, give strength for our present, and instill hope for our future.

3

Across Cultures

Looking at other cultures and traditions, some of the most compelling stories about great ideals and dreams are found in the Abrahamic or Judeo-Christian-Islamic traditions. There are several stories that these three major religious traditions have in common. The stories take us back to a glorious past that is believed to have existed, provide strength for our present, and offer hope for our future. The stories tell us about the vision of life that God has set for us. And they speak to the human longing for peace and harmony, and righteousness and goodwill.

The account of Paradise (Ge 2) is a stunning story shared by the Jews, Christians, and Muslims, with some minor differences in each of their Scriptures regarding how the story unfolded. According to the Judeo-Christian and Islamic traditions, God is the creator of all that is. He created the universe with all its wonder and beauty. He set everything in perfect order. And then he created the most magnificent thing of all: human beings. He created them male and female, and they came to be known as Adam and Eve. They were the first parents of all human beings. He placed them in the garden of Eden, a perfect world, or Paradise.

According to the Biblical account, God walked hand in hand with Adam and Eve. He gave them dominion over all animals and plants and commanded them to cultivate the land and take care of it. He also commanded them not to eat of the tree in the middle of the garden lest they die. Satan, the evil one and God's enemy, saw an opportunity in God's command to trick Adam and Eve and tear them away from God's company. Coming in the form of a serpent, he persuaded Eve to try eating the fruit of the forbidden tree. He told her that she would not die as God had suggested. She ate the fruit, and brought it to her husband, Adam, who did the same. They did not die; they were still alive. But they were dead in another sense. The death that God had indicated was an inner death: a death of friendship, a death of love, and a death of communion with one another. With their disobedience to God's command, they had died internally. The sense of peace and joy had begun to go out of them.

Having given into Satan's deception and disobeyed God's commandment, they began to experience fear, guilt, and shame. They were terrified and hid themselves from God. They lost their favor with God and began to blame each other for the fall. They became aware of their nakedness and stitched fig leaves to cover themselves. Although the story says that God banished them from Paradise, it would make more sense to think that having chosen to follow the words of Satan rather than God, they banished themselves from Paradise. They sought Satan's allurements rather than God's love.

The story of Paradise is a story of perfection and imperfection, success and failure, good and evil. It is a story that has seen innumerable interpretations. Some interpret it literally, while others look at it as a metaphor with a deeper meaning about God, the world, and the human beings. Several subplots are woven into this one uniform story. The subplots are as follows: God as the creator of all that is, the godly nature of the human beings and their glorious and guileless past, the curious nature of the human beings to know the unknowable and to get to forbidden things, the never-ending longing for a perfect life and perfect world, the fear and shame associated with human frailties, the blame game that human beings engage in, the constant struggle between our longing for pleasure and longing for perfection, the depiction of woman as the temptress and man as the victim of her viciousness, the prohibitions associated with the genital and sexual dimensions of human life, and the fate of man to toil and do hard labor.

The telling and retelling of this story generation after generation points to people's hope of seeing the life in Paradise reenacted one day.

For some it is an eschatological reality, while others conceive of it as an imminent earthly experience. It points to people's unflagging spirit and confidence in our God-given ability to return to a harmonious life with God and one another. There is a longing for a righteous, prosperous, peaceful, and Eden-like life. We may have messed up, but we are capable of doing better. But the story is also a reminder to us that if we want things to change, we need to start taking responsibility for what we do. We might blame each other for our falls and faults, but none of us can totally absolve ourselves of the evils and sins we find in our world. The story takes us back to the glory of our past, gives strength for our present, and instills hope for our future.

Another story that is found in the Bible and shared by the Judeo-Christian traditions is the story of Exodus (Ex 12). It is the story of a people breaking free of slavery in Egypt and marching toward the Promised Land of milk and honey. Having experienced a famine in the land of Canaan, the Israelites had gone to Egypt seeking food and shelter. They prospered and flourished there for some time, and then their good fortunes were turned upside down. They were forced into slavery by a new pharaoh. Many generations passed, and they struggled and suffered much. But they trusted in God and kept their faith. They hoped to someday return to Canaan, the land of their forefathers. As they hoped, God noticed their misery, and they were saved from their slavery. Under the leadership of Moses, they were led back to Canaan, the Promised Land. They are said to have traveled for forty years before they reached their destination. Many of them perished on the way. Many of them never saw the Promised Land. But as a community, they kept alive their hopes and dreams, and marched on with faith.

Several subplots are incorporated into the single story of Exodus. They are as follows: the sudden change in the destiny of the immigrants, the Israelites, who came to the prosperous land of Egypt with a hope to build a better future; the cruelty of Pharaoh to the immigrants and their descendants; the unexpected rise of Moses into a leadership position, the unwillingness of some of the Israelites to heed to Moses' call to march to freedom; the desire of some of the Israelites to stay as slaves rather than fight for freedom, the enormous task of Moses to lead an uncouth and disunited people; the faith of the community in the providence of

God; the complaints and grievances of the people against Moses and his leadership; the desire of the people to stay with the familiar rather than facing the unknown, the struggle between the individual's destiny and a community's destiny; and the depiction of God as supreme and powerful and yet as the God of a clan or a particular group. Although all these subplots are present in the one story of Exodus, the core theme of the story is the unbreakable faith and spirit of a community. They trusted in God's providence and kept alive their indomitable spirit. They were determined to build a better future and live a life of freedom and prosperity. They were hopeful of returning to their glorious past. They were resilient and resolute. And they passed on the story to subsequent generations.

The story of Exodus is a story of faith and hope. It reminds us that although today looks gloomy and sad, tomorrow could be bright and shiny. It is a story that calls for respect for our fellow human beings. It is a story that tells us that we are all sojourners on this earth and we need to find ways to coexist peacefully. But it also tells us that despite the discouraging elements of our life, we still have the God-given capacity to rise up and shine. With God on our side, we can march on fearlessly. The Pharaohs in us might try to enslave and subjugate others, but no evil goes unnoticed in God's sight. The ultimate victory is with the good and not the evil.

The Christians, in general, have a concept that conveys a message akin to those found in the stories mentioned above. It is the concept of the kingdom of God (Mt 13). Although the kingdom of God is interpreted in different ways, there is a general agreement among Christians that it refers to a perfect state of life in which God is the center and we are all united with him. This experience is envisioned as internal and external, and imminent as well as eschatological. As an internal reality, it is conceived as God making his home within a person, or a person becoming totally God-filled (Jn 14:23). It is more of a spiritual reality than the physical establishment of a kingdom. Externally, in a more physical sense, it is conceived as a world that is characterized by features, such as peace, harmony, justice, and love.

Some conceive of the kingdom of God as something that is going to happen here and now, while others think of it as an eschatological or end-of-time reality. To most of the early Christians, the imminent and external manifestation of the kingdom stood prominent in their expectations. Because they were subjected to gruesome persecutions and tortures by the Roman emperors and others, they expected the establishment of a just and peaceful kingdom by Jesus in their lifetime. Such a faith sustained many of them. Although none of them personally saw the imminent establishment of such a kingdom or world, they continued to share in that one story and passed that story on to subsequent generations.

The concept of the kingdom of God represents people's deep faith in the providence of God and their God-given capacity to build a better future. People might try to break our spirit through persecution and torture, but with God on our side, we will be able to overcome our troubles and live a joyful and peaceful life not only in eternity but also on this earth.

Just as with the story of Mahābali, these stories and ideals in the Abrahamic tradition also need to be seen on two levels: physical and spiritual, and actual and symbolic. They have a surface level meaning and a deeper-level meaning. In most of the stories presented in the Bible, we have to see both these levels of meanings or message. We have to understand what actually may have happened, and we have to understand what God is trying to tell us through these stories. There is a reason why the Biblical authors chose to put certain stories and not others in their writings. We read at the end of the gospel of John, "But there are also many other things that Jesus did; if every one of them were written down, I suppose that the world itself could not contain the books that would be written" (Jn 21:25). John could have put in his gospel many other stories about Jesus, but he chose to include only those that we find. Each of those stories that found a place in his gospel has a specific message for us. He not only tells us what actually happened but also points to what God is trying to tell us through each of those stories. There is the real story, and then there is a deeper story behind that story.

Some of them may not be historical, and not all of them refer to the same reality when they speak of certain things, but legends and stories that communities keep alive generation after generation are manifestations of deep-seated human longing for something better.

First, they can be understood as the community's collective projection of the ideal self, the ideal other, the ideal community, and the ideal world. They encapsulate the community's longing for the ideal. Whether they reach it or not, communities have an ideal that they want everyone to focus on. If not them, they hope that their future generations make it a reality.

Second, the legends and stories can be seen as affirmations of the noble, glorious, and divine features that human beings possess. By focusing on those features and freeing ourselves from all jealousy and evil—of our own or of others—we will be able to establish a world of peace and prosperity, righteousness and truth, and love and brotherhood. People desire and look forward to such a reality not only in the eschatological times but also here and now.

Third, these stories and legends reveal the great truth about us that we are not mere isolated individuals but rather a community of persons. We journey together, counting on each other's support. We share in a common story and a common destiny. We form one family with God and others.

Fourth, the stories and legends are a proclamation that there is more to life than meets the eye. There is something in all of us that longs for something more than what this world or this life can offer.

Fifth, the stories tell us what Saint Paul tells us in the letter to the Corinthians—that we are all pilgrims on this earth, putting up temporary tents (2Co 5:1). Our ultimate destiny is our union with God and others in eternity.

Sixth, the legends and stories are a gentle and yet powerful way of telling us certain truths that we otherwise may not pay attention to. Telling certain things through the medium of a story may result in those things being better received than when communicated or commanded directly.

Seventh, the stories and legends tell us that the power and presence of God in our lives and in our world are much more than the power and presence of evil. The ultimate victory lies with the good and not the evil.

And finally, these stories tell us that a life that keeps away God and others is not a real life. We can pretend that God and others don't matter, but in reality they do. Closing our eyes does not make the whole world dark. It simply puts us in darkness.

Characters and characteristics might vary, but it appears that almost every community and culture across the world has and needs such stories and legends to fall back on. The story may have a religious, political, or cultural origin to it. It may be found in sacred texts or folklores. It may or may not have a historical backing. Whatever may be its source or shape, the story offers the community a path and a purpose. The story ensures the community's continuity and cohesion. The story keeps the community together. The story instills in them a sense of humility, encouraging them to learn from their past. The story inspires them to march on with unflagging spirit. The story tells them to live with faith and hope, trusting in God's providence and having faith in each other's goodness. The core message in all such stories seems to be "Let us not lose hope; let us strive to makes our lives and our world better. Let us not lose our focus and get stuck with all the rigmarole of our life; let us get to that which is bigger than ourselves." They may not see the complete materialization of the ideals and dreams contained in these stories, but they keep them alive and never stop telling them to their children and grandchildren. The hope is ever kept alive, and life moves on.

Although a community's ideals and dreams expressed through legends and stories may have a cultural, religious, or political origin, when it comes to their core message, most of them go beyond these considerations. Most people in all communities and on all continents desire a righteous, peaceful, and prosperous life. The legends and stories that we carry and pass on often have a universal appeal. As an extraordinary species, we have achieved many things. And as an ever innovative and insatiable group of seekers, we set for ourselves great goals and ideals, and they are often immortalized in our stories and legends.

4

A Different World

Although we have immortalized our ideals and dreams in our stories and legends, in the day-to-day affairs of our lives, we see ourselves far removed from them. The ideals and the actual are often far apart from each other. Peace and prosperity are hard to find. Righteousness and respect are hardly mentioned. "Extraordinariness" is a term that we find hard to identify with. We are engaged in unrighteous and acrimonious lifestyles. We promote atrocities and intolerance. We wage wars and unleash violence on to each other. We nurture hatred and aggression. We become parochial and territorial in our thinking and dealings. We are smothered by inequalities, intolerance, injustice, corruption, and deceptions in our communities and societies. We are caught up in extreme individualism or its opposite, the denial of individual rights. And we pass the buck and point fingers at each other.

In many communities across the world, we see this great divide between the ideal and the actual. We do things that make our goals and ideals remain as great showcase pieces or memorabilia that we take out occasionally to dust off or reminisce about. We simply become a link in the long chain of generations that kept alive these stories and legends and passed them on to the subsequent generations. The past generations kept alive their stories and legends and dreamed of a fantastic future. They made some progress, but they did things that made that progress look insignificant. They fought and they perished. They regressed faster than they progressed. We follow suit in many ways, with the exception that we have become more sophisticated in the way we fight or deceive each other. We make progress, but we also do things that make our progress look dispensable and dismissible. Our regression is sometimes quicker than our progression.

I often wondered why we experience this great dissonance between our ideals and reality. For a long time, the answer seemed to escape me. And then one day my attention was turned to one of my own experiences that I thought hit the nail right on the head. Let me share it here.

When I first came to the United States, I was confronted with a difficult problem: my accent. I had a different accent, and that made my communication with the natives a little difficult. Many of them were not used to the Indian accent.

Let me first clarify the terms "native" and "Indian," because these terms don't mean the same everywhere. I gradually realized that these terms, "native" and "Indian," meant different things in America. In the United States, "native" could also refer to the Native Americans, the indigenous people of the land. When I refer to the accent of the natives, it refers to those who use the American accent or American English as opposed to British English or other derivatives of English used in other countries. When I use the term "Indian," it refers to a citizen of India or a person of Indian origin. Sometimes the Native Americans in the United States are mistakenly called American Indians or simply Indians, a misnomer given to the native tribesmen and their families by the European explorers.

Now let me get back to what I was explaining. Until I came to the United States, I believed that when I spoke English, people could understand me. Not to be boastful by any means, but by the normal standards in India, I thought I was proficient in English because I had somewhat of a rigorous training in the language in the seminary. But the problem was not with my proficiency, but rather my accent. I had a different accent, and it did not match with that of the natives. The American accent was much different from my Indian accent. I was entering a very different world.

The "Indian flavor" in my English was natural. It took a while for me to recognize how different I sounded to the natives. Not wanting to feel like a total alien among my new acquaintances, I had to improve and refine my language skills. In a frantic effort to meet the expected standards of the natives, I began to adapt to the American accent, but unfortunately, more often than not, I got the American, British, and Indian accents mixed up.

Many English-speaking Indians who move to the United States for work, study, or permanent residence are often confronted with this difficulty. Indian-accented English sounds foreign to an American, and often there is great difficulty for each in understanding what the other is saying. This may be true of people from several other countries that move to the United States as well.

In India, speaking even not-so-perfect English is considered a great achievement, as it is a hard-to-learn language for many. Those who are English speakers are often bilingual or multilingual as well. English is the second language for the majority of Indians. There are three hundred or more languages in India, and many of them have their own alphabets. Indian English (if at all there is a usage so unique) has attained the flavors of many of these languages, and each person adds something of his or her style to it when it is spoken. It is like the same pan or pot being used to prepare many dishes without bothering to clean it after each item is prepared. Each dish gets some flavor from the dish or all of the dishes that came before it.

Present-day American English may not be too different in its history either. The British, the Irish, the Germans, the French, the Italians, the Norwegians, the Polish, and people of all other nationalities and ethnicities who moved to the United States did not have a single accent or style of speaking English at one time. What we call American English today is the current product of many combinations. Before that, they all spoke with their own accents, and some still continue to do so. As America is considered a melting pot of many cultures, American English could be thought of as a dish that came out of that melting pot. Indian English is no different. It is a dish that came out of the melting pot of many cultures and languages in India.

Even after it established its uniqueness, how does American English sound to the British, the original claimants of the language? I could be causing a world war here, but a couple of years back when I visited London, I had a seemingly true and patriotic Englishman comment to me, "Americans don't speak English." The British find the American accent strange and unfamiliar. And the Americans feel the same about the British. Listen to how the Americans and the British pronounce words like "God," "body," "laboratory," "doctor," "mobile," and "mob." They may sound like people from two planets. If you put an Indian with them, you wouldn't have to look for the Tower of Babel (see Ge 11:1–9) far away.

Although my accent was primarily Indian, when it came to the English accents of other countries, I was more attuned to the British accent than the American one. Hence, when I first came to the United States, I was pretty much new to the natives' style. I had great difficulty in understanding many Americans when they spoke.

We differ in the way we speak English. The difference becomes all the more pronounced if English is the second language and the speaker has a different mother tongue. When I learn another language, I might think that I have mastered that language perfectly well and that I can speak it like any native would. Unfortunately it is a false belief. I may come pretty close to how the natives speak, but it still will not be the same. I may not recognize the difference, but a native can feel it. It is even difficult for them to say how it is different. They can tell me only that I sound different.

The term "mother tongue" refers not only to vocabulary and grammar but also to the mother (and father) who has passed on to the child some inexplicable flavors of the language and culture that an outsider may not easily obtain. I may learn the meaning of a word in a foreign language, but I may not capture fully the culture and feeling that go with it as a native would. The cultural and emotional component of the word is not as easily accessible to me as it is to a native.

Some time back, someone asked me whether I think in English or in my mother tongue. I responded that when I converse in English, I think in English as well. But later, I thought about it further and came to realize something new. When I started learning English, I used to think in Malayalam, my mother tongue, and then translate it into English. Later, when I became more proficient in English, I started thinking in English as well. However, I realized that although I was thinking in English, I was not "feeling" in English. Feeling in English was yet another level that I had not moved into. I may speak, think, and write in English, but I may not be feeling in English. The feeling component comes easy for the natives, but not so for a foreigner, because the "mother/father" part of the language is missing for him or her. When one is speaking a language other than his or her mother tongue, the cultural and emotional component of the language is not easily accessible. An instructor may be able to give me only the meanings of words and not the feelings that go with them. With passage of time, immersion in the culture, and proficiency in the language, one may move into the feeling component of the language as well. A total immersion into a language involves speaking, thinking, feeling, and writing in that language. In this sense, many of us are outsiders when it comes to a different language or culture.

The variations in accents exist not only in terms of different nationalities but also with respect to different groups, regions, and states within the same country. Thus, in the United States, we have the Caucasian, the African American, the Hispanic, and the Asian versions of English. Within the Hispanic and Asian versions, there are still many differences based on the country or place of each person's origin. Then we have the Missourian, the Kentuckian, the Georgian, the Floridian, the Californian, the Illinoisan, and all such derivatives of American English depending on what state one comes from. And then we have the southern, the midwestern, the northeastern, and the western styles of the American English. Some time back, while spending a weekend at a church in Kentucky, I heard an interesting observation from the pastor there. Commenting on the differences in the way English is spoken in the United States, he said, "In one week I celebrate mass in English, and in the following week I do it in 'Kentuckian.'"

In the United Kingdom, there are variations in accents depending on whether one comes from England, Scotland, Wales, or Northern Ireland. Then there are differences in accents between those who live in the city and those in the countryside. In India, the Malayalis, Tamils, Kashmiris, Bengalis, Hindi-speaking Indians, and all other Indians representing other states or languages have their own versions of English. Although the introduction of English in India goes back to the colonial times or even before, Indians don't follow the British accent either. During the British rule, only very few Indians spoke English. Present-day Indian English evolved over the years after independence, and it has absorbed elements and styles from the many vernacular languages of the land.

Whether it is in the United States, Great Britain, or India, the truth is that English has become a regional language as much as it has become an international language. There is a great deal of difference between American English, British English, Indian English, Australian English, and Canadian English. Many people don't realize that English is not just what we hear on BBC or CNN. Considering the individual variations of English spoken in different countries and regions, we might even wonder who actually speaks the "correct" English.

We may assume that we all speak the same language, but we don't understand each other. We differ in our accents. Hence it is not surprising that sometimes we find ourselves somewhat strangers in someone else's territory.

So there it was, the answer to my question about why there was so much dissonance between our ideals and actuality. It is our "accent." As individuals and groups, we differ in our accents. This refers not just to our language but also to every aspect of our lives. We differ in many ways, and sometimes we get stuck in our differences. Our attachment to our accents or ways is often coupled with ignorance and biases about other accents and ways. We tend to think that our way is the only way, and that stands as a major hurdle in moving toward the realization of our ideals and dreams. We find it difficult to transcend our accents and develop a language that is understandable for all.

It is even difficult to comprehend how much and in how many ways we differ as individuals and groups. We differ in our physical, mental, social, and spiritual abilities. We differ in our looks, acts, and speech. We differ in our personalities and styles. We differ in our feelings, thinking, and execution of things. We differ in our occupations and interests. We differ in our races, ethnicities, religions, and languages. We differ in our customs, traditions, beliefs, and practices. We differ in our ideas, ideologies, opinions, values, and worldviews. We differ in our cultures and nationalities. We differ in the problems and issues that we face in life. We differ in the way we see, hear, and perceive things. We differ even in the way we see our differences.

If there are so many variations and difficulties with regard to our accents in language, how much more complex and complicated are our lives and relationships because of the individual and group differences that we bring? Our difficulties in understanding each other because of the differences in our accents is representative of the difficulties we experience in our lives and relationships because of the personal and communal differences and peculiarities we possess. We may do things that we think are perfectly fine, but they do not make sense for others. We perceive and understand things in certain ways, but often we don't realize that others don't see the same things in the same way. We think in certain ways and think that other people also think similarly. As we said about languages, we may think that others understand us, but often they don't. We don't realize that our accents do not match those of others.

These differences can cause enormous difficulties in our lives and relationships. When our accents do not match, we might get into confrontations or begin to avoid each other. In either case, our personal growth and development get stunted, and our interpersonal relationships are compromised. The difficulties in relationships do not necessarily have to be between two people representing two languages or cultures. It happens within our own homes, communities, and neighborhoods. Mismatched accents and the consequential problems could occur in any context of life.

When it comes to different accents in language and the difficulties arising out of them, some people might think that it is better to associate with their own kind than mingle with people who are different, so that they don't have to expend their energy in finding compatibility with those with different accents. Or some might say, "Why bother at all; you remain in your territory and I will remain in mine, and we will have no need to worry about each other's hard feelings." That might work in the case of a language. But we can't do that with our life and relationships. It is not just about me or my territory and culture. It is much more than that. It involves a great deal of other people and things. We can claim our individuality, but we cannot separate ourselves from others or the rest of the world.

5

Our Headlines and Primetime News

It is not a shocker anymore that all the primetime news and headlines on our TV, radio, and other electronic and print media are about the enormous amount of mismatches in people's accents all over the world. Our lives and relationships do not look pretty all the time. People get into conflicts and problems. There is a great mismatch in our accents. We don't understand each other. Differences in our accents that lead to problems in our lives stifle our growth and development.

Here are a few headlines and stories that I picked up from the *New York Times* in its November 26, 2014 Columbia, Missouri, edition that speak to this reality of mismatched accents and conflicted relationships between people and communities:

"Governor to Triple Guard Presence in Ferguson" (Davey & Fernandez, 2014): Our city, St. Louis, has been in the news for several weeks now. It all began with the fatal shooting of an unarmed black teenager by a white police officer in Ferguson, a city in St. Louis County. Demonstrations and violent protests have been going on in and around Ferguson for several weeks now, with people seeking justice and fairness. Racial tensions have been resurrected with this event, and when the decision of the grand jury not to indict the police officer was finally released, the anger and frustration of those who were waiting to hear the opposite were fanned into flames. They resorted to arson, looting, and riots in the St. Louis area, and angry protests have been reported in several other cities across the country. The governor of Missouri and the law enforcement agencies looked for ways to contain the violence and rising emotions. The shooting case and its aftereffects pointed to the still unhealed tensions and mistrust between people of different races and law enforcement agencies. There is a mismatch of accents between all the parties concerned.

"US-Led Raid Rescues Eight Held in Yemen" (Schmitt, 2014): The United States commandos and Yemeni troops are reported to have rescued eight hostages taken captive and kept in a cave in a remote part of Yemen by a militant group associated with al-Qaeda. Militant groups operating with extremist religious and ideological views have claimed innumerable lives all over the world in their efforts to outdo their opponents or make their voices heard. They declare war on governments and opposing groups and cause immense suffering and colossal damage to life and property. They vow not to give up their fight until they implement their agenda in the community or nation that they intend to overtake. It is a mismatch of accents between the general population and religious and ideological extremists.

"At European Parliament, Pope Bluntly Critiques a Continent's Malaise" (Higgins, 2014): Addressing the European Parliament in Strasbourg, France, Pope Francis is reported to have given a gentle and yet introspective address to the members. He reminded the parliamentarians about how the world today views Europe. He also reminded them about how their own citizens viewed the institutions they had built up. In both cases, the pope said, there appeared to be a disconnect—a disconnect between Europe and the rest of the world, and a disconnect between the citizens of Europe and their union's bureaucracy. The pope urged the members to become more embracive of the world and its citizens rather than keeping themselves aloof and elite. The pope pointed to a deep-seated problem that plagues not only Europe but also many cultures and countries across the globe. There is a disconnect or mismatch of accents between the government and the governed, institutions and the general population, and cultures and communities.

"Breaking Silence, Top Leader Says Iran Is Standing Up to West in Nuclear Talks" (Erdbrink, 2014): Negotiations have been going on for several years between Iran and countries in the West regarding Iran scrapping its ambitions to build nuclear weapons. Although the deadline for concluding the negotiations was extended for several more months, Iran's supreme leader, Ayatollah Ali Khamenei, is reported to have taken a tough stand with the Western negotiators. Nations have been at loggerheads on the international arena regarding various issues, and there is a widespread mistrust between several of these countries even when they come to the negotiating table. There is a large amount of mismatch in accents between many countries and leaders.

"Clashes Erupt in Hong Kong as Police Try to Clear Part of a Protest Camp" (Buckley & Wong, 2014): Prodemocracy protests and demonstrations have been going on in Hong Kong for several weeks now. Most of the protestors being students, the police have been cautious and yet forceful in their strategies to disperse the crowd and weaken the spirit of the protestors. The protestors demand that the Chinese government allow free and fair elections in the metropolis rather than forcing their chosen candidates on the electorate. With the Tiananmen Square incident of 1989 remaining as a black spot in its history, the Chinese government also appeared to be cautious in its approach to the present protests in Hong Kong. In any case, the incidents pointed to a serious mismatch of accents between the government and the governed.

"U.N. Extends Help for South Sudan" (Baquet, 2014): The Republic of South Sudan has been reeling under fights between government troops and rebel forces for several months. The rebels are reported to have seized major cities. The conflict has taken the country to a bloody civil war. Several lives have been lost, houses and properties have been destroyed, and thousands of people have been forced out of their homes. Although the conflict is between the government and the rebels, essentially it points to a mismatch of accents between rival ethnic groups and communities.

"Two Suicide Bombers Kill Dozens in Nigeria" (Idris & Gladstone, 2014): Scores of people have reportedly been killed in a suicide attack in a crowded market in Maiduguri in Nigeria. Although no one took the responsibility for the carnage, the militant group Boko Haram was suspected to be the culprit. The said group has been fighting the government for several years, and they have been engaged in fatal attacks and mass abductions of people. There is an intense mismatch of accents between the rebel group, the government, and the general population.

"After Obama's Immigration Action, a Blast of Energy for the Tea Party" (Peters, 2014): President Obama's decision to bypass Congress and use his executive power to overhaul immigration policy is reported to have emboldened the Tea Party movement, the conservative base within the Republican Party that has been opposing any change to the current immigration policy. The Republicans and the Democrats have been at loggerheads for years with regard to overhauling the immigration policy of the nation. Although a bipartisan group of senators had proposed sweeping changes in the policy, making it easier for the 11 million illegal immigrants in the United States to obtain legal status or citizenship, the issue still remains unresolved. There is a lot of mistrust and many differences of opinion between all the parties concerned. There is a clear mismatch of accents between the opposing political parties as well as between the illegal immigrants themselves and those who oppose the granting of legal status to them.

These are just a few of the story lines in a day's news in a single newspaper. Imagine what we would have if we were to scan all the other circulations of all the media all over the world. We would have thousands of such story lines of mismatches of accents and the consequent conflicts and problems in all intensities and forms in people's lives. A closer look at them will tell us that it is the mismatch of accents and the resultant conflicts and problems in people's relationships that get the most coverage in all the news media all over the world. By the time this book goes into print, people will have moved past many of these stories. But new stories of mismatched accents and the resultant problems and issues in people's relationships keep coming every day.

6

On Our Home Front

Scanning through newspapers and other media, we get a glimpse of the mismatches in accents and the resultant problems and issues that are out there. But the media grabs only the sensational pieces. They may report about mismatches in accents and problematic relationships leading nations to wars and communities to violence. Or they might talk about mismatched accents and conflicted relationships between groups with opposing ideologies leading to militant fights and terrorist activities. But how about the state of affairs on our home front?

We don't need to turn to newspapers and TV; we can find mismatched accents and the resultant problems and issues in our own ordinary, everyday lives. Mismatched accents lead people not only to big problems, as seen in newspapers and on TV, but also to small disruptions in their everyday lives. It happens in our families, schools, neighborhoods, and communities. Spouses don't get along with each other, parents and children don't understand each other, and siblings fight with each other or keep to themselves. Mismatches in accents and conflicted relationships drive couples to divorce attorneys and courts, parents and their children to therapists and mental health professionals, adults and adolescents to psychiatrists, teens and others to drug courts and treatment facilities, teachers and students to school counselors, employers and employees to grievance redress forums, and providers and consumers to consumer courts. Families and friends part ways when they differ in their accents and issues are not contained.

We can think of thousands of instances in our daily lives where our accents don't match with those of others. Family life, for example, is beautiful, but often it is disrupted because of mismatched accents. If everyone gets along with each other, things go well. But sometimes that doesn't happen very easily. They argue and fight. They nag and irritate. And they harass and humiliate. Think of a woman who walks around upset and angry all day because she had an argument with her husband about some family matters. They don't talk, and no one bothers to cool their tempers down. "How can he be so insensitive?" she asks. "Why is she so sensitive?" he asks. They both find each other unreasonable. The environment is tense, and there is a clear mismatch in their accents.

Another woman finds her husband cold and uncaring and engages in a verbal fight with him. She takes out her anger on her children and things in the house. The situation is tense, and no one is talking. In another family, the husband—who is a chronic alcoholic—comes home kicking and screaming every day. His wife and children have had enough of his drama. "How can he come home drunk like this every day?" she asks. "Why can't I have a drink?" he asks. Their thoughts look reasonable in their minds, but their accents don't match.

Families with young children are often a school for learning patience. Think of a woman's day beginning with a lot of yelling and screaming as she gets her children ready for school. The kids test her patience as they make a fuss over their breakfast, uniforms, lunch boxes, toys, school, teachers, friends, etc. The tension is high, and the mother and her children are on the verge of explosion. They find it difficult to understand each other's accents. The mother later feels sorry for her emotional outbursts, but this becomes a daily routine. It drains everyone of strength and energy.

Sometimes the kids' priorities and adults' priorities in families are different. Consider the situation of a family where a little girl wants to play with her mommy, but her mommy is watching her favorite TV show and does not want to be disturbed. When the kid persists with the demand, the mother gets irritated and says, "For crying out loud, can't you see what I am doing; can you leave me alone for a moment?" The mother is not able to understand the daughter, and the daughter is not able to understand her mother. They are not too happy with each other.

Handling teenagers is not an easy task for many parents. They don't know what hurts and what helps. Think of an adolescent picking a fight with her mother and her mother yelling at her: "You are the worst daughter I ever had!" the mother shouts. The mother later feels sorry for saying that, but she has had enough of her daughter's attitude and acting out. Their accents often do not match.

Think of another family where a young man begins using drugs and alcohol, and engaging in other destructive behaviors. His father goes ballistic in his outbursts toward him: "I wish I never had a son like you!" Later he regrets saying that, but he has no clue about how to deal with his son. The accents of the father and son often do not match.

There are families in which members cut themselves off from each other. They stop communicating and blame each other for it. They don't talk for years. No one bothers to take the first step in melting the ice. They think keeping away from each other will solve the problems, but it doesn't. It is like a brewing kettle waiting for its lid to burst open. In some families, the pent-up emotions and feelings come out in the open in the form of denigration and contempt. They berate and attack each other. A mother-in-law, for example, makes a scathing attack on her much-disliked daughter-in-law in front of everybody at a family get-together: "She is so obnoxious," she says. And the daughter-in-law does not mince her words about her mother-in-law either. "She is so disgusting," she retorts. The mismatch of accents between the two women is no more a secret.

Teachers and students sometimes do not understand each other's accent. Think of a teacher who is punitive or a student who is disruptive in the class. They both see the other as the problem. What kind of teacher is this? What kind of student is this? They each have the same question directed at the other.

Good neighbors are a blessing, but sometimes we don't get to choose them. There are neighborhoods where people are constantly in fights with each other. They fight over their boundaries and fences, their kids and animals, and their races and beliefs. They use curse words and abusive language. They fight verbally and physically. And they maintain a tense relationship that could collapse any time.

Places of work can be refreshing or depressing. For some, their work environment is positive and healthy, while for others it is negative and burdensome. Think of a supervisor who finds it hard to work with some of her subordinates because the latter are critical, lazy, and gossipy. Or think of a supervisor who is bossy and too demanding. His subordinates and coworkers find it hard to work with him. In such places, they are not the best of friends and they try to avoid each other as much as possible. Their accents do not match, and they create an unhealthy work environment for each other.

While driving or shopping, it is not uncommon to see people trying to outdo each other. Crazy drivers are not rare on the roads. They cruise along the highways, cutting in front of everyone. In shopping malls or other places, people cut in line to place themselves in front of others. Negative reactions and responses from others are immediate in many such instances. People let out mouthfuls of nasty words at perpetrators of such rude behavior. Their accents do not match, and their days do not go well.

There are several other instances in everyday life that we can think of in which our accents do not match with those of others. Family members, friends, coworkers, and community members fight and fume over things they do or say. People fight over property, prestige, and power. They keep grudges and hatred in their heart. They dominate, exploit, and abuse. They cheat and lie. They see others as objects for their pleasure. They dislike and denigrate others because of their racial, religious, and regional differences. They allow their emotions to take over their reason. They speak words that hurt, and do things that harm. They get into a pattern of relating with others in a wrong way. They think that they are behaving perfectly well, but it doesn't make sense for others.

Sometimes our accents are so mismatched that we have to either disengage or remain in perpetual conflict. When our accents do not match, or when we are not able to go beyond our accents, our personal growth and relationships get disrupted. We don't see eye to eye, and we don't understand each other. In many of these instances, things may not escalate to a point where they make it to the front pages of newspapers. But they disrupt our daily lives. These mismatches in accents take different forms and shapes individually and communally, and they keep our ideals and actuality far apart from each other.

7

Two Drives

If the differences in our accents cause so many problems in our daily lives, it is important to understand how we develop them and how they scuttle our personal growth and interpersonal relationships. There are two concepts that I wish to introduce here to aid in the understanding of this problem. They are the drive to survive (DTS) and the drive to thrive (DTT).

Language has its own limitations. Certain words may not capture the whole experience or phenomenon that we are trying to communicate. I feel that limitation when I use the word "drive." "Drive" is a word that has been used much in psychology and other fields. Hearing the word itself may make some people associate it with what they have heard or learned before. Generally, the word "drive" is associated with the drive theory in psychology, in which it refers to impulses and urges. Sigmund Freud, the father of psychoanalysis, used this term in his theories. In my use of the word "drive," it means much more than an urge or impulse. It could be a need, an urge, a desire, a push, a motivation, a capacity, an ability, a right, or a duty, and sometimes all of these. It is both psychological and physical. It has a neurological basis, as the brain's functioning is an integral part of the operations of the drive.

Drive can sometimes be an instinctual and unconscious desire, while at other times it might operate as a rational and conscious desire. Sometimes it may feel like an effort, while at other times it may seem like a natural course of action. Sometimes it is limited to the physical and psychological realm, but at other times it extends to the spiritual realm. Sometimes it appears to be a right, but at other times, it feels like a duty. In short, a drive, as it is conceptualized here, is a physical, neurological, psychological, social, and spiritual phenomenon that is operational in a human being, sometimes consciously and at other times unconsciously. That having been established, let us look at what the drive to survive and the drive to thrive are.

The Drive to Survive (DTS)

The drive to survive, which from now on I will mostly refer to as DTS, is basically a need of an organism to survive or stay alive. An organism first needs to stay alive to accomplish whatever it is meant to accomplish. Without being alive, it cannot accomplish the task. But to stay alive is not easy, because of the challenges that come the organism's way and threaten its survival. The threats can be internal and external, physical and psychological (although psychological threats apply more to human beings than other organisms). A terminal illness is an example of an internal physical threat. A deep depression that ultimately leads to suicide or other forms of death is an example of an internal psychological threat. An example of an external threat is a natural disaster, such as an earthquake. A fear of an inimical person or group is an example of an external psychological threat. An organism has to battle all these challenges to stay alive. Some have to fight hard, while others may not need to do so much. Whether they succeed to stay alive or not is altogether a different matter. Almost all organisms put up a good fight to survive and stay alive. Some win and some lose.

In this battle to survive, sometimes it is not even a consciously thought-out action. It comes across as an instinctual motivation to stay alive. Sometimes it would seem to be one of the most basic instincts. However, each organism fights for its survival according to its nature. That would mean that the way a human being fights to stay alive is different from how an animal of a different nature tries to stay alive. The way a cat fights to stay alive is different from how a mouse fights to stay alive. Each employs tools that are available and specific to its nature to accomplish this task. When it comes to human beings, we may employ our thinking and imagination to find ways to stay alive, and it could be a conscious and rational act. For the lesser forms of beings, since such tools are not available in their nature, they have to purely depend on other instinctual cues that are available to them.

The drive to survive is primarily geared toward physical survival. A conducive emotional and psychological environment will undoubtedly enhance physical survival. Physical survival requires many things. It requires adequate bodily nourishment by way of food and drink. It involves protection from inclement weather or the fury of nature by way of finding or creating a comfortable shelter and clothing. Protection from life-threatening diseases is another requirement necessary for an organism's survival. Safety from the attack of predators, wild and violent animals, or other human beings is necessary for any organism's survival. In the case of human beings, along with the physical facilities and facilitators, if they are provided with adequate emotional and psychological support, their survival becomes easier. In any case, these basic requirements must be more or less met for any organism to survive.

DTS often operates in a person without much fanfare. Unless there is a real threat to our survival, we don't even become conscious of the operation of DTS in us. But when we do come under some specific threat to our survival, we become more conscious of its operation. When something or somebody threatens us, we realize how we immediately move into a heightened state of survival mode. All our energy is concentrated on this one motive—that is, to stay alive or survive.

Researchers such as Tom Smeets and his colleagues, and Erno Hermans and his companions, have suggested that when our survival is threatened, our whole system comes under acute stress, and the stress, in turn, creates changes in our brain function and physiological responses. The critical situation that creates stress and threatens our survival could be an accident, an illness, a natural calamity, an attack from a violent animal or person, or acute hunger and thirst. These situations could leave us in a heightened state of emergency. We immediately move into a survival mode. Our brain activities change instantly. Even without us being aware of it, our brain engages in an instant strategic reallocation of resources that is necessary for our survival. A supplementary dose of energy becomes available to us. We enter into a fight-or-flight physiological response. The hypothalamic-pituitary-adrenal axis gets activated. And various hormones and neurotransmitters, such as cortisol and noradrenaline, are released.

All these activities and responses in our system, particularly in our brain, happen in a matter of seconds. Our system accesses everything that helps its survival. We know how our body reacts when we have a panic attack or feel anxiety. For those who work out in a gym or in the open, it takes about fifteen or twenty minutes of working out to break a sweat, but it doesn't take even fifteen seconds to sweat profusely when shaken by anxiety or panic. Our system responds to threats quickly and in full force.

But once the threat disappears, we begin to relax and distribute our energy to other tasks that help us to move to higher levels of growth and development. After the threat subsides, for some time—or until the next emergency occurs—we don't pay much attention to DTS operating in us. That doesn't mean DTS stops operating. DTS ensures our survival around the clock.

For all organisms, this battle for survival is a lifelong process. Until death puts a natural end to that survival, each organism fights to stay afloat. Young or old, born or in the womb, sick or healthy, every single individual is driven by this need for survival. We see sick children or children who are threatened by some impending danger fighting tooth and nail to protect themselves and stay alive. Older men and women are no exception; they do the same. People who are threatened by predators, violent animals and human beings, deadly illnesses, and natural disasters all long for one thing—to stay alive.

Some organisms keep fighting, while others give up the fight after they reach a certain age or a certain point. Some give up the fight happily, while others do it out of frustration or helplessness. DTS is necessary for our life. It keeps us alive and going.

The Drive to Thrive (DTT)

The Drive to Thrive, which from now on will be mostly referred to as DTT, is the phenomenon that facilitates our growth and development. It is a drive that is present in all of us and is necessary for our life. You may have seen children or adults who have a condition called "failure to thrive." Failure to thrive is a condition of significant failure to gain appropriate weight and height as per the recognized norms for age and gender. It is a condition seen more commonly in children than adults. It often results from malnourishment, and in some cases it may have a psychological basis. The failure to thrive is more in reference to a child's physical state than his or her mental or emotional condition.

DTT refers to an individual's overall functioning. It has a particular emphasis on the mental, emotional, social, and spiritual processes that take an individual to higher levels of growth and development. DTT is not just about physical survival; it is rather about the overall progress and development of an individual. It is not just enough to survive; the person wants and needs to thrive as well. It is not just enough to stay alive; the person wants and needs to live well. The person wants and needs to grow and develop.

To describe it a little more specifically, DTT focuses on bringing the best out of a person. It refers to physical growth and intellectual development. It includes spiritual advancements and the emotional and psychological well-being. It consists of personal and professional excellence. It includes the person's social life and growth in interpersonal relationships. It is all of these. It is a power that is in us that takes us to higher levels of growth and development. It helps us to do well with our life and become a blessing for others. It ultimately helps us to be in union with God and others. Thriving is not real thriving if we don't get to this ultimate goal.

These days, when people think of growth and development or speak about bringing the best out of themselves, sometimes only a few dimensions, such as the physical, intellectual, and economic realms, come to their mind. But such a compartmentalized approach neglects the other areas of our life. DTT is not limited only to a few realms of our life, but rather to our overall development. It undoubtedly manifests itself in very visible ways in some of these realms, depending on each one's strength and ability. For example, DTT takes the individual to higher levels of physical functioning. It builds on the accomplishments of DTS and provides adequate stamina, strength, and ability to the individual to perform complex physical tasks and functions. In the intellectual realm, it helps the person to acquire knowledge and skills that are required for carrying out the various tasks of everyday life or a career. Spiritually, DTT helps the person to go beyond himself or herself and find communion with God and others. But the real scope of DTT is comprehensive and wide-ranging. It includes every aspect of our lives. The physical and the psychological, the economic and the emotional, the social and the political, the religious and the spiritual—all of these come under the purview of DTT.

Focusing on only a few dimensions of our life does not develop us to our full potential. Certain persons, groups, or communities may limit the operations of their DTT to only a few of these realms, but that does not bring the best out of them. One may be excellent in his or her professional work but terrible when it comes to interpersonal relationships. No one may be able to relate to that person because of his or her unfriendly attitude, behavior, and personality. One may be very intelligent and skillful, but very disorderly and messy when it comes to personal life, morals, and values. One may be on the top of the economic ladder in society, with money and materials flowing in unlimitedly, but he or she may be at the bottom of the ladder when it comes to human qualities. One may appear to be very religious and spiritual, but he or she could be a divisive and unhealthy force in the community or neighborhood.

The drive to thrive (DTT) is about bringing the best out of every possible dimension of one's life. It is about finding a balance between the social and political, physical and psychological, economic and emotional, and intellectual and spiritual dimensions of our lives. It is a way to reach perfection as a human being. It is a life force that takes the individual to this perfection, to higher levels of overall growth and development. It is a power that is in us that helps us to do well. When our life is conceptualized as going beyond the physical realities of this world, DTT becomes the springboard for life eternal. It helps us to find a union with God and others in eternity. DTT's scope and purview, in other words, are over and beyond what is physical and temporal. But whatever can be envisioned as transphysical and eternal has to be an extension and continuation of what we truly manifest in our temporal and physical life here on earth.

The drive to survive (DTS), as mentioned, is a phenomenon that we see throughout our lives. We need to stay alive to move from one moment to the other, from one stage of our development to the other. Every organism does its best to meet the goal of this drive with a zest for life and a longing to stay alive. Until the last breath departs from us, we all fight a good fight to stay alive. And this is not peculiar to human beings; it is the same for all living organisms. Fortunately or unfortunately, some make it and some don't. The departure of some might be viewed as good for the survival of the rest. For example, the death and disappearance of disease-causing germs and organisms, predatory animals and birds, and criminals and terrorists might be viewed as a blessing for those who are subjected to their attacks. However, when it comes to life, every living organism, good or bad, gives a good fight to stay alive.

Being tired of this constant fight, or because of some other reasons, some human beings might give up the desire to stay alive. However, that is usually not because they don't want to stay alive, but because they see the futility of the fight and the weak prospects of making it much further. Some take their disappointments and anger out on themselves and end their lives. Suicide and self-destructive behaviors are not too uncommon these days. However, for the vast majority of people, surviving and staying alive are of utmost importance.

The drive to thrive (DTT), on the other hand, is a much more complex phenomenon. It is not peculiar to human beings. Nonhuman living beings also manifest a movement toward growth and development and have a sort of urge to realize their fullest being. But there is a distinction. Simply as a movement for growth and development, DTT may seem common to all living beings. But as a phenomenon that is open to one's conscious awareness, it is unique to human beings. The unique faculties of human beings, the faculties that make us who we are, make me draw a line of distinction between human beings and other living beings.

The specific constructs that make us up as human beings—such as the will, intellect, emotions, intuition, imagination, reason, memory— are alien to other living beings. Our ability to think, feel, and fantasize, and the ability to think about our thinking, feel about our feeling, and fantasize about our fantasies are uniquely our own. The goodness and the inner beauty that human beings possess, and the ability to be aware of them, are alien to all other beings. Human beings can choose to be either destructive or nondestructive in their survival and thriving. The ability to choose and the capacity to become conscious of DTS and DTT are not conceivable for nonhuman beings. Other living beings are incapable of making a conscious choice about the direction that they should or want to take. The ability to love and the ability to be conscious about one's ability to love are not conceivable for nonhuman beings. The ability to be the subject and object of one's reflections and thoughts is not conceivable for nonhuman beings. The ability to love God and others, and the ability to know that we are being loved by God and others is special to us.

Our hearts not only pump blood but also burst with love and goodness. Our brains not only coordinate the complex communication system in our body but also emanate the rays of goodness and inner beauty that can transform everything and everyone around us. So while I acknowledge an instinctual urge toward growth and physical development in all other living beings, I credit only human beings with this specific phenomenon of the drive to thrive (DTT).

DTS and DTT are universal. Whether one is young or old; rich or poor; man or woman, Christian, Hindu, Jew, or Muslim; educated or uneducated; from this nation or the other; from this race or the other; from this language or the other; from a village or town; a president of a nation or a peasant; a healthy person or sick; religious or secular; married or single; of this caste or that caste; or enslaved or free, everyone wants and needs to survive, and everyone wants and needs to thrive.

DTS and DTT are more prominently manifested in some than others; nevertheless, they are present in everyone. Some stay alive; others perish. Some thrive and bring the best out of themselves, others do not thrive much, and still others bring the worst out of themselves.

In the movement toward the higher levels of growth and development, DTS plays an important role. DTS ensures that the individual stays alive so that he or she can thrive. In other words, DTS is an antecedent as well as a constant for DTT. To put it simply, we need to survive to thrive. We need to stay alive to make progress. As and when DTS does its job, DTT unfolds its operations. When survival is ensured or is not under threat, a person can invest his or her energy in the operations of DTT, which takes him or her to higher levels of growth and development.

Although both DTS and DTT are important in a person's growth and development, in the case of certain people in certain situations, all that matters is DTS. DTT does not appear much on their radar. For example, children or people living in war-torn areas do not and cannot think of anything except staying alive. Their survival is constantly under threat. They live in the midst of gunshots and bombings. They don't have the luxury of desiring or longing for growth and development as understood in terms of DTT. They desire just to stay alive. Similar things could be said of people living in extreme poverty or living with life-threatening diseases. They cannot think of anything except trying to stay alive. It is not that they don't have a desire to thrive, but they cannot have that luxury as long as their physical life and survival are under threat. In those circumstances, survival becomes primary. They need to stay alive to thrive.

8

Divergent Operations

Both the drive to survive (DTS) and the drive to thrive (DTT) are necessary for a person's life and growth. DTS ensures the person's survival, and DTT takes the person on the path of growth and development. However, both these phenomena could generate mismatches in accents and consequent problems and difficulties in people's lives. On the one hand, they are good and necessary, but on the other, they cause trouble for oneself and others.

DTS is a natural generator of mismatch in accents and consequent problems in people's lives. When a human organism comes into being, there is already way too much deficiency in meeting the basic requirements for his or her survival. Starting from the prenatal stage and continuing through the different stages of their lives, many are deprived of things that are necessary for a healthy life and growth. They are exposed to things that constantly threaten their survival.

There is no adequate bodily nourishment for millions of children and adults all over the world. There is way too much poverty in many parts of the world. Poverty and injustice can make people resentful toward unjust systems and those who live in luxury and abundance. It becomes a vicious circle of one leading to the other. Neglect, injustice, and exploitation make people resentful toward perpetrators of those crimes, and those people might resort to robbery, violence, and revenge. Robbery, violence, and revenge, in turn, make the victims of such crimes resentful toward those who perpetrate them, and those people might resort to violence and revenge in return. They all end up speaking with mismatched accents.

Children who are victims of neglect and abuse in families might turn against their parents, family members, and others. They become a threat for each other. Protection from the fury of nature or inclement weather is always a daunting task for many. Floods, tornadoes, hurricanes, cyclonic storms, snowstorms, drought, lightning, deadly cloudbursts, earthquakes, tsunamis, mudslides, and all such occurrences in the nature pose a threat to people's need for survival. All these natural disasters destroy and displace people and leave them frustrated and angry. Protection from life-threatening diseases is an unfinished work and will continue to be so for ages to come. Attacks of predatory, venomous, and violent animals have always been a problem for many. Deficiency in the availability of the required resources for survival is a given, and many people are born into this deficient environment. Such an environment is a natural generator of mismatch in accents and consequent problems and conflicts.

And then there are others who think that their survival would be better if others did not survive. So they exterminate or silence those whom they see as a threat to their survival. Violence and aggression unleashed by human beings on their fellow human beings provides the top captions in daily news. Gunmen appear from nowhere and shoot and kill people at random. Frenzied mobs pounce on innocent people and turn villages and towns into battlefields. Tens and hundreds are killed mercilessly in war-torn countries and regions. Women and children are abused and assaulted in many families and communities. In many places people live in fear. Most of these victims are unprepared for these eventualities and attacks when they occur. And when they occur, people run for their lives. They try to defend themselves and stay alive. The first instinct for all the victims and survivors is to guard against the enemy and ensure their survival. To protect themselves, they might get hold of anything they can find: guns, swords, arrows, etc. If provoked, they may become aggressive and violent in return.

There are many such factors that threaten people's survival. We want to stay alive and survive, but there is way too much threat against that instinct all around us. Because there is already this deficiency and disequilibrium on all these fronts, everyone is guarded against all possible threats. Many people are in constant readiness to fight the enemy and stay afloat. It is like a person drowning and fighting to the best of his ability to come up to the surface so that he can breathe again. In that fight there is only one motivation and that is to breathe and stay alive. Those who can fight the odds and challenges may survive; others perish. When it comes to survival, everyone is vulnerable.

The phenomenon of DTS does not necessarily have to create a mismatch in accents and problems, but it has the potential to trigger them. The injuries people absorb into their bodies and psyches in the process of ensuring their survival have an enormous negative impact on how they relate to others.

The operations of DTT are more complex and complicated. Thriving can mean different things to different people, and hence its capacity to generate mismatch in accents and problems is multilayered. Even when the needs of DTS are satisfactorily attended to, DTT could generate problems in our lives. In itself, DTT is an amoral phenomenon; it is neither good nor bad. It is a phenomenon that goes with our "human-beingness."

We all want and need to thrive. But this need or urge to thrive unfolds in people in multiple ways. In general, it can take two distinct routes in its manifestation in a person. It can either be positive or negative. The person can thrive positively or negatively. It can also operate in the person on these two levels simultaneously. The person driven by the positive dimension of thriving will show a genuine interest and passion for living a good life, free from negativity and destruction. His or her life will be marked by a desire for growth and development and a passion for realizing his or her fullest being. The person may take the route of excellence through hard work, honest and respectful interpersonal relationships, and an uncompromising stand on life-promoting values and principles. He or she may strive to bring the best out of himself or herself and become a blessing for others. Such individuals keep their eyes focused on giving their best and finding a union with God and others. The person driven by the negative dimension of thriving, on the other hand, will show the least interest in living a good and honest life. He or she will try to thrive by becoming aggressive, manipulative, destructive, deceptive, and extremely narcissistic. Such individuals bring the worst out of themselves. They live for themselves and care less about God and others. Although negative and destructive, they also might claim that they are thriving.

Both the positive and negative operations of DTT can be ongoing in the same person simultaneously. In some, the positive dimension dominates, while in others the negative dimension may be prominent.

Thus the goodness or badness of DTT depends on the way this phenomenon is channeled and manifested in a person. It is like a flame from a lamp or candle, which can bring light and warmth to people but can also burn and destroy. The effect depends on where it is placed and how it is handled. If it is placed in a secure place and guarded with caution, it fulfills its function of giving light and warmth to those around it. And when its mission is accomplished, it extinguishes itself silently. But if it is left somewhere carelessly and no one bothers to guard it, it may begin to spread fire to things around, destroying the whole place. Someone will have to extinguish it violently or with much effort.

To determine whether a person's DTT is positively or negatively operating, we have to look at its effect on him or her and others. How do we qualify this as good or bad? We do so by evaluating its manifestation and impact on a person and others. A simple thing such as honey can be good and bad. Most of us like honey and enjoy its sweetness. We consider it good. But the same honey can be bad if the doctor has told us that it is detrimental for our health and has forbidden us from eating it. If we ignore the warning of the doctor and go ahead with eating the honey, it could turn out to be a bad material for our body. So the goodness or the badness of something is often based on its impact on others and ourselves. But that is not the only criterion in determining the goodness or badness of something.

We also evaluate the goodness and badness of something on the basis of certain fundamental moral principles and accepted norms of behaviors prevalent in human cultures and communities. When narrowed down, we realize that these fundamental moral principles are also based on certain value judgments about the impact of human behaviors—that is, whether our behaviors have a negative or positive impact on others and us. Some of these principles are universally accepted, while others are particular to each community or society. The Ten Commandments in the Bible (Ex 20:1–17; Dt 5:6–21), for example, is one of the foundations for Christian morality. Summing up these commandments to two, Jesus said, "'You shall love the Lord your God with all your heart, and with all your soul, and with all your mind.' This is the greatest and first commandment. And a second is like it: 'You shall love your neighbor as yourself.' On these two commandments hang all the law and the prophets" (Mt 22:37–40).

These commandments basically boil down to finding a balance between the love of God, love of neighbor, and love of oneself. Anything that damages this love for God, others, and oneself is thus bad. Another foundation for Christian morality is the Sermon on the Mount, particularly, the Beatitudes (Matthew 5–7). The goodness or the badness of one's actions can be based on these teachings of Jesus. Although sometimes people debate the universality of some of the universal moral principles, most societies and communities have certain norms by which they determine what is good and what is bad. Even if some try to justify their acts as not bad, if they go against these accepted norms of the community or society and have a negative impact on their lives or the lives of others, they would be considered bad.

In its true sense, DTT is meant to help a person to grow, develop, and bring the best out of himself or herself. DTT helps people to bring out their goodness and beauty, and abilities and talents to further their personal growth and development as well as to be a source of support for others in their development. It is meant to help a person to find communion with God and others. They will not see others as a threat or as an object for their self-aggrandizement. They will rather strive to make others' lives better and make this world a better place. They will live by the universally accepted fundamental moral principle of finding a balance between the love of God, love of neighbor, and love of oneself. Such individuals will remain open to God's ways so that they will "have life, and have it abundantly" (Jn 10:10).

Those who are driven by the negative dimension of DTT will exhibit behaviors that are contrary to healthy living and relationships. They are not driven by a true love for God, others, and themselves, but rather a false sense of thriving. Sometimes they might care more about themselves and less about God and others. They will follow their ways rather than God's ways. They will exhibit extreme narcissism and individualistic endeavors without any regard for anyone else. They rarely show any empathy for others' feelings. They will have no regret in causing injury or harm to others. They don't develop a sense of remorse or guilt.

When extremely negative, DTT in a person can take a monstrous form, causing the person to desire, plan, and execute the total annihilation of others. It is like a degenerative disease. It eats into the whole person and makes the person sick. It makes the person constantly speak with wrong accents and engage in conflicts with others. It has a ripple effect on every aspect of his or her life. It brings the worst out of that person. Sometimes the person's sickness spreads to others in the community and the whole system becomes ugly.

Sometimes people in this situation might not care about anybody, even themselves. They become negative and destructive toward all, including themselves, or simply waste away. They will cause great damage to themselves. They don't truly love themselves. Instead of bringing the best out of themselves, they bring out the worst, which leads to their own destruction.

As in the case of DTS, DTT doesn't have to necessarily cause mismatches in accents or problems in relationships. However, when negatively oriented, it does. It is not difficult to imagine that the injuries that people absorb into their body and psyche, particularly in the early stages of their life, could have enormous negative impacts on the manifestation of their DTT in later life. Injustice, exploitation, and abuses could sow the seeds of negative DTT in people who are subjected to such crimes. Negatively oriented and self-focused individuals bring the worst out of themselves.

Both DTS and DTT are necessary for our life, but they have a potential for triggering mismatches in our relationships as well. The irreparable conflicts in interpersonal relationships, divisions in families and communities, and wars and violence between groups or nations point to the intensity of mismatch of accents and consequent problems in people's lives. In their mad rush for thriving or frantic effort to stay alive, some people threaten and exploit others, while others resent the state of affairs they find themselves in. Both DTS and DTT have the potential to take a person either to a healthy growth and development or to conflictual relationships and self-destruction.

PART II

The Battle for Survival and Growth

9

Origin and Development

If the major source of the mismatch in our accents and the consequent problems in our lives can be traced back to the operations of DTS and DTT in us, we need to understand these phenomena in greater detail. We need to understand how and when exactly these phenomena originate in us. We need to understand how they gain the potential for troubles and problems. A short exploratory journey into the various developmental stages of our life might help us to understand the origin and the operations of these two phenomena.

In terms of an individual's physical development, theorists often break down the whole life span into different periods or milestones. These periods of development often range from the prenatal stage to old age. Breaking these down into specific stages, Benjamin J. Sadock and Virginia A. Sadock in their book, *Kaplan & Sadock's Synopsis of Psychiatry*, included the following in an individual's life span: the prenatal period (conception to birth), infancy (birth to 15 months), childhood (end of infancy to 12 years), adolescence (11 to 20 years), and adulthood (age 20 to death). Some of these stages could be further broken down into substages. Childhood, for example, consists of toddlerhood, preschool period, and middle years. Adolescence consists of early (11 to 14 years), middle (14 to 17 years), and late (17 to 20 years) periods. And adulthood consists of early adulthood (20 to 40 years), middle adulthood (40 to 65 years), and late adulthood or old age.

When considering the origin and development of DTS and DTT, I propose that these two phenomena are present in human beings from the very beginning of their life to the end of their life, from conception to death. However, to keep the exploration of their operations simple and easy, I divide our whole life span into five broad periods. They are the prenatal stage (before birth), the postnatal stage (0–2 years), the school age (3–10 years), adolescence (11–20), and adulthood (21 and above). Although I have assigned certain ages to these different stages, the exact time of transition from one stage to the other could vary depending on factors specific to each individual. DTS and DTT manifest their operations in very specific and distinct ways in all these stages of life.

As far as an individual is concerned, the unfolding of his or her DTS and DTT starts with the sexual union and reproductive activity of his or her parents. The sexual union of the parents leads to the conception and inception of the individual. In sexual reproduction, the male gamete (sperm) fertilizes the female gamete (ovum), and it results in the formation of a zygote, the beginning of a new and unique human organism. But before this extraordinary union takes place, there is the unfolding of the two phenomena of DTS and DTT. Let us look at that for a moment.

The genital union leading to the deposit of tens and millions of sperm by the man into the woman's reproductive organs sets in motion a race for survival and thriving. While the woman releases only one egg from the ovary to be fertilized, the man releases millions of sperm. Out of the millions of sperm only one beats all odds and stays alive, fertilizes the egg, and survives, while all the rest disintegrate in a matter of days. To fertilize and survive, a sperm has to reach the egg at the right time and in the right place—as the egg makes its way to the fallopian tube. The sperm also has to reach the correct fallopian tube where the egg is, since the egg will be present in only one of the two fallopian tubes. Hence, for the sperm, reaching early or late or entering the wrong fallopian tube means losing the race or rather endangering its own survival and thriving.

This whole process of sexual union and subsequent fertilization of the egg by the sperm is a fascinating drama of both the male and female gametes engaged in the twofold drives of survival and thriving. The phenomena of DTS and DTT bring the sperm and the ovum toward each other. Unless they come together and unite, they cannot survive and thrive.

The unfolding of DTS is very evident in the race that the male gametes engage in. They all want to survive; they all want to fertilize the egg and stay alive. But only one, if fortunate, makes it to the finish line. All the rest disintegrate and die after the victorious one penetrates the nucleus of the egg or before they even get to the fallopian tube. The female gamete or ovum also needs to survive. It needs a sperm to fertilize it so that it can survive and stay alive. If no sperm fertilizes the egg, it disintegrates and dies. Hence it is a race for survival for both. DTS is already operational even before the sperm and the ovum unite.

This activity of the male gamete fertilizing the female gamete is a fascinating and dynamic start to the manifestation of DTT as well. We don't need to think of this process in terms of a conscious act of two adults, but it is fascinating to think about how both the male gamete and the female gamete meet and unite. Left to themselves, the gametes are incomplete. If they don't meet and unite, they die. The need for survival and the need to grow and develop bring them together. They want not only to survive but also to thrive. They are not dead materials floating around, but rather seeds of human life infused with the power to grow and develop. Their need for survival and their thriving process reach the first milestone in their union. They are on the path of bringing the best out of themselves. When I say DTS and DTT are already operational in the process of the union of the sperm and the ovum, it has to be understood partly as a need for survival and thriving and partly as a push for the formation of a new life. The word "drive," as I said before, could mean a need, a desire, a capacity, a push, an urge, etc.

When the male and female gametes come together, a new life is formed. The male and the female gametes have their own individual drives to survive and thrive, but they are incomplete by themselves. Only in uniting with each other can they survive and thrive. If they stay apart, they survive and thrive for a while but soon disintegrate and die. When united, they stay alive and thrive. Does it not point to a larger truth about our life? I would think that just as the male and female gametes have their own individual drives to survive and thrive but are incomplete by themselves, we all have our own drives to survive and thrive but are incomplete unless we are united with each other. In a marriage or family, for example, the spouses or all the members have their own individual drives to survive and thrive, but for the good of the marriage or family they need to work hand in hand. The same thing applies to other relationship settings, whether they are regional, national, or international in nature. If we are united, we can grow and develop and bring the best out of ourselves. Left to ourselves, we might survive and thrive for a while, but we may not be able to bring the best out of ourselves.

The union of the gametes or the fertilization of the egg by the sperm is a milestone in the life of each gamete. That is the point when each of the gametes, according to its nature and property, reaches its optimal development. After the union, they are no longer the same. They take on a new identity. They are no longer separate. As individual gametes, their optimal development is to reach and unite with the partner gamete at the right time and in the right place. As mentioned above, reaching at the wrong time or in the wrong place makes the sperm and the egg disintegrate and die.

This fact of the gametes reaching and meeting at the right time and in the right place or failing to do so also speaks of a greater truth about our life and relationships. The sperm reaching the fallopian tube at the wrong time or reaching the wrong fallopian tube is equivalent to people who speak with wrong accents and who do not connect with others in a healthy way. They either do not connect at all or connect in a wrong way. Likewise, if no sperm reaches the egg, the egg will disintegrate and die. The gametes never meet, they never see eye to eye, and they never unite. In a matter of a few days, they disintegrate and disappear. That is what happens to those people who speak with wrong accents. They do not connect with others or connect in the wrong way. They communicate or relate with people at the wrong time, in the wrong place, and in the wrong way. The sperm that fail to reach and fertilize the egg, and the eggs that never get fertilized by a sperm, are representative of people who are caught up in their own world and wander in all directions without a purpose.

Just as the sperm and eggs stay alive and move for a while and then disintegrate, people who speak with wrong accents stay alive and thrive for a while and then disintegrate and die. While they stay alive, they might wander around without any clear purpose, engage in a tough race of life, and compete with everyone. They might never connect with anyone in the right way. They live a lonely life. They are caught up in their own world, ideas, and ideologies. They might appear to be successful for some time, but gradually they disintegrate and disappear. They don't grow and develop. Left to themselves, they are incomplete. They don't bring the best out of themselves, and they never let anyone else do that either.

Once the fertilization is complete, it is a new and completely different journey for the joint gametes. They are no more separate with their individual DTS or DTT. They are not gametes anymore. They are formed into a new being. Fertilization brings into being a new human organism with a unified DTS and DTT. It is no more two separate drives for survival or two separate drives for thriving. It becomes one and is unique in its own way. It includes DTS and DTT of both the sperm and the egg, but these are not the same; they are a new DTS and DTT.

I would consider this union of the gametes giving rise to a unified DTS and DTT as representative of many relationships in our life. In a marriage, for example, both the husband and wife come with their own individual DTS and DTT. They come with their own uniqueness. But once married, they become one. They turn their two drives into one. In the case of gametes, it is a complete union, including physical union. In the case of a marriage, the union of the partners is more in terms of their emotional and psychological relationships. Physically they remain separate. They don't amalgamate or blend in the physical sense. But in all other respects they need to unite to make it a successful marriage. They need to move forward with a single purpose. They can have their individual DTS and DTT, but they also need to find some sort of integration of their drives. Otherwise they will function like two separate islands.

In many marriages this integration does not happen. The two parties come into the marriage with their individual drives, and they continue to be directed by their individual drives without finding a common path. If they go in separate ways, as two individual drives to survive and thrive, spousal relationship becomes difficult. They may not see eye to eye and never become one emotionally or in other ways. They may live under one roof but function as two rails that never meet. Left to themselves, they remain incomplete.

When we think of DTS and DTT in each of the gametes, we should also remember that they connect us with a long chain of relationships in history. They don't come to us from nowhere. The sperm and the egg derive their DTS and DTT from their respective producers, the parents. Each gamete, in its own way, carries the attributes of its individual parent's drives along with other genetic characteristics that come with his or her DNA. And those parents, who were the products of the union of another set of gametes, received their respective gametes from their parents. The chain of connection thus goes back to thousands and thousands of people in our ancestry. The gametes, or the sperm and the egg, of our parents that brought us life may not have all the characteristics of DTS and DTT of the past generations, but they may have some of those characteristics that connect us with this unfathomable number of ancestors.

As mentioned, once united with each other, the gametes or their drives are no more separate. The new human organism appropriates and organizes its drives in its own unique way and attains an individuality of its own. Although it carries the characteristics of both parents and the past generations, it has its own identity. Thus DTS and DTT of the new human organism are similar to those of the parents, and yet they are different and unique in their own way. The new organism's accent is similar to and yet different from that of its parents.

This fact of the new organism developing a new accent different from that of its parents speaks of a larger truth about human families and relationships. When a man and a woman get married, a new family begins. Beginning that new family means separating from the old family in many ways. The Bible says, "Therefore a man leaves his father and his mother and clings to his wife, and they become one flesh" (Ge 2:24). To become one flesh, they have to detach from their father and mother, from their family of origin. To become one flesh, they have to unite their DTS and DTT. Detaching from the father and mother can be representative of letting go of the past and starting something new, letting go of the two separate drives and turning them into one.

Detaching from the father and mother can mean letting go of the past wounds, negativity, and unhealthy characteristics. Detaching from the father and mother and becoming one flesh can be representative of letting go of past accents and developing a new accent that is understandable for all. Sometimes it does not happen that easily. Some individuals find it difficult to detach from their father and mother, from their family of origin, and from their past accents. They may detach from their parents physically, but emotionally they still carry a lot of things that belong to their parents or past generations. They carry with them past wounds and hurts, negative memories, and debilitating accents. So even after they start a new family life, they act as though they are with their mother or father, aunt or uncle, grandfather or grandmother, and so on and so forth. They deal with their spouses as they dealt with their father or mother, brother or sister, or aunt or uncle. Or they see their spouses as a reincarnation of their father or mother, uncle or aunt, or grandfather or grandmother.

As Glen Gabbard and Sallye Wilkinson said, marital relationship becomes a repetition of past relationships. People come into marriage with a lot of baggage from their past. Detaching completely from one's past or individual drives is not possible for anyone. People carry the characteristics of their parents and past generations in many ways, and they will continue to show those characteristics in many ways even after they form their own family.

Murray Bowen, a pioneer in family therapy, discussed this fact of intergenerational transmission of relational characteristics in his natural systems or family of origin theory. Bowen held that chronic anxiety and negative interactional patterns are often re-created and repeated across generations.

Bowen discusses this idea of intergenerational transmission of relational characteristics through eight key concepts. The concepts are as follows:

1. *Differentiation of self:* This is a person's ability to operate on clearly defined beliefs, opinions, convictions, and life principles

without being excessively influenced by the characteristics of the family of origin or past generations. A person with low differentiation is overly influenced by the characteristics of the family of origin or past generations. Such persons make faulty and unhealthy choices on the basis of emotional pressures.

2. *Multigenerational transmission:* This is the transmission of emotional responses and chronic anxiety from generation to generation. In many families we see grandparents, parents, and children exhibiting chronic anxiety or a particular way of responding to certain situations. Children act just like their parents or grandparents.

3. *Emotional triangle:* When two people have problems, one or both will turn to someone else to try to fix it or take sides. Turning to someone else can be an unconscious act. For example, a woman having problems with her husband may turn to her mother or friend to discuss all that is going on with her husband. The mother or friend may not come into the picture physically, but he or she can be emotionally involved in the couple's issues and influence the thoughts and emotions of the woman. The involvement of a third person forms a triangle and further destabilizes the system. Many families get into this unconscious act of triangulation.

4. *Nuclear family emotional fusion:* Persons who are fused with their family of origin tend to marry others who are similarly fused, and the marital fusion leads to reactive emotional and physical distances. For example, it is not uncommon to see children of alcoholic parents marrying alcoholics.

5. *The family projection process:* Undifferentiated parents transmit their lack of differentiation to their children, crippling the children emotionally. Children become an extension of their narcissistic injuries or longings.

6. *Sibling position:* Children develop personality characteristics based on their sibling position in the family. The oldest children, for example, tend to become like the parents, assuming authority and responsibility and expecting loyalty and trust.

7. *Emotional cutoff:* People separate (physically or emotionally) from their family to reduce anxiety. Although relationships may look better when separations are enacted, problems remain unresolved.

8. *Societal regression:* Society itself sometimes becomes an extension of the family system caught up in a downward spiral of regression rather than progression with its own chronic anxiety, emotional triangles, cutoffs, projection process, and fusion/differentiation struggles.

As individuals, couples, or families, we are unique in our own ways, and we carry our own unique characteristics, but as an integral part of a long chain of connections and systems, we share and transmit intergenerational characteristics. We sometimes repeat or carry the styles and accents of the preceding generations.

Having said that, it should be once again noted that the zygote or the new human organism that comes into being with the union of the male and female gametes has its own individuality and uniqueness. It has its own DTS and DTT, different from those of the parents or preceding generations.

Once the fertilization process is completed and the zygote is formed, the unified DTS and DTT take the human organism to the next level of survival and thriving. To survive and thrive, the zygote has to find an adequate environment. It moves through the fallopian tube and attaches itself to the uterine wall. As mentioned before, at this stage it is very difficult to differentiate between the operations of DTS and DTT and the biological processes that go with them.

As a new human organism, the zygote is unique and different from the mother and the father, but it is not independent. The tiny human organism primarily needs nurture, nourishment, care, and protection from the mother. To survive and thrive, it needs the support of the mother.

The growing organism is so tiny and fragile that its primary focus is on its optimal physical development. At this stage, we don't notice a fully expressive unfolding of DTT as we would see in an adult. Thriving at this stage is not diversified into the emotional, social, intellectual, spiritual, and all such aspects. But every little push for growth is a sign of the presence of these two phenomena, the need to survive and the need to thrive. DTS and DTT are pretty much undifferentiated at this stage.

The new human organism makes its presence and its need for survival and thriving known to the mother in many ways. To start with, morning sickness and bodily changes experienced by the mother could be an indication of the new human organism making its unique presence known. The obvious message is, "It is no more you alone; now it's two of us." The bodily changes also might signal the new organism's announcement to its mother that she needs to be attentive to herself and the new member. The mother has her own drives and accent, and the new human organism has its own drives and accent. Being totally dependent on the mother, the new organism needs the mother to tune her ears, heart, and mind to hear and understand its accent. Most mothers get this message and attend appropriately to the new member growing in their wombs. They are attuned to the accent of the baby. They are reliable and attentive. They become what Donald Winnicott called the "holding environment" for the baby. Mothers who fail to provide this environment or refuse to tune their hearts and minds to the accent of the baby cause great damage to his or her DTS and DTT.

As the new human organism goes through the developmental stages of becoming an embryo, a fetus, and so on, it further makes its presence known to the mother in many ways. A healthy and proper development of the organism requires the mother to be in sync with the baby's accent. At this prenatal level, the effort to find the sync or understand the accent is mostly one-sided. Being totally dependent on the mother, the embryo or the fetus is incapable of tuning into the accent of the mother. The embryo or the fetus needs the total commitment of the mother to understand its accent. Winnicott said that mothers usually know accurately what the baby needs, and they ensure that it is provided. He suggested that most mothers identify with their children growing in their wombs and care for them as they would care for themselves.

But some mothers don't care for themselves in the first place. They engage in behaviors and actions that threaten their own survival and thriving. When they do that, they also threaten the survival and thriving of the embryo or fetus growing inside of them. For example, consumption of alcohol and the use of tobacco and other drugs during pregnancy are proven to be potentially dangerous to the fetus as well as the mother. These unhealthy behaviors cause miscarriages, low birth weight, birth defects, fetal alcohol syndrome (FAS; a group of birth defects including physical and cognitive abnormalities), and other health risks for the child in later life. It is common knowledge that pregnant mothers who are subjected to physical and emotional stress, traumas, injuries, and violence are risking not only their own lives but also the lives of their children in their wombs.

The phenomena of DTS and DTT continue to unfold in many ways as the organism continues its multicellular development and transition from one stage to the other in its prenatal development. While DTS ensures the survival and continuation of the baby from one stage to the other, DTT ensures the full blooming of the individual in all possible ways at each of the developmental stages in the prenatal period.

10

Anticipation, Anxiety, and Ambivalence

The conception and birth of a child is a story mixed with anticipation, anxiety, and ambivalence. It is both fascinating and frightful for both parents and children. While the conception of a child is exciting for some parents, it creates anxiety and ambivalence for others. Some wait for the birth of the child with great anticipation, while others do it with a lot of anxiety and ambivalent feelings.

These days, many couples speak of conception and pregnancy as a joint act rather than a woman's own responsibility or prerogative. For example, they say, "we are pregnant," "we are expecting," "we are carrying," or "we have conceived." Once they have conceived, they wait with great anticipation to see the face of this child who is the flesh of their flesh and bone of their bones. They have desired and decided to be fathers and mothers, and they can't wait for the moment when they can hear the voice of their little one.

However, there are others who do not have any such desire or decision to be fathers and mothers. And they find ways to avoid conceptions and pregnancies. There are others who do not decide and desire to be fathers and mothers and yet end up conceiving a child. If they conceive without having desired or decided about it, they would call it an "accident," "unexpected," or "unplanned." If they happen to conceive thusly, they react to it in different ways. Some resent it; others accept it.

If they resent the pregnancy, this has many negative repercussions for both the baby and the parents. For the baby, the parents' resentment marks the first instance of rejection in his or her life. The negativity of that resentment is passed on to the baby emotionally, and it may be the first of the many messages, which tells the baby that his or her survival and thriving processes are not going to be easy. Resenting the pregnancy, the mother might consciously or unconsciously refuse to be in sync with the baby. As mentioned earlier, the baby and the mother have individual accents. Since the baby is totally dependent on the mother, he or she needs the mother to tune her heart and mind to understand the accent of the baby. The baby does not know whether the parents desired or decided to conceive. The only thing that the baby needs to know is whether the parents are tuned into its accent, whether the parents are helping the baby's survival and thriving.

Some parents resent the pregnancy and decide to terminate it. Abortions and all forms of termination of pregnancies are topics of heated debate in many cultures and countries. My discussion here does not include a discourse or debate on those topics. The discussion here is limited to how the decisions and desires of the parents impact the survival and thriving of their children.

Some parents resent their pregnancy but decide to keep it. For various reasons, they avoid the prospects of terminating the pregnancy, but they go through feelings of anxiety and ambivalence. If they decide to keep the baby and yet resent it, it may still do great harm to the development of the baby and the normal progression of his or her DTS and DTT. Every major hurdle they encounter during the pregnancy and during the postpartum years may make them resent the "unwanted" child again and again. And the negative emotional messages of this resentment continue to be passed on to the child in many ways. Tessa Baradon, in one of her articles, speaks of a patient in therapy who described the fetus in her womb as a "parasite" living off the mother. Although from an anatomical or physiological standpoint the fetus is a parasite, the patient's feeling toward her child was much more than an anatomical conceptualization. In some ways, she resented her pregnancy. This patient felt guilty for feeling that way, but that is how she felt about her pregnancy.

The resentment gets passed on to the child directly from the mother. However, the resentment could also very well come from the father, and the negativity can be passed on to the child. The father may pass on the resentment more prominently in the postnatal period. However, he can negatively influence the behaviors of the mother during pregnancy with his negative attitudes and opinions about the pregnancy. There are cases where the mother wants to keep the pregnancy but the father does not want it. Some men might force their partners to terminate the pregnancy. Some might tolerate it and yet resent it for months and years. This may give rise to the mother always needing to defend her decision. When things get tough, even she might begin to wonder why she decided to keep it. Thus, in many ways the father can cause negative emotional messages to be passed down to the child in the womb. Largely, it is the negative messages coming from the mother that get passed onto the child both prenatally and postnatally.

Even if a child experiences such negative emotional messages from the parents, he or she may survive and thrive well to a great extent if there are other caregivers who can stand in for a caring parent. However, the ideal for a child's normal development and positive progression of DTS and DTT is the total and unqualified support of caring parents.

The resentment of pregnancy has many negative repercussions for the parents as well—especially for the mother. Besides the usual discomforts associated with pregnancy, she may experience and display overwhelming and negative emotions. This could debilitate her personal life, daily functioning, and relationships with others. These dynamics become more intense if she is a single mother without the support of the father.

Whether it is planned or unplanned, desired or resented, once the parents or the mother decide to take the pregnancy to its full term, the baby continues to grow and develop in its mother's womb. Remaining true to the basic goals of DTS and DTT, the baby constantly moves toward realizing its fullest being. The two phenomena help the baby to accomplish this task at every step of its development. This push for staying alive and realizing one's fullest being continues for several months in the mother's womb. And then comes the time for the baby to leap into the next stage of its development. The moment it is ready to move into the next stage of growth and development, it begins its battle to ease out of its mother's womb. And that battle, which we call the labor, causes enormous discomfort to the mother. When the environment is most appropriate, the baby eases itself out of its mother's womb. We call that phenomenon birth.

The term "birth pangs" refers to the contractions and consequent intense pain experienced by a woman who is about to give birth. As the baby begins its exit from the uterus and passes through the birth canal to the final exit point, these episodes of contractions and pain increase with frequency and intensity. It is a fascinating and yet stressful experience for both the mother and the baby. It is a stressful experience for the mother, as she has to go through intense pain and contractions. Although these days some epidurals that help to avoid such pain are available, a delivery without such aids might involve a lot of anxiety, fear, and pain for mothers. It is a stressful experience for the baby as well. Leaving the comfortable uterine environment, the baby has to ease out of its mother's womb through a narrow canal. Tremendous pressure is exerted on the infant as it goes through the contractions involved in the birth. These days, with the availability of state-of-the-art facilities and excellent doctors, the anxieties connected with childbirth may be minimal for mothers and their babies. However, such facilities are either not an option or are a luxury for millions of mothers and children in several countries.

The birth of a child is fascinating and frightful for both the mother and the child. On the one hand birth can be seen as a process by which the mother brings forth a new life into this world. But on the other hand it is a dynamic process through which the baby leaves its constraining environment and comes forth into a world of freedom and space. Constraint is not necessarily negative. For a human organism, the mother's womb or the amniotic sac is both nurturing and constraining. The baby needs the nurturing environment of the womb, but at the same time, it is in the process of breaking free from all its restrictive environments. It is constantly looking for ways to give greater expression to its DTS and DTT. So birth is not merely a physical phenomenon in which a mother brings forth a new life into this world; it is also the process of a new human organism seeking to give a new expression to its DTS and DTT.

The baby has an urge and need to live and thrive outside the walls of the amniotic sac. It has an unconscious urge to seek freedom and further growth. In this sense, the mother—specifically the amniotic sac—is a restrictive environment. The baby is not seeking independence and freedom from the mother because she is bad, but rather because there is a push in the baby to move beyond the amniotic sac. This is in no way meant to minimize the sacred role of the mother in the conception and birth of a baby, but rather to acknowledge with equal importance the presence of the phenomena of DTS and DTT in a human organism right from the beginning of his or her life. Thus birth is a process where the organism comes forth and seeks a wider spectrum of movement, a spectrum wider than the restrictive amniotic sac.

11

Becoming Parents

If the phenomena of DTS and DTT unfold in such extraordinary ways in a child in the prenatal stage, how do they manifest in the parents? Although I will be discussing the unfolding of these drives in the adulthood stage later on, I shall take a quick look at their operations in the mother and the father. Just as they unfold themselves in varied ways in a child, DTS and DTT show their operations in the father and the mother in multiple ways.

There may be many opinions about when exactly the actual mothering begins for a woman. Some might say that it begins at conception or from the moment the new human organism begins its life in the womb of the mother. Others might push it back still further and say that the actual mothering begins at the start of a desire in the woman or the would-be mother to have a baby. In other words, she conceives the child in her mind and heart before she conceives him or her in her womb. Some others might say that real mothering begins only after the birth of the child. But here we shall think of the beginning of mothering with the beginning of a new human organism's life in its mother's womb—that is, with conception.

The sexual union that leads to the conception of a new human organism also marks the birth of parents. The conception makes a man a father and a woman a mother. The conception makes them parents.

When the mothering role begins for a woman from this stage, her life and activities get a new orientation. They are thereafter oriented toward the care of the new human organism growing inside of her and the maturation of her role as mother. There is an urge and desire in her to protect the child, nurture it, and assist its growth in all possible ways. There is an urge to bring forth this life into the world so that the baby can grow into its fullest being. There is also a desire in her to see her own maturation as a mother. As much as she desires to see the birth and growth of her child, so much more does she desire to see herself becoming a mother. The mother's desire to have the baby is so strong that sometimes it would seem as though the baby's own need to survive and thrive is secondary to the urge of the mother to materialize her desire to be a mother. So the question would be, which is the primary urge for a mother—to fulfill her desire to be a mother, or to fulfill the baby's need to survive and thrive? It is very difficult to differentiate and say which is primary and which is secondary. The woman likes being a mother, but she also would like to see her baby surviving and thriving. They occur simultaneously. They are different but inseparable.

For a woman there is a genuine urge to be a mother. To be a mother is part of her desire to thrive. But she cannot fulfill that desire without the baby. Donald Winnicott said that there is no infant without maternal care. The same thing could be said about the mother. There is no mother without the baby. The baby makes the woman a mother. And to take care of the baby is another part of the mother's desire to thrive. Taking care of the baby and ensuring the baby survives and thrives is an expression of her DTS and DTT. Her desire to be a mother and her desire for the baby to survive and thrive are mutually dependent. The baby has a genuine urge and need to survive and thrive, but the baby cannot survive and thrive without the mother. The baby has to allow the woman to materialize her need and desire to be a mother. For the mother to materialize her desire and need to be a mother, she has to allow the baby to survive and thrive. These are different expressions of the mother's and the baby's DTS and DTT, but they are mutually dependent. The mother and the baby help each other in fulfilling the goals of their DTS and DTT.

From another point of view, the phenomena of DTS and DTT manifest themselves in a mother in a totally different manner. The woman has a desire to be a mother and a desire to have a baby. She carries the baby in her womb for weeks and months. But at the same time, the mother feels an urge to be freed of the baby. When the baby is born, there is great relief for the mother. She rejoices for both reasons: for having given birth to her child and at the same time for being relieved of all the hardships and struggles associated with pregnancy.

So it is a two-way battle for freedom. On the one hand the mother is restricting the baby, but on the other hand the baby is restricting the mother. The baby has an urge to come forth and be freed from the restricting environment of the mother's womb, and the mother has an urge to be freed of the baby. Thus the mother can be a restricting environment for the baby and the baby can be a restricting environment for the mother. Each of them is in a constant push for freedom from that restricting environment. Again, this push for freedom is to be understood not in any negative sense, but in the sense of the natural operations of DTS and DTT. Since the mother has a nondetachable connection to the baby and the baby's life depends on the mother, the baby ends up restricting the mother. Left to herself, the woman probably would not want anyone, even her baby, to restrict or control her. But in the case of a mother and a child, except for those who resent the pregnancy, it is usually a happy restriction for both.

The fact that the baby has a controlling effect on the mother leads to the consequent effect on the mother in her being limited in her movement, relationships, and the urge to satisfy her needs for pleasure.

Society in general portrays pregnant women as happy mothers. Without denying the fact that there are many happy elements connected with pregnancy and being a mother, it is important to also acknowledge the not-so-happy elements connected with pregnancy. When pregnant, a woman may have to live in constant anxiety because of the fear and uncertainty regarding how everything will go with her pregnancy. She has to be watchful of her mental and physical stress, lest she cause harm to herself and the child. The mother has to take care not only of herself, but also of the baby in her. She has an added responsibility. She has to watch what she eats and drinks, lest her own health and the baby's health and growth be compromised. Her body structure and looks change, and she has to live with an ever-protruding belly, which often may not look and feel comfortable.

Do physical looks matter to women and men? Yes, they do. Does a protruding belly cause discomfort to the woman? I suppose it does. She is constantly carrying an extra person. The woman has to deal with all the other discomforts as well, such as morning sickness, nausea, fatigue, fear of miscarriage, fear of labor, and fear of all other risk factors. Many of her personal needs have to become secondary because the primary concern is the welfare of the baby. Margaret Mahler conceptualized this mother-child relationship as symbiotic in the sense of the child living off the mother like a parasite living off its host. Although this idea of the child living off the mother might sound very negative, the truth is that the child cannot help but live that way. The child is not independent; it is unable to take care of itself. But because the child is putting the mother under this responsibility, the former restricts the latter in many ways.

If we think of pregnancy as a restriction, the sooner the baby is eased out of her womb, the freer the mother will be to pursue other dimensions of her DTT. But most mothers don't think of their pregnancy as a restriction. They don't just wait for the day when they can push out their babies from their wombs. And if some mothers have a desire to be relieved of their babies as a passing thought, they feel guilty for feeling that way. Most mothers take utmost care to ensure the full growth of the child before it is ready to enter into the extrauterine world. For most mothers, being a caring and a supportive mother to the baby is a sign of the fulfillment of their DTS and DTT at that stage in their life. DTT in particular takes on a new appearance by turning a woman into a mother. That is the fulfillment of DTT for that woman at that stage of her life. Her DTT is very much connected to caring for the child. She is adding another jewel to her record of perfection as a human being by being a good mother and caring for the baby.

In one sense, the pregnancy, childbirth, breast-feeding, mothering, and all such functions of a woman could be viewed as curtailing the freedom of a woman. But in another sense, these are the ways in which a woman advances in her DTS and DTT. Not all women choose this path, but most women do. The baby is, in fact, assisting his or her mother to realize her fullest being by helping her to become a mother. Just as the mother is helping the baby to move toward realizing its fullest being by caring for it, the baby is indirectly helping the mother to actualize her drives to survive and thrive. It is difficult to differentiate one from the other and make any judgment on who is helping whom. The only difference is that one is dependent and the other is independent; one is not conscious of DTS and DTT and the other is conscious of it, or at least capable of being conscious of it.

A fine balance between the mother's DTS and DTT and the baby's DTS and DTT is a prerequisite for a normal and healthy development of the child and the maturation of the woman as a mother. They have different accents, yet they have to match. They have to move beyond the peripheral concerns of who is restricting whom and find a common language. How is that possible, given the fact that in both these individuals DTS and DTT are operational? It becomes possible when the mother steers her drives in such a way that it not only brings to fruition her role as a mother but also assists the full blooming of the baby. The independent and conscious mother makes an extra effort to tune her heart and mind to understand the language of the dependent and not-so-conscious baby.

The focus of the mother is not so much on her needs for pleasure or independence from the baby, but rather on the full fruition of her role as mother. Although desiring her independence from the baby and seeking pleasure might look like normal and justifiable expressions of her DTS and DTT, when these things are done at the expense of the dependent and fragile baby, it could result in a negative manifestation of her drives. The positive manifestation of her drives occurs when she has no concern other than the full fruition of her mothering role and the growth and development of her child. So the focus is more on the mothering dimension of her drive than on the freedom-from-the-baby dimension of the drive. When it comes to her DTT, she consciously makes a choice for the positive manifestation of her drive. The dependent and not-so-conscious baby needs that extra consideration from the mother, who is independent and conscious. (Note that when I use the terms "independent and conscious" or "dependent and not-so-conscious" I don't use them in their absolute senses. Nobody is absolutely independent or absolutely conscious. In short, her own maturation as a mother and the baby's life and welfare begin to be the ultimate goal of the mother.)

The same things could be said of the father. Just as the mother has DTS and DTT, the father also has these drives. The father's DTS and DTT unfold themselves in his desire to be a father and to care for the baby. The question is, which is his primary drive—the desire to be a father or the desire to see the growth and development of the baby? It is hard to distinguish between the two. But both are manifestations of his DTS and DTT. Just like a mother, the father has an urge to be freed from the restrictive environment that the baby indirectly puts him in. The baby restricts the father by putting him under the responsibility of caring for the baby rather than seeking his own pleasure. Although this responsibility does not affect him as much as it does the mother, the arrival of a baby affects his movements and relationships. He has to be attentive and available to the mother and the baby. He cannot have his partner completely to himself, because she has to be available to the baby as well. So he has a double duty, caring for the baby and the mother. But like the mother, being independent and conscious, he steers his drives in such a way that it leads to the fruition of his role as father and the growth and development of the baby, who is dependent and not-so-conscious. He makes an extra effort to tune his heart and mind to understand the language of the dependent and not-so-conscious baby.

Both the father and mother experience the blossoming of their DTS and DTT in different ways in their experience of becoming parents. On the one hand, becoming a father or mother is another dimension of the actualization of their DTS and DTT, but on the other it is a restriction of their own selves by their children. As noted previously, in most cases, mothers and fathers see it as a happy restriction. They make a great sacrifice in putting the welfare of their children before their own desire to survive and thrive. The parents will function as stabilizing agents in a child's life to the extent that they themselves are able to experience that stability in their own individual lives and their life together as a couple. When parents fail to be a stabilizing factor in the baby's life, they can cause much damage to the baby's ability to survive and thrive, and that, in turn, can cause problems in the child's accent in the future.

12

The Postnatal Stage

If the prenatal period is filled with novelty and nostalgia about the operations of DTS and DTT, it gets even more complex in the postnatal period. The operations of these phenomena become more diversified. The transition begins with birth. Birth is a significant milestone in the life of the parents and the baby. It is another step of accomplishment in the operations of their DTS and DTT.

When a baby is born, the mother and the father accomplish a significant goal in their life. They become a mother and a father in a more concrete way, and together they become parents. They bring a new life into this world. Both of these are significant events. Becoming a mother or a father is a significant goal in their drives to survive and thrive, especially if it is their first child, as they have never been a father or a mother before. They have had parents, but they have never been parents themselves. With the birth of the child, they move from being simply a man or a woman into becoming a father and a mother. All that they have read or heard about being a father or mother or being a parent may look trivial when compared to what they really experience with the birth of the child. Books, articles, and lectures do not convey the actuality of parenthood. It has to be experienced. With parenthood, their roles gain an additional dimension, their family structure changes with the addition of the new member, and their relationship dynamics change, particularly from a dyadic relationship to a triadic relationship.

Birth is a significant milestone for the child. The child survives all the odds and challenges of the prenatal period and moves toward becoming a mature human being. With birth, the child launches out into a new stage of growth and development.

Birth brings the child an experience of relief as well as discomfort. The experience of relief comes from the fact that it is no more constrained by the amniotic sac. The child eases itself out of the restricting environment of the amniotic sac into a freer extrauterine world. The womb has its limitations. Remaining within it, the child cannot grow any further. It has to come out for further growth and development.

But leaving that comfort of the womb is painful. The experience of discomfort comes first of all from being out of the comfortable amniotic sac and cut off from the umbilical cord. The new environment of the outside world is larger and wider than the amniotic sac, and the child can have more freedom, but the measure of comfort in the extrauterine world is comparatively much less than the comfort level in the amniotic sac. The line of uninterrupted supply of oxygen and nutrients from the mother is disconnected. The physiological connection with the mother now has to be replaced by an emotional connection or other forms of attachment. Once out of the womb, the infant has to breathe the cold air, experience a strange world, and encounter a new environment. None of this ever existed before for the child. The child sees people and things. The child sees the mother herself for the first time.

What do all these things mean for the child? There is bright light, loud sounds, and an overwhelming environment all around. The newborn has a very limited capacity to cope with all such excessive and overwhelming sensory input and stimuli. Maia Szalavitz and Bruce Perry, in their book *Born for Love*, state that human babies might be the most fragile of babies among all animal species. Most of our brain development takes place after birth, and it takes several years for our brain to mature and for us to gain mastery over our motor, emotional, and cognitive functions. Many animal babies are able to stand and run soon after they are born, but human babies take months to crawl, walk, and run. We need the continued support of our mothers and others for many months and years.

The extrauterine world might look like a larger and freer world, but the level of support we receive in that new environment is different from what we have in the amniotic sac. There is no uninterrupted comfort and support in the postnatal world. The possibilities of constraints and restrictions are also greater in the new environment. Prior to birth, the amniotic sac is the only restricting environment. With birth, that equation changes; the restrictive environment becomes more elaborate, with an extra figure in the person of the father. Then there are other relatives, such as grandparents, great-grandparents, older siblings, uncles, aunts, and all other significant people connected with the family. In the womb, the amniotic sac is both a nurturing and restricting environment. The mother is both a nurturing and constricting agent. Similarly, in the extrauterine world, the rest of the family is both a nurturing and a restricting environment. The child experiences more space and freedom, but he or she has more heads to reckon with. The child thrives into the new realms of growth and development, but he or she faces restrictions from a larger family circle.

The most important of all the discomforts may be the discomfort coming from the sense of being cut off from the mother. Prior to birth, the mother facilitates a physical and an emotional connection. The sense of being connected to the mother gives the infant a sense of belonging, closeness, relatedness, being wanted, being loved, etc. That connection is a given before birth. It is probably the most intense stage of feeling "at home." After birth, that feeling fades little by little. It may appear that the child has to earn that connection. The mother may not be able to give that sense of constant connection to the child. The ideal is to give the child an uninterrupted sense of connectedness, security, and well-being. But given the fact that the parents have to negotiate between many interests and needs, even the best of mothers and fathers cannot offer the ideal environment for the child.

In the case of a mother, she may be away from the child for significant periods of time. She could be busy with many things. She could be spending time with her husband, attending to other children if she has more than one, working away from home if she is employed somewhere, or busy in the kitchen preparing food for everyone. She could be self-absorbed, depressed, or overwhelmed by some emotional turmoil. In so many ways, a mother could be absent or away from the child physically and emotionally. She may not be available to the child around the clock. Thus the warmth of the mother may be limited to certain hours. The child is left to hold on to a warm bed, cradle, or blanket, which are all artificial and have no human touch. The baby wants the whole of the mother. While in the womb, the baby had the mother totally to himself or herself. But after birth, the mother's availability becomes more and more sporadic.

The child might express his or her anxiety, frustration, and distress about the mother's absence in many ways. He or she may engage in behaviors such as crying, drooling, hiccupping, sucking his or her fingers, and burping to bring back the mother's attention. On hearing the baby crying or seeing the baby drooling, most mothers would run to the baby and give the needed comfort. The mother will repair the damage that is caused by her absence and reconnect with the baby. The presence and the touch of the mother have a tremendous emotion regulating effect on the child. But again, after a while, the mother leaves the baby and engages in other things. Some mothers who are too self-absorbed or emotionally absent due to emotional turmoil, influence of drugs, or some other reason might ignore these behaviors of children and might not give much attention to them at all.

Difficult experiences, especially consistent disconnection from the mother, can have many negative repercussions on the child's sense of self, others, and the world. If the mother does not adequately respond to the child even after repeated efforts, he or she may give up the hope of ever getting the mother's attention. The child may have to begin to self-soothe. The experience might make the child conclude that the mother is bad, cold, and unreliable. The child might also develop an image of himself or herself as bad or unlovable. The child's feeling might be *Mother is not coming because she doesn't like me* or *I am not lovable.* Of course, these are not well-calculated and thought-out conclusions, but the child looks to the mother for any signs of its own self-worth and position in the world.

Donald Winnicott emphasized the crucial role that mothers play in the development of children, particularly in their "mirroring role." The mother functions like a mirror to the child. Winnicott suggested that when a child looks at his or her mother, what he or she sees on the mother's face is himself of herself. The mother's face will reflect what and how she thinks and feels about the child. For most mothers, their face will reflect their pride and joy in their children. This is most important in infancy, as the child is in a preverbal state and is totally dependent on the empathy of the mother. The gaze of the mother is a significant cue for the child to know how she feels about the child. For some mothers, especially for those who resent their children, their face will reflect their disappointment, displeasure, anger, and all such negative affects regarding the child. If the mother's face shows a sense of joy, delight, satisfaction, and pride, the child will get a feeling that the mother loves and prizes him or her very dearly. The child then gets a feeling that he or she is likeable, lovable, and precious. Such mother–child relationships are akin to what Daniel Stern called the "affect attunement." The mother is attuned to the child.

According to Stern, "mirroring" or "empathic response" is more or less the same as interaffectivity or affect attunement. When we speak of empathic response, for example, we often mean that we are able to feel what another person is feeling. But how do we do that? How do we get "inside of" other people's subjective experiences? And how do we let another person know that we are feeling what he or she is feeling? How is this possible when one partner is an infant? How can a mother get inside of the infant and feel what he or she is feeling? How can the mother let the infant know that she is experiencing what the infant is experiencing? How can they have an intersubjective experience? Through the concept of affect attunement, Stern tries to answer some of these questions.

Stern opined that simply imitating the behaviors of the infant would not create the intersubjective experience or affect attunement. There are several processes involved in creating intersubjective experiences or affect attunement. He lists three of these processes. First, the mother should be able to read the infant's emotional state from his or her behavior. In other words, the mother should be able to read the infant's affects. Affect is a combination of a sensation or experience of pleasure or displeasure and an idea. Usually affects are demonstrated nonverbally in facial expression, voice prosody (tone, inflections, pitch), gestures, and posture. Looking at someone's face, for example, we can often tell whether he or she is angry, afraid, happy, or sad. Each emotion has its specific affective expression, and emotions often appear on a person's face and in his or her voice, gestures, and posture.

The second requirement for affect attunement is that the mother should be able to match the behavior of the child in some manner without making it look like a strict imitation. The modality that the mother uses has to be different from the modality that the infant uses. An example that Stern used is that of a boy who is trying to reach a toy and is frustrated. He looks at the mother, and the mother tries to match that frustration of the boy by using a vocal expression such as "Uuuuuuh." The boy's frustration is evident in the stretching of his hand, and the mother matches that frustration using another modality, her voice.

The third requirement for affect attunement is that the infant should be able to read the mother's behavior (her voice, facial and bodily expressions, etc.) as connected to her own feeling state, which matches with the infant's own feeling state. So the mother's response should not be read as a mere imitation of the infant's overt behavior, but rather as an expression of her feelings, which arose as a response to the infant's feelings.

When a mother is able to accomplish these three tasks, we can say there is an affect attunement and intersubjective experience. When attuned, the mother will be affectively and cognitively present to the child. The child will feel that the mother is really in sync with him or her.

Attachment theorists, such as John Bowlby and Mary Ainsworth, consider affect attunement as essential for children to develop attachment bonds with the mother or caregiver. Attachment bonds, according to them, are essential for the child's growth and development. In other words, affect attunement that leads to the formation of attachment bonds enhances the operations of DTS and DTT in a child, and helps him or her to survive and thrive well.

Most mothers develop an affect attunement with their children. They are in sync with their children. Usually we know that when faced with the overwhelming emotional experience of the child, it is very difficult for the mother or a parent to remain totally unaffected by the emotion of the child. Simply imitating the external behaviors of the child is not what we see. If the child is feeling sad, the mother also feels sad. The emotional experience of the child generates a matching emotional experience in the mother, even if it does not happen in the same intensity. Matching the external expression of the child's emotion without connecting with his or her internal experience may be hard for many mothers.

Recently I was talking to a young mother who said that she could "feel it" when her child was hungry. Parents often feel what their children feel. This may not apply to all emotions, but it does to some. For example, if a child is angry, the mother doesn't need to be angry to be attuned. The child's anger may not generate a matching anger in the mother. But when it comes to other emotions, such as sadness or happiness, the mother may feel sad and happy in some way. Thus, to be attuned, the mother should be able to join the child's emotional state in some way without getting overwhelmed by those emotions. Remaining totally unaffected by such emotions of the child is a near impossibility unless the mother is totally emotionally absent because of drugs, alcohol, depression, or some other reason.

In most cases, the mother will feel the sadness of the child and yet remain as a stabilizing factor for the child because of her ability to contain the overwhelming effect of that emotion. "Containment," according to psychoanalysts such as Wilfred Bion and Lucy LaFarge, refers to the process by which a mother or caregiver receives the overwhelming "unmetabolized" emotional experiences of the child and transforms them into digestible and nonthreatening experiences, just as a psychoanalyst or psychotherapist would do for his or her patients. As a "container," or stabilizing agent, the mother will be sensitive to the painful negative affect that the child is experiencing and will assist the child by coregulating the affect through empathy and comfort.

Children also engage in affect attunement with their parents sometimes, although they may not have the same ability to contain and stabilize that parents do. When a mother is sad or crying, it is not unusual to see her child come to her and ask, "Mommy, are you sad?" In some way the child feels what the mother feels and matches her affect. If we see sadness on the face of the mother, we will see sadness on the face of the child. It is not necessary to experience all that the other person is experiencing, but the possibility of joining the other person's emotional state and experiencing that emotion in some way is part of attunement.

In everyday conversations, we hear people express their frustrations about lack of affect attunement and intersubjectivity. They say, "You don't get it, do you?" Such comments indicate that there is not much affect attunement or intersubjectivity going on between the two parties. A mother who is not attuned to her child may hear a similar message. Looking at the mother, the child might say, "You don't get it, do you?"

A consistent failure on the mother's part to give the child an attuned response causes great damage to the child's development and sense of self. I am not talking about the mother's absence or lack of response for just one or two days, but rather about a repeated experience of lack of attunement over weeks and months in the early years of one's life. Such repeated lack of attunement, according to Daniel Hughes, leads to the development of negative self-meanings. The child will begin to form such images of himself or herself as "I am bad," "I am lazy," "I am stupid," "I am selfish," "I am unlovable," "I am burdensome," "I am boring," and "I am mean." And such negative self-meanings create in the child all sorts of negative affects, such as shame, guilt, fear, and anger. And these negative affects, in turn, can cause great damage to his or her accent in the future. He or she may have great difficulty in connecting with others and understanding their accents.

So we see how important affect attunement or mirroring is in the development of a child. What the affect attunement, mirroring, or empathic response from the mother does is enhance the operations of the child's DTS and DTT. The mother matches her accent with that of her child, and it helps the child to survive and thrive well. When the mother or caregiver is affectively attuned with the child, the child will have no threat of survival, and the child will thrive well, making steady progress in his or her growth and development. The mother will show this in her facial expressions, tone of voice, gestures, and postures, and the child will experience these things as impetuses for his or her survival and growth. If the mother's face, voice, gestures, and postures, on the other hand, consistently reflect displeasure and disappointment toward the child, the child might develop a negative sense of self, others, and the world. Such dynamics negatively impact DTS and DTT of children.

The child may not feel safe and secure, and his or her survival may be threatened. The behaviors of the mother might make it difficult for the child to thrive, stunting his or her growth and development. The child will then experience a disconnect between his or her accent and the mother's accent.

Children who experience such a mismatch of accents with their mothers or parents might survive and thrive to some extent, but the unmet needs might resurface in many ways in later life. Their accents may not match with those of others in the future. For example, in a marital relationship, a person might begin to look to his or her spouse to satisfy the unmet needs of his or her childhood. Of course, the person is not directly telling the spouse things like "Take care of me because I was neglected in my childhood" or "Fulfill the unmet needs of my childhood, because my mother did not do it." The person rather looks to the spouse to see whether he or she is different or just a replica of his or her mother, who was cold and uncaring or whom he or she perceived as cold and uncaring. The person will hear the spouse's words and see his or her actions through this filter. If the spouse appears to be a replica of the person's mother, he or she might begin to view the spouse as cold, uncaring, and emotionally unresponsive, just as he or she experienced his or her mother. The person might begin to view himself or herself as bad and unlovable, and distance himself or herself from the spouse as well. Most of these dynamics might be going on in the person unconsciously. The person could be either too clingy or too disconnected, but he or she may not realize it. The marital partner might find it hard to connect with such a spouse. If both spouses come into the relationship with many such unmet needs, it is already open to many problems, conflicts, and disappointments. Their accents will hardly match. They would be constantly frustrated and disappointed with each other.

The same relationship dynamics that happen between a mother and child could play out in the child's relationship with the father and other family members or caregivers. They all play a mirroring role in the development of the child. In the early stages of life, the child's DTS and DTT are very fragile. The child needs the optimum support from the mother, father, and other significant caregivers to survive and thrive.

The mother, father, and other significant caregivers need to tune their hearts and minds to understand the accent of the child. A mismatch of accents from the mother, father, and other caregivers can threaten the survival and growth of the child, and subsequently cause great damage to his or her accent.

Having said this, it is to be noted that even if the mother is not adequately responsive and reliable to the child, and if there are other caregivers who can fill that gap and provide the child with a safe and secure environment, reliability, affect attunement, responsiveness, and healthy mirroring, the child will survive and thrive without having much damage done to it.

So the paradox in all this is that while birth brings the joy of thriving in a new world and experiencing wider space and freedom, there is the sadness of encountering the hard reality of a strange and cold world and gradual disconnection from the mother. The extrauterine world might look like a wide space and freedom to the child, but he or she is not equipped well enough to be totally free. The child needs a caring, responsive, and reliable mother or caregiver. The inevitable disconnectedness that comes with birth sometimes seems to be a heavy price that one pays for the enjoyment of freedom that the extrauterine world offers. At every step of the accomplishment of DTS and DTT, there is a loss and a gain. And if the loss is greater than the gain, it can negatively affect the child's survival and thriving, and consequently do damage to his or her developing personality and accent.

13

The Joy and Pain of Letting Go

Just as a child experiences a sense of relief as well as discomfort when birth occurs, the parents, particularly the mother, also experience similar dynamics. After a child is born, there is greater freedom for the mother. However, she experiences a sense of disconnectedness and separation as well. There is a sense of relief as well as remorse. There is a gain and a loss.

The feeling of freedom and relief comes from the fact that the baby is no longer restricting the mother completely, although she continues to care for the child. After the child's birth, she can attend more to her needs for pleasure. Her sense of relief also comes from the fact that after birth the care of the child becomes a shared responsibility. The father and other significant others assist and participate in the caregiving task. Although she will continue to be the primary person in charge of the baby, the shared responsibility will help her to be much freer. With that new freedom, she can concentrate on other aspects of her DTS and DTT, which she might not have been able to focus on while she was pregnant.

The birth of the child brings the mother a sense of powerlessness, remorse, and loss of control as well. When the child separates from her, the mother could experience a feeling of no longer being needed. Erna Furman speaks of this experience of mothers through a concept called "to be there to be left." The concept originally goes back to Anna Freud, Sigmund Freud's daughter and Furman's teacher. What is meant by this is that mothers often have to accept the painful fact that they are meant to be there for their children with the awareness that their children will leave them and go away- As much as they want to cling on to their children, so much more will their children separate themselves from them. But that is the job of the mothers; they are there to be left. They make themselves available to their children even though their children will leave them and go away.

This painful experience of being there to be left, according to Furman, begins as early as the weaning stage, and it continues in the subsequent stages of the child's development. But I would push it back even further. I see this painful experience beginning even from the moment of the child's birth. The child leaves the mother's womb—leaves her literally—and declares his or her independence or separateness. The mother's first feeling of being not needed begins there. The child disconnects himself or herself from the mother. Physically, the mother doesn't have the child all to herself anymore. The mother is no more the sole caretaker of the baby. The caretaking is thereafter shared. The father and other family members or caregivers come into the picture. The mother sees the prospects of her child separating from her more and more. She is there to be left.

Even from a purely physical point of view, we know that many children survive and thrive even when they are deprived of their mother's care for different reasons. We are not referring to "test-tube babies," but in the normal conception and birth of a child, a mother is needed at all the stages of its development. She is the life source for the baby. But once the baby is born, the whole dynamic changes. She is no longer needed as before. The child could survive and thrive without her. The mother's first feeling of being there to be left begins there.

This feeling of being there to be left and the consequent sense of powerlessness and worthlessness could affect the mother in multiple ways. She could become depressed. This feeling of being separated and being left is a contributing factor for postpartum depression in many women. Feeling disconnected, the mother could become indifferent and disinterested in the care of the child. The mother could become jealous and envious of others to whom the child begins to reach out.

Given the circumstances, the mother reckons with the new environment. She takes pleasure in being relieved of the baby and at the same time mourns the experience of disconnectedness. She absorbs the pain that arises from the fact of being there to be left and takes comfort in the fact that the child is still within her reach. Mothers who are able to integrate this pain of separateness in a healthy way will recognize that the child is not rejecting them but rather moving into another phase of his or her DTS and DTT. Such mothers will continue to take pleasure in being the primary caretaker of the child.

Although they are not in complete control of the care of their children after their children leave the womb, mothers continue to enjoy giving their attention and love. A sense of power, though not completely satisfied, continues in a good measure. This need to have power and control is to be understood as a normal course of action in the parenting process. The mother does not try to control the child with any malice in mind. Taking pleasure in being relieved from the baby is also to be understood as a normal part of the process. The mother is not taking pleasure in the sense of the baby being a burden. It is only a result of the dance between the mother's urge to be the primary caregiver for the child and her equally powerful urge to be freed from the hardships of caregiving. It is a result of the dance between the operation of the mother's DTS and DTT and the child's DTS and DTT.

However, there are mothers who take immense pleasure in being freed from the physical constraints and the responsibility of caring their children put on them. There are other mothers who make their children a narcissistic extension of themselves or try to control and use their children with malice in their mind. Such mothers, who focus primarily on meeting their needs for pleasure rather than caring for their children, might end up hurting their children in many ways, but they are to be seen as exceptions rather than the norm. Most mothers love their children. They find a fine balance between their need for pleasure and the responsibility of caring for their children.

Similar processes happen in the father as well, although not in the same manner or intensity as in the mother. When parents tune their minds and hearts to understand the accents of their children and continue to focus primarily on their parenting role, they fulfill the tasks of their DTS and DTT at that stage of their life. The child who is dependent and not-so-conscious needs all the support he or she can get from the parents or caregivers, who are more conscious and independent.

The restrictions and responsibilities children put on their parents continue in subsequent years after birth. The mother and father continue to invest a lot of their time and energy in the welfare of the child. The parents have to feed the baby, hold the baby, rock the baby, and soothe the baby. They have to live with interrupted sleep for many months and years. They have to go through anxious moments when the baby gets sick or is in some danger. The baby continues to keep the parents occupied and alert. Some babies keep their parents on their toes. They look very upset and agitated if their parents are not at their beck and call. They call the shots. They demand and dictate. They want to act like little adults.

However, most parents do not feel intimidated. They in fact enjoy watching every new, innovative act of the child unfolding before them. The complex processes going on in the child's mind mesmerize them. They take pleasure in meeting the needs of the child. Maia Szalavitz and Bruce Perry contend that parents and other caregivers not only give themselves to their children but also receive a sense of satisfaction in that giving. They feel rewarded in meeting the needs of their children. Parents enjoy caring for their children. There is a pleasure involved in that caring. In that sense, children are not only demanding and dictating; they also help the parents to gain a sense of self-worth and satisfaction. Children indirectly help parents to move a step further in their DTS and DTT, a step closer to bringing the best out of themselves.

As the child develops further, he or she explores new ways of maneuvering the world and manifesting his or her DTS and DTT. The child still needs the care and protection of the parents or significant others, but he or she also wants to independently explore the world and thrive still further. The child goes through what Margaret Mahler and her colleagues call the separation-individuation process. The child wants to be with the mother, but he or she also wants to move away from the mother. It is a dance in which the child's song ranges from "hold me" to "don't keep me." The child wants the mother to watch him or her, but at the same time he or she does not want to be constricted or controlled. The mother should be in sight, but she should not constrain the child's movement. The moment the mother or father tries to hold and keep him or her, the child wriggles out of the mother's or father's hands. Any controlling act from the parents is frowned upon and resisted by way of temper tantrums and victim-like expressions.

Parents often set limits and boundaries to ensure that children don't hurt themselves. Children don't like those boundaries. They don't understand why those limits and boundaries are set, and they tend to resent them. However, the parents who know better stay put and function as their children's buffer zones, stabilizing caregivers, and springboards for further growth and development. Parents function as a thermostat for their growing children. They keep the temperature steady. The irony of the relationship is that as much as children want the protection and care of their parents or caregivers, they look for autonomy from them even more so.

Even if they are not given the best or most ideal parenting or caregiving, if children are provided with a "good-enough" environment, as Winnicott phrased it, they will continue to grow physically, emotionally, and intellectually. They will survive every hurdle that comes their way and thrive more as they move into new realms of growth and development. An absence of such an environment can be a threat to the child's ability to survive and thrive, and it can negatively influence his or her future relationships.

14

School Age

Cultures differ in the way they define school age. In some cultures, children get a long time to spend in their home with their parents and others before they begin school, while in others, children have to move into school-like centers such as crèches, or day care centers, early in life. Crèches function as stepping-stones to the school environment. But the age of children sent to crèches could vary anywhere from one to three. Not all children are sent to crèches. Parents who are working away from home and who have no one else to take care of their children while they are gone often seek the help of such facilities. Larger families with grandparents or other relatives residing in the house or in the vicinity do not find the need to send their toddlers to crèches.

The actual transition into school age begins with preschool or nursery or kindergarten; these institutions are known by different names in different countries. Not all communities have such systems either. In some places, their school system may begin with the first grade or first standard at the age of five or six. But considering how even the preschool systems have become internationally standardized, we could consider the preschool or nursery or kindergarten as the beginning of school age. Although we might find variations even in this, the usual age of children when they transition into school age is three. From age three, children begin a new phase of their DTS and DTT. They have to survive and thrive in the new environment.

Moving into school age is the reenactment of the drama of the postnatal period all over again, except that life becomes more complex for the child and the parents. A new set of actors in the form of teachers and school staff are added to the play.

The school environment can be a pleasurable and painful place for a child. School presents a child with many novelties that promote the progression of his or her DTS and DTT, but it may also pose challenges and hurdles that discourage and disappoint the child. Transitioning into the school environment is an overwhelming experience for most children. Leslie Koplow, in her book, *Creating Schools That Heal*, describes in detail the unnerving experiences of children as they move from their homes to school. It is a transition from a small family home to a big environment. Big buildings, high ceilings, huge windows, long hallways, the voices of many other children, the intimidating gazes of many grown-ups, a sense of being thrown into a crowd—everything overwhelms the little kid. Many children hold tight to the hand or dress of the parent or adult who brings him or her to the school. Occasionally they look to the faces of teachers or school staff for signs of trustworthiness. It is a big, new world, and the first task for the child is to become comfortable with the new environment and feel connected. Sometimes comfortable and at other times scary, the school presents to the child a replica of the novelties and scariness of the larger world. Most children, if the environment is not excessively scary and negative, learn to appreciate the novelties and tolerate the frustrations that arise from the new experiences.

From the time they move into the school environment, children have two sets of people who function as their thermostat—parents and teachers. The parents are still in control, but a greater part of children's time is spent with teachers and the school staff. A new dance between the operations of the teachers' DTS and DTT and the children's DTS and DTT begins to emerge.

Children go through a new phase of constraints and freedom. Although they continue to need the nurturing environment of their parents and families, they are not under the control of their parents all the time. They are freer now. But they have only moved into a new set of controls in the school environment. They feel restricted in many ways by the teachers, by the rules and regulations of the school, by the boundaries and expectations set by the cliques and peer groups, so on and so forth. However, the school environment opens up new possibilities for relationships and interactions. It is no more the small family of parents and siblings but a wider world of friends and peers. Children learn new things about themselves, about others, and about the world. They develop physically, emotionally, cognitively, and intellectually. They move from toys to more complex activities and calculations. There is restriction, but there is also a greater freedom. They resent the constraints, but they tolerate it for the sake of the freedom that is offered. The school environment gives them opportunities to accomplish another phase of the tasks and goals of their DTS and DTT, in bringing the best out of themselves. Teachers and others assist them in accomplishing this task.

The teachers and the school staff also go through a phase of constraints and freedom when dealing with their students. They accomplish the tasks of their DTS and DTT by being good teachers and staff to their students. They feel rewarded in fostering a supportive and nurturing environment to their students. They meet the educational, emotional, and other needs of the children. It gives them a sense of satisfaction and fulfillment. The students, in fact, become the agents of these fulfillments for the teachers. They help the teachers in taking their DTS and DTT a step further, in bringing the best out of themselves. But the teachers also feel constrained by the students. In some sense, students are the masters. They keep the teachers employed and occupied. Just as I mentioned about parents, there are no teachers without students. The students make teachers, and vice versa. The students hold the teachers accountable for their development and learning. And in the immediate circumstances, they hold the teachers and the school staff responsible for their safety and satisfaction. The teachers and the staff experience some relief when the children go back home.

The transition of children into school age brings about both relief and distress in parents. The relief comes from the fact that the child is no more constraining them completely. At least during the school hours, the parents are free from their children. They don't have to concentrate all their attention and energy on the care of the child; it is shared, as the school and the teachers have come into the picture. The parents can thereafter take more time to attend to their needs for pleasure and personal development. The teachers step in to teach the children whatever the parents are not able to teach. The school opens up the larger world for the children. Parents are spared the task of disciplining the children around the clock. The teachers and the school staff share that responsibility.

However, children's transition to school age is also an experience of pain for the parents, because a child moving into school is another instance of parents losing complete control over their children. The mother's sense of no longer being needed or "being there to be left" returns in a big way. From then on, a series of separations and painful moments follows. Some mothers cannot tolerate this sense of being there to be left. Erna Furman gives some details about the experiences of mothers who sadly watch their children leave for school. These mothers watch their children with tearful eyes as they run to meet their teacher or peers. The mothers wait for a return kiss or "bye-bye," and sometimes they will have to return home without getting one. In their excitement at seeing the teachers or peers, the children forget about their mothers, at least for the moment. The mothers wait for the children at lunchtime or when it is time for the children to return from school. The children sometimes do not read the distress of their mothers and take their time in returning home. The children may hang around or play with their friends, look at the novelties of nature on the way, or engage in adultlike conversations with anyone they find on the way. Some of these things might apply only to children who go to school or live in the countryside.

The more such a child is separated, the more the mother becomes anxious and worried. She is worried not only about the physical safety of the child but also about her child's "need" for the mother. Her sense of not being needed gets increasingly affirmed as the child explores new avenues of thriving and independence. She once again feels that her job is to be there to be left. On the one hand she is happy that the child is growing and going to school, but on the other, she is sad that the child is leaving her.

Every now and then we hear some parents expressing this sense of sadness and loss of power and control when they speak about their children. They may say, "He is already a big boy" or "She is already a big girl" or "Only a few years more and then they will be gone." They already foresee the day when their kids will be independent and separated from them. They foresee the empty nest. For some parents, this experience of their child leaving them or seeking more independence and separation as he or she matures becomes a motivating factor for conceiving or having another child. They make up for that sense of emptiness or loss by having another child. And this process might get repeated for a third, fourth, fifth, or sixth time.

Some mothers make their children feel guilty for making them feel that way, blaming the child for her feeling not needed. Separation from the mother or the parent is part of growing up. Children who don't have to feel guilty for growing up, Furman says, will survive and thrive well. They will continue to develop physically, emotionally, intellectually, socially, and spiritually. They need their parents and teachers to continue to function as the thermostat.

Knowing that children transitioning into school age and seeking greater freedom is part of their normal growth and development rather than a rejection of parental care, parents can continue to facilitate a healthy environment. Parents who continue to provide a nurturing and containing environment will promote a balanced growth of the children. If they tune their hearts and minds to understand the accents of the children, they will see the amazing growth that happens in their children.

When children reciprocate this benevolence of the parents, life becomes easy for both parties. Children enjoy their freedom and yet stay under the watchful care of their parents so that they can survive and thrive uninterrupted. In other words, both parents and children match their accents and understand each other's language. It is akin to a child running ahead of his or her parents in a park to catch the first glimpse of the beauty that lies ahead, but at the same time not going so far as to be out of sight of the parents. Teachers and the school staff become an additional resource for the parents and children in this survival and thriving process. If parents and teachers focus more on their needs for pleasure rather than on the needs of the children, the latter will find themselves ill-prepared for the subsequent stages of growth.

When accents are not matched, life becomes difficult both at home and school. The direction that our DTS and DTT take depends not only on our inherited characteristics but also on the measure of nurture and support that we receive from our parents, teachers, and other caregivers. Children and students who grow up without a healthy environment for survival and thriving will have great difficulty in personal growth and interpersonal relationships in the future. They will find their accents mismatched with those of others.

15

Adolescence

The operations of DTS and DTT become more complex as children move into their adolescence, which begins at about age eleven. Having been exposed to a whole new world in the school environment, children develop new friendships and relationships. They form their own little groups or cliques and get involved in extracurricular activities. As they move into their teenage years, they experience a plethora of changes physically, mentally, emotionally, sexually, and socially. Little by little, they begin to squeeze out of the control of the biological family and solidify their support among friends and peers.

For some, entry into peer groups is preceded by a long struggle to break free from the constraining environment of the family. They want to test their ability to survive and thrive without the control of their parents. Many adolescents consider their parents and other caregivers in the family as agents of restraint and control. Often they find their parents not understanding their accents. They look for opportunities to break free from this constraining environment and launch into a control-free world. They want to be left free to do what they like and to explore the world of unlimited freedom. Although the parents themselves have gone through these developmental stages, they are already at another level, and it makes it hard for some of them to understand the accents of their adolescent children.

Breaking free from the constraining environment of the parents or family is not always a negative phenomenon. It could be seen as a normal developmental need to associate with people of the same age group. Just as little toddlers would like to play with their counterparts, many adolescents wouldn't find it too interesting to spend excessive time with their parents or older persons. They may not find much pleasure in spending too much time with their younger siblings either. They differ in their accents. Adolescent boys and girls do not think, feel, or act like their parents or younger siblings. They look for counterparts who speak the same language or speak with the same accent.

However, this launching out into the new realm of relationships is not without problems either. Their cortex in the brain that helps with self-control is not fully developed yet. They often are impulsive, careless, apprehensive, fearful, skeptical, self-focused, and emotionally volatile. They are careless about whom they pick and choose as their friends. They are careless about the behaviors and activities they get themselves into. They develop an arrogant attitude, believing they know everything. They become violent and destructive. They are bitter and full of rage toward others, and they see the whole world as inimical. Because of many of these behaviors and attitudes, sometimes a normal and healthy unfolding of their DTS and DTT is compromised or scuttled. They threaten their own survival, and they cause problems in their interpersonal relationships because of the negativity in their thriving.

Adolescence is an age of emotional, physical, and sexual changes. During this time, children go through hormonal changes and notice visible changes in their body. They become aware of a more pronounced change in their biology and physical growth. Most adolescents see themselves growing physically into the size of mature adults. They stand next to their parents or other adults and compare their height. They compare their body muscles with those of adults. They notice changes in their sexual organs, voice, body hair, and so on. They transition into sexual maturity, and nature prepares them for reproduction and continuation of their species.

Boys and girls are often curious about why and how these changes happen, and a natural course of action is for them to explore these changes. The bodily changes are accompanied by emotional changes that drive the adolescents to seek love, support, and pleasure outside of one's biological family. Although they are present throughout life, there is a surge in desires, imaginations, and fantasies, particularly in the direction of sexual expression, at this stage. They become romantic. They look for other individuals who speak their language and understand their accents. Their peers often meet these needs and provide avenues to explore the "limitless world of freedom."

When young boys and girls go through their adolescence, they experience a substantial change in their sense of self. They become more and more aware of their "self" and their position in relation to other "selves" in the community or society. They realize that they are no more little children to be coaxed and coached by parents and others. They know they are separate and different from others, but they are not sure who they are. They go through moments of questions, doubts, crises, and frustrations. Erik Erikson refers to this stage as a time when young men and women are conflicted about their ego identity. They don't know who they are. They are confused about where they belong. Their association with other like-minded adolescents is often a way to solidify their sense of self or ego identity. If properly oriented, these associations will help them solidify their sense of self. The peer groups, if chosen well, will help them move steadily in their growth and development. They will then survive and thrive well.

The peer group is a powerful incentive and intoxicant. Many of them might seem to speak the same language and understand each other's accents. The group support might seem to be a much better alternative than the support of the family. However, for some, the curious exploration of the world of their peers takes them to extreme behaviors and practices. They see themselves getting involved in destructive and violent behaviors, substance abuse, chemical dependence, alcohol dependence, and promiscuous sexual behaviors, and they may develop belligerent attitudes. These behaviors often give them a sense of mastery. They may also exhibit these behaviors to make up for the sense of helplessness that arises from the lack of coherence and solidity they feel about their self. Although they are driven by a desire for freedom and curiosity, they end up being dependent and controlled by these behaviors and habits. When these things happen, their DTS and DTT get stunted in some way. Unless they have an adult person(s) who is capable of seeing the bigger picture of their life and guides them in ways that are more constructive and healthy, these adolescents might end up in serious danger of destroying themselves and others.

Peer relationships are not without discord and conflicts within the group either. As much as one wants the support of the peers, so much more does he or she resent peer pressure. A few in the group might dominate and even turn aggressive toward others. Bullies and self-focused individuals are part of any such group. They might drag everyone to unhealthy and risky behaviors. It is a dance between seeking the peer support and resenting the constraint that arises from that support. Although the peer group provides a certain amount of security, the pressure to remain with the group and act according to the dictates of the group is a controlling factor. If some resist the pressure and resent the actions, it might give rise to conflicts.

Adolescents may break free from their parents or biological families and end up with peer groups or cliques, but sooner or later they might realize that a totally unlimited freedom is a fantasy rather than a reality. They may escape the supervision of their parents, but they bump into more hurdles regarding societal norms and rules. Sooner or later, they come to realize that life is not just about themselves, but a whole lot of other people in society as well. Society has certain expectations and standards that everyone is expected to abide by. They cannot simply have a "limitless world of freedom." Soon they might also realize that moving out of the restrictions of the biological family means moving into the restrictions of the peer group. The dynamic is more or less the same; only the players in the game change. Moving into a peer group might mean coming into contact with like-minded people, but sooner or later the adolescent might realize that it also means coming into contact with equally disoriented and disenchanted people. Often the group has a collective mentality and is left without the advantage of a guiding figure who can see life and the world in a different way.

Adolescents and their parents differ in their accents and in the way their DTS and DTT operate. Unless each of them makes an honest effort to understand the other, growth and forward movement become near impossible. Although a teenager is at a much higher level of understanding and perceiving things than a toddler or young child, his or her worldview is still small. Besides, each child comes with a different temperament and personality structure. As it happens in childhood, the adolescent might resent the boundaries and restrictions because he or she is looking for opportunities to break free from all constraining factors. The resentment might be expressed through destructive behaviors, social and emotional withdrawal, rebelliousness, belligerent and combative actions and attitudes, acting out, etc. Some adolescents stay out partying and hanging out with their friends way past their curfew time, making their parents worried and angry. Being fed up with these behaviors of their adolescent children, some parents tighten the rules and limit their freedom. This leads to more mismatches in accents and consequent conflicts. Some parent might also wish that they would be freed from the responsibility of caring for their adolescent children.

Some of these behaviors and relationship dynamics, of course, do not apply to all cultures and societies. Curfew, for example, is an order or requirement for children or guests to return home at a specific time after they have gone out in the night to party or hang out with their friends. This kind of system is usually seen only in individualistic cultures and specific places, such as hostels. Wherever such systems exist, most adolescents abide by the rules. However, some stretch it a little further and aggravate their parents or guardians.

Another example is the exploration of avenues for romantic and sexual relationships among adolescents. Not all cultures approve of such relationships or behaviors. Certain cultures and communities frown upon such behaviors and put a cap on them. Even the typical age-appropriate adolescent behaviors may not find adequate avenues for expression in such cultures and communities. That doesn't mean that such longings for exploration disappear. They might resurface at a later stage, as far as ten or fifteen years later, when the individuals are freer and are on their own. When they reappear, it may seem strange, as those individuals look like adults but behave like adolescents. It is not uncommon to see married men and women behaving like adolescents, making their spouses to wonder when they will "grow up." Lack of appropriate avenues for growth and development and undue restrictions from parents or the larger society can stunt the growth and development of adolescents, and that can negatively impact their future life and relationships.

Not all cultures see too much stress and storm in the lives of their adolescents either. In some cultures, the adolescents generally do not act out, become aggressive, or cross the sexual, gender, or generational boundaries. They seem to be much calmer and put together. These differences may have something to do with the overall culture of the society.

In cultures where the adolescent phase is stormy and stressful, both parents and children sometimes find it hard to understand each other's accent. Parents who have had unhealthy and negative experiences during their own childhood and adolescence might find it difficult to deal with the wayward behaviors of their adolescent children. It might trigger in some parents memories of their own teenage years. Many of them might emulate their own parents in dealing with the wayward behavior of their "incorrigible" adolescents. They might become dictatorial and intimidating, or excessively loose and neglectful. Some parents might take the rebellious and destructive behaviors of their adolescent children as a sign of their failure, powerlessness, and poor parenting. Some parents use and abuse their adolescent children to deal with their own personal, marital, or family issues. The adolescent might become the recipient of the parent's anger or frustrations that arise from the marital discord or other issues going on in their personal, family, or professional life.

As they wish that their incorrigible adolescent children leave their house at the earliest opportunity, parents also mourn the prospects of being disconnected from their children. The adolescent children distance themselves from their parents little by little. They find satisfaction outside of their family and spend most of their time in romantic or peer relationships. They feel awkward in sharing with their parents what they are going through. They become less communicative and pull themselves away from the parents. The parents often are taken by surprise by such behaviors. "What happened to my son?" a parent of such a child might say. "All of a sudden he has become silent. He doesn't communicate anything to us." Such parents are at a loss about what is going on with their adolescent children. This shift in relationship once again makes the parents, especially the mother, return to the feeling of not being needed. They return to the sense of being there to be left.

Adolescence is a time of high volatility in emotions for both parents and their children. For parents, all of a sudden they realize that their little boy or girl has grown so big and adultlike. In one moment they become teary eyed because of their joy at seeing the amazing growth and development of their child. In another moment they become teary eyed for a different reason: their child has become uncontrollable and rebellious. They feel disrespected and ignored. Their joy is turned into sadness and anger. In one moment they want to kiss their child. In another moment they want to kill their child. They hate themselves for feeling that way, but that is how their relationship dynamics make them feel. The adolescents also go through similar emotions. All of a sudden they come to a new realization that their parents, who were so good and loving, have become insensitive and controlling. They feel disrespected and abused. The earlier they break free of that restrictive environment, the better, they think.

If the parents are "good-enough" parents, as Winnicott (1953) termed it, and live a rather healthy life, they will realize that these changes and shifts in relationships and behaviors are normal characteristics of the operations of DTS and DTT and that they do not always occur because they are bad parents or their children are bad children. When their teenage son or daughter tells them, "I hate you," sometimes he or she means it, but most of the times they hate not the parents but the situation that has arisen between them. If they are referring to the situation, the hatred will dissipate when the situation changes.

Parents are more independent, conscious, and experienced than their adolescent children, and they have a better and more complete picture of the world and life. Being aware that DTS and DTT are actively operating in themselves and in their children, if the parents can respect and acknowledge the changes taking place in the adolescents and take the responsibility of setting certain healthy boundaries and limits, they will steer their adolescent children onto the path of further survival and growth. Being more independent and experienced than their teenage children, the parents take the responsibility of setting certain healthy boundaries for the growing teenagers to ensure that their DTS and DTT do not escalate into negative and harmful expressions, threatening their own and others' survival and growth.

Although it might be viewed as constraining and controlling, the parents need to set those boundaries and limits as they would do for a toddler to protect him or her from getting hurt. It is a combination of discipline, respect, and love. Instead, if the parents fail to be cognizant of the physical and emotional changes the adolescents are going through, neglect their responsibilities, fail to set appropriate boundaries, fail to contain the stirred-up emotions of their adolescent children, or act in irresponsible ways, they will do more harm than good to their adolescent children and others who are connected with them. Having been left to deal with their adolescent issues or childhood issues on their own, these adolescents sometimes turn into little monsters, causing trouble wherever they go. It will negatively affect their ability to survive and thrive, and will cause great damage to their lives and relationships. They get stuck in their ways, and without proper guidance, they may not know how to transcend their accents and connect with others.

The parents may not understand the accents of their adolescent children entirely, but if they tune their hearts and minds to understand the language of their children and gently guide them in recognizing the operations of their DTS and DTT, their children will appreciate the environment. When parents steer their DTS and DTT in a way that helps them to realize their parenting or caregiving role and support the development of their adolescent children, not only will they grow, but they will also help their children to move to new levels of growth and development.

Please note that this environment of discipline, respect, and love has to be built up right from the beginning of a child's life. The parents cannot simply introduce or expect such an environment as soon as their child has moved into adolescence. If the parents have been disrespectful, neglectful, unloving, and excessively loose or strict in the early stages of their children's development, they cannot expect any miraculous changes in their children when they become adolescents. A healthy environment for healthy survival and thriving is needed all through one's life. A healthy life is developmental rather than a one-time occurrence. Sometimes the parents are not able to do all this by themselves. They might need to seek the support and counsel of families, friends, and professionals to create such an environment and deal with their children's issues.

Adolescent children may want to associate with their peers and distance themselves from their parents in some way. There is nothing unusual about that. The truth is that they have a different accent. However, both parents and their adolescent children require a healthy understanding of all these dynamics. Parents need to look beyond the threats and rejections and see the new developments as another phase in the unfolding of their children's DTS and DTT. Adolescents also need to realize that they are not completely independent or self-sufficient. They need the continued support and supervision of their parents or caregivers. Ignoring this fact, if they become excessively rebellious and violent, disrespectful and disobedient in their dealings with their parents and others, the operations of their DTS and DTT will be stunted or pushed back rather than making a healthy forward movement. Such adolescents will find their accents mismatched with those of others.

If parents find a fine balance between discipline, respect, and love, and children reciprocate those efforts of the parents by following their directions and guidance, it leads to a healthy unfolding of DTS and DTT and the consequent agreement in the accents of both parties.

16

Adulthood

DTS and DTT continue their operations through the adulthood stage. The young adult survives the volatile and dramatic stage of adolescence and thrives forth into a calmer and settled stage of life. Although it may not be exactly the same across all cultures, adulthood, by and large, is a stage in which one moves out of one's biological family to start one's own family. That also means that the individual begins to make his or her own decisions with regard to what he or she wants to do with his or her life. In other words, those moving into adulthood expect their parents and others not to interfere too much in their personal life and decisions. That is what really separates one generation from another. That is what really ushers in independence from the parents and caregivers. A person at this stage assumes the mantle of self-determination and self-reliance and disengages from the parent generation. He or she is ready to start a family or life of his or her own. This disengagement or separation occurs not because of any disregard or dislike for the parents or caregivers, but because time has come for this person to give a new thrust and orientation to his or her DTS and DTT.

Although we can assign a certain age to this transition to adulthood, it is not necessarily age-determined. Some reach this stage earlier than others. The exact time of this switchover is not universal either. It differs from culture to culture. In some cultures people move into this stage earlier than people in other cultures. But to give this stage of life some distinction, it could be considered as a phase that starts at age twenty-one or thereabout.

Adulthood is a significant stage in one's life. The adult children (it is ironic to call them that; they are adults, but they are children as well) take different directions in their relationship with their parents. Most adults want to free themselves from the constraining environment of their family and begin a life of their own. Their DTS and DTT look for freer avenues and opportunities so that they can bring the best out of themselves. Parents have limitations regarding what they can provide for the full realization of one's potential. Refusing to leave that parent realm automatically stunts the growth of a person. People need to leave the amniotic sac of their biological family to survive and thrive further. By working toward their independence and self-reliance, they give new thrust to their DTS and DTT. By doing that, they also free their parents from the additional responsibility of providing for them. They see it as their responsibility to settle down and allow their parents to be free from the obligation of taking care of them, which they themselves are capable of doing to a great extent.

Once sprung forth from the family environment, the first task for the person is to ensure his or her survival in the new environment. The world out there can be wonderful and yet scary and challenging. The parents can assist their children in the process of switching over from the secure environment of the home to the challenging environment of the home-free world. The parents are in a more independent and privileged position than their children, who are just springing forth into adulthood. The parents can assist them to become responsible and strong adults like them. The children can seek support from their peers and other adults in finding their space as distinct and responsible individuals in the world.

Once a person survives the initial challenges and hurdles and normalizes his or her DTS, DTT will begin to unfold in multiple ways. It might find its expression in the adult trying to achieve excellence in a professional field. It might show up in the form of a desire to get married and settle down with a family. It might show itself in the form of the desire to be a leader in society, be it a leader of a group, political party, government, nation, or community. DTT could express itself in the realm of scientific, technological, and intellectual researches, innovations, and discoveries. It could express itself in poetical and artistic ways. It could unfold itself in a personal or institutional framework. It could find its expression in many of these ways in the same individual. DTT unfolds itself in an adult in multiple ways.

These different routes that the adult person takes in the manifestation of his or her DTT don't have to wait for the adulthood stage for their inception. In some, some of these begin while they are adolescents or even before, but they get perfected more and more as they move into adulthood. And this process of the unfolding and accomplishment of the tasks of DTT continues to the end of one's life. In all things, when channeled in the right direction, the goal of DTS and DTT is to bring the best out of the person. DTS continues to ensure that the person stays alive and fit, and DTT continues to bring the best out of the person.

There are some adult children who do not wish to separate from their parents and begin a life of their own. These are exceptions, but they do exist. They find the constraints of the parents more comfortable than the terrors that they fear would occur if they lived life on their own. They are afraid of the prospects of looking for self-reliance and independence. Some children are so strongly fused with their parents or other family members that they find it difficult to separate and individuate. They could be categorized as what Winnicott called "mother-fixated" individuals. They would find all kinds of excuses for not separating from their parents.

Continued dependence on parents ensures continued security and care, but it scuttles their growth and development. They don't really move into adulthood. They survive, but they don't thrive. It is like desiring to continue in the amniotic sac, not wanting to be born into the extrauterine world because the amniotic sac is cozy and comfortable. They allow themselves to be continually controlled by the parents, even if they have outgrown such an amniotic state. Remaining in the amniotic sac, the individual has nothing to do except be resigned to the rhythm of its functioning. Of course, it is cozy and comfortable, but the amniotic sac is a constraining environment. It does not allow the individual to spring forth and thrive beyond certain limits.

Besides, refusing to leave the amniotic sac can endanger the growth of both the infant and the mother. The amniotic sac has a limit to its expansion. When overstretched, it can cause damage to the mother as well as the infant. Some adults continue to enjoy the cozy environment provided by the parents, and they have no desire to spring forth and give a new impetus to their DTS and DTT. They generally do not demonstrate much zest for life. They live as parasites, sucking all energy out of their parents. They don't survive and thrive well, and they don't allow their parents to do that either. Even if they move out of their parents' home, they will continue to show signs of that unhealthy fusion in their new relationship settings.

Parents, in their turn, could take different directions with regard to their relationships with their children who become adults. Some parents may want to continue to keep their children even if they are adults. This is typical of parents who are afraid of losing their control over their children. They are overcontrolling or they are too strongly fused with their children. For them, their children become a narcissistic extension of themselves. They refuse to acknowledge their children as adults and continue to treat them as children. They deny the individuality and separateness of their children. The development of their own self, separate from that of the mother or parents, becomes a difficult task for such children.

Some parents refuse to part ways with their money or power, lest their adult children become independent or take control of them. Some parents favor some children over others, which leads to a tilt in the balance of family relationships and sibling rivalry. Some parents are afraid to let their adult children go because they find it intolerable "to be there to be left." Their feeling of not being needed returns to them in a big way. The moment their children show signs of distancing themselves, they feel agitated. They cannot tolerate their children leaving them. As they age, this feeling of not being needed might become more pronounced.

There are other parents who might want their children to move out because they see their children as parasites, sucking all energy out of them. They indirectly feel controlled by their children. They look for relief and freedom from their responsibilities of caring for their adult children. Most parents, especially in individualistic cultures, do not allow adult children to remain under a passive, effortlessly earned security and sufficiency even if the children want to continue under their care. They force them out into their own world and make them look for self-sufficiency and self-reliance. Some parents, of course, go to an extreme position of desiring complete freedom from their children. They want to rid themselves of all responsibilities of caring for their children.

When I first came to the United States, I was surprised to hear some parents telling me that they were just waiting for their son or daughter to turn eighteen so that they could ask them to leave the house and find their own place to live. And if the children continued to stay in the parents' house, they would have to pay rent. Boy, I was glad then that I was not born in the United States! But I was quick to remind myself that people born in the United States might find something similarly surprising about our family system in India. In some families in India, adult children stay with their parents even after they turn forty and fifty. An American might say exactly what I said, "Boy, I am glad that I was not born in India!" Cultures differ in the way these things are perceived and handled, but in every culture we find parents and children who go to extremes with regard to separation and dependence.

There are other parents who try to find a middle ground, whereby they continue to care for their children but at the same time wish that their children become self-reliant and independent. Such parents know how to recognize the unfolding of DTS and DTT in their own lives and in the lives of their children. They realize that their responsibility in caring and providing for their children is minimal now and the children need to spring forth into the world, making the best out of their lives and realizing their fullest being. Although it is painful to lose control of their children, they steer their DTS and DTT in such a way that they promote the independence and self-reliance of their adult children.

Although the children are freed from parental control, the healthy maturation of their DTS and DTT will depend on how well they are able to balance their independence from and connection with their parents. Healthy adult children will find ways to build up their own lives and yet continue to stay connected with their parents. They will offer assistance to their parents when necessary, especially when their parents reach old age and are on the decline with regard to health and energy. When parents age, adult children are in a more privileged position, and they assist their aging parents in taking care of their needs. The adult children stand by their side to provide them strength and support. Even if they become self-reliant and independent, they cannot divorce themselves from the rest of their family. They have to find a balance between independence and connection, individuality and collectivity.

Thus, when both parents and children manifest their DTS and DTT in a mutually strengthening way, their actions and efforts become life giving. Although they differ in their accents and in the unfolding of their DTS and DTT, they will be able to complement each other because they have learned to grow into deeper levels of relationship. Such a relationship will help the adult children to understand the accents of other people in society. They will be able to launch out confidently into the larger world and become responsible citizens for their own good and the good of society. They will not only be focused on their own survival and thriving but also on assisting those around to survive and thrive so that they can also bring the best out of themselves. Whether in family life, professional life, or leadership positions in society, they will be able to survive and thrive well, and help others to do the same.

If adult children marry and begin their own families and raise children, they become a link in the intergenerational dynamics of DTS and DTT. A healthy unfolding of DTS and DTT in their own lives and in the lives of others in their family means that they become a support system for each other in their spousal relationship, a support system for their children in their parental role, and a support system for their own parents in their role as children. They become responsible parents, building a strong and healthy family and laying a strong foundation for the healthy development of their children. They survive and thrive well as a couple, and they become a support system for their children and others. Such adults become a blessing for any community and society.

If adult children decide to achieve excellence in a professional field or in the area of art, science, or technology, a healthy unfolding of their DTS and DTT means that they give their best in what they do and help the development of the society. They make use of the intelligence and abilities that God has given them and do things to help people live better. Adults who decide to become leaders in the community—whether political, religious, or social—focus on working hard to make this world a better place. They become the voice of God in the community, helping everyone to follow good and godly ways and uniting them as one family. Adults who invest their time and energy in commerce and business do the same. They follow honest ways in trade and transactions. Thus, all these men and women who leave their parents and start lives of their own work hard to survive and thrive well, and they help others to do the same. When positively oriented, they are able not only to bring the best out of themselves but also to assist others to do the same. They are like the seeds that fell on good soil in the parable of the sower that Jesus related. They would produce rich results, "some a hundredfold, some sixty, some thirty" (Mt 13:8).

The responsibility for providing an adequate environment for such positive and healthy adult expressions of DTS and DTT rests primarily upon parents and families. Whether or not a person survives and thrives well in his or her adult life depends on how much the parents and families have groomed him or her for it. As with adolescents, adults don't turn out to be good just like that if the preceding stages of life are not healthy and stable. Exceptions are always possible, but in the normal course of life, a healthy life is developmental, and it has to be built from early on. If parents neglect or fail to bring up their children in a loving and caring environment, they cannot expect them to undergo a miraculous change when they become adults.

Children who grow up in unstable and unhealthy family environments do not know how to survive and thrive in a healthy way when they become adults. They might find their accents often mismatched with those of others. If they had dominant and controlling parents, for example, they might in turn become dominant and controlling toward others. If their parents were too rigid and strict, they might become just like them or become the opposite. They might become messy and disorganized. They might become extremely fearful, submissive, and dependent, or they might become rebellious and destructive. If they did not have a healthy attachment experience, they might become too distanced or too clingy. If the family had no order or structure, they might become too disorganized and show disregard for the structures and systems in society. If they were abused and ill treated, they might become perpetrators of the same crimes. If they were deprived of the basic necessities of life, they might view others and the world as uncaring, cruel, and hateful. As a result of all these factors, they might do things that destroy themselves and others. Their growth and development would then become stunted, and they might become a problem for others.

The unfolding of DTS and DTT in adult life can be varied and complex. Although the primary responsibility of providing a healthy environment to children to launch confidently into this stage of life falls on parents and families, the community and culture in which these children grow also have vital roles to play in this matter. Why and how people do things depends a lot on how much the community or society favors the healthy survival and thriving of its members and provides avenues for them.

PART III

The Wrong Direction

17

The Two Sides of the Coin

Looking at the unfolding of DTS and DTT in the various developmental stages of our life, we see how complex and complicated their operations can be. Our survival and ability to thrive involve much effort and energy. Many people and things are involved in ensuring our healthy survival and thriving. When positively oriented, DTS and DTT take us on the path of growth and development. They help us to bring the best out of ourselves. We will find our accents matching those of others, and that helps us build healthy interpersonal relationships. We will not only grow and develop but also become a blessing for others. Positive survival and thriving help us to find communion with God and others. But our DTS and DTT also have a great potential to create debilitating accents in us and cause problems in our life. When negatively oriented, we will be led to attitudes and behaviors that are not very healthy for others and us. Negative DTS and DTT make us take a wrong direction. They make us speak with wrong accents, or they cause us to find our accents mismatched with those of others. When such mismatched accents arise in our lives and relationships, we will find our personal and communal lives difficult.

In the early stages of life, DTS and DTT exist pretty much undifferentiated and uncontaminated. We simply survive and thrive without much negativity. But as time passes by, and as we pass from one developmental stage to the other, the operations of DTS and DTT get more and more differentiated. They operate differently in different people, depending on who the people are, where they come from, and what they do. For everyone, the focus is to survive and thrive, but as life takes us through different routes and directions, survival and thriving begin to mean different things to different people. The emergence of will and the freedom to choose play major roles in the direction we take in our survival and thriving.

We saw that DTS can be a natural generator of mismatches in accents and consequent problems and conflicts in our lives. When their survival is threatened, people might begin to threaten in return. When abused and neglected, they might view others and the world as inimical and unsafe. They might become demanding, retaliatory, resentful, and destructive. They might rob and cheat. They might fight and threaten. They might become antagonistic and antisocial. When their survival is threatened, people look for different ways and means to defend themselves and ensure their survival. Some of those ways being negative and destructive, people for whom this occurs often find their accents mismatched with those of others. Conflicts and problems in their personal lives and relationships are a natural outcome of such mismatched accents. However, if and when their survival is assured, they might soften their stand and try to match their accents with those of others.

The power of DTT in causing mismatches in accents and consequent troubles in our lives is much more extensive, because thriving means different things to different people. Both parties, those who manifest their DTT negatively and positively, might call the direction they take "thriving."

Positive thriving means that the individual makes choices that enhance his or her growth and development, which ultimately brings the best out of him or herself. The person strives to excel in whatever he or she is without being a threat or pain to others. Such persons don't feel the need to grab and accumulate things or exploit and cheat others. They don't run after money and power. They feel content with who they are, what they do, and what they have. They seek harmony with God and others. They also assist others to bring the best out of themselves. They become a supportive environment in which others may survive and thrive.

Negative thriving means that the individual makes choices that are unhealthy and destructive. Such persons are never satisfied even if they have enough to ensure their survival and growth. They actively pursue the path of power, prestige, and pleasures. "Enough" is not a word in their dictionary. They grab and are greedy. They don't mind exploiting or destroying others to expand their empire. They rob because they are never satisfied. They become extremely self-focused. They bring the worst out of themselves. They focus only on a few aspects of DTT and ignore other aspects that are important for their overall development. The few aspects that they choose may favor their advancement in some sense, but they may be bereft of any positive energy or life. As mentioned earlier, a person can be an extremely successful entrepreneur or businessman but can also be destructively and painfully narcissistic when it comes to interpersonal relationships. Besides destroying their own lives, such people will end up destroying the lives of many other people.

Although DTS and DTT should work hand in hand to keep the person alive and thriving, DTT could sabotage the working of DTS. In other words, DTT could threaten and end one's own survival. When a person's DTT is negatively and destructively channeled, he or she is self-sabotaging his or her own life and survival. Some people dig their own graves, and in the process they bury many others too.

Talking about what negative survival and thriving can do to us, Jesus told a parable of two sons (Lk 15:11–32). Although it is often referred to as the parable of the prodigal son, the story is about both sons taking the negative route. The younger son took his inheritance from the father, went to a faraway country, and squandered his property. He survived and thrived negatively, leading to his own destruction. He separated himself from his father and brother, and lived a totally self-focused life. The older son stayed with the father, but he was full of rage and held a grudge. He didn't truly love his father or brother. He also survived and thrived negatively. His suppressed anger and disappointment came into the open when he saw his father forgiving and welcoming back his younger brother. Both sons survived and thrived negatively, but each one had his own way of doing it. They were cut off from the father and from each other. They did not really live healthy and happy lives. Their negative survival and thriving left the family divided. One was narcissistic and wasteful, and the other was passive-aggressive. Both were destructive for themselves and their family. Jesus cautions us about all kinds of negativity in our survival and thriving. If not prudent, we might see our own destruction, and in the process we might do great harm to others.

DTS and DTT manifest themselves in us in different ways. Sometimes we may see both the negative and positive dimensions simultaneously present in us. But most of the time, we may have one of these dimensions dominating. It is like the two sides of a coin. What we see, the head or the tail, depends on how the coin is held or placed. Just because we see only one side of the coin, it doesn't mean that the other side is nonexistent; but the side that is visible to us is what affects us most. The impact of DTS and DTT on us depends on how frequently and consistently we allow one of these two dimensions, the positive or the negative, to dominate in our lives.

We could recognize them in our own lives, but the best way to identify the positive and negative manifestations of DTS and DTT and their great impact on our lives is to recall some prominent names in our history. When names of certain well-known people are mentioned, most people can associate them with the positive or negative manifestations of DTS and DTT. By their lives and actions, these people of renown have shown the world what it means to positively or negatively survive and thrive.

For the positive manifestation of survival and thriving, I consider names like Abraham Lincoln, Peter Damien of Molokai, Mother Teresa of Calcutta, Martin Luther King Jr., Mahatma Gandhi, B. R. Ambedkar, Helen Keller, and Nelson Mandela. The list is not exhaustive, but a lot of people in the world recognize these figures. They all attract or attracted a lot of attention and public adulation, but most of that attention and adulation came uninvited and unsolicited. They didn't ask for it; it came to them because of who they were and what they did.

All these men and women, I believe, had their own drives to survive and thrive with immense possibilities, both positive and negative. They had their flaws, but they made honest and conscious efforts to channel their DTS and DTT for things that were life-promoting and liberating. Many of them, in the accounts of their own lives, state that they had to constantly battle against their own flaws to stay away from all negativity and stay focused on what was positive. They show us how we can fight our flaws and follow the path that God has traced for us. They had a passion for life and not death, a passion for construction and not destruction, and a passion for good and not evil. They looked into themselves and saw something beautiful within. They allowed it to grow and develop. They showed us what it means to follow God's ways. They brought the best out of themselves. They did it with hard work and sincerity. They didn't see the need to hate or harm, to grab or be greedy. Instead they endured hatred and hurt, and they shared with others what they had.

They not only allowed their DTS and DTT to bloom and shine but also helped others to do the same. They looked beyond themselves and looked at the world around them. And they saw thousands and millions who had an equally powerful longing for survival and thriving but were less privileged, less independent, or less able-bodied, for whatever reason. Some of them were less privileged and less independent as a result of their own imprudence. Others ended up in that position because of the selfishness and greed of those around them. But whatever may have been the reason for their hapless state, they all had a desire to survive and thrive but had no one to assist them in bringing them to their fruition. So these great personalities, driven by their own lives promoting DTS and DTT, came to lift them up. They made a conscious decision to steer their DTS and DTT in such a way that it would light fires in those hapless folks. Their focus was not manipulation and enslavement but enrichment and emancipation. They showed to the world that humanity had the capacity to bring out the best in themselves. They showed that there is something noble, glorious, and heavenly in all of us. They showed that we could live in harmony with God and others. They bent down to lift others up. And by doing that, they were not losing anything but were rather gaining an immeasurable honor and glory. They survived and thrived well, and they helped others to do the same.

By surviving and thriving well and helping others to do the same, they played their parts in setting in motion the materialization of the great ideals and dreams encapsulated in our legends and stories. They demonstrated that love was more powerful than death and evil. Even though they did so only for a limited number of people, their actions ushered in a situation of peace, prosperity, and freedom for those hapless people. Their influence and inspiration reverberate throughout the whole world.

These are only a handful of people who came into the limelight, thanks to the media and others who were connected with them. But there are millions of other people who have not come into the limelight but still try to survive and thrive well and help others to do the same. They are in the unknown world of our homes, communities, and neighborhoods. We see their faces in a woman who silently toils in the kitchen for love of her family; a daily-wage laborer who pulls a hand-drawn rickshaw to provide for his family; an unassuming child who smiles at people even when they show their grouchy faces; a doctor, nurse, or firefighter who runs to rescue someone at any time of the day or night; a soldier who does not want to hurt anyone but risks being hurt while on duty; a sweeper who cleans our rooms or offices and disappears unnoticed even before we get to our desk; a teacher who quietly spends her time in the classroom imparting her knowledge and example to her students so that they can grow up; and a committed volunteer or missionary in an unknown land who attends to the lost and lonely, the hurting and the rejected. They all have a drive to survive and thrive, and they do it in a noble and constructive way. They don't demand gratitude or recognition for being the lifeline of our society; they go unnoticed. They are the hidden steel in the pillar of any strong society or community. They find their accents matching those of others. Everyone can understand their language. They connect with everyone.

At the same time, we have seen in our human history, particularly in the past few decades, how certain persons and systems have manifested their DTS and DTT in negative ways as well. They wanted to survive and thrive at the cost of others. Not only have they doomed themselves, but they have also annihilated millions in the process. They looked at everything and everyone as objects for their survival and thriving. They controlled and manipulated people to realize their objectives. They brought the worst out of themselves. Holocaust, slavery, racism, apartheid, colonialism, and the caste system are some of the prominent negative manifestations of DTS and DTT in recent history. These are dark and monstrous manifestations of people's desire for survival and thriving at the expense of others. Those who promoted these institutions mutilated and dehumanized their fellow human beings beyond description. They had an accent that no one could follow. They spoke a language that their victims and the rest of the humanity could not understand.

Miniature and extensive manifestations of negative survival and thriving continue to pop up every now and then in our communities and societies. Wars and violent clashes between peoples and communities continue in many parts of the world. Dictatorial leadership and the subjugation of weaker folks continue to threaten the peace and harmony among people in many societies. People who have taken a wrong direction in the manifestation of their DTS and DTT walk over others without any regard for human values and dignity. They want to survive and thrive at any cost. They are bothered little about what it does to others.

The negative manifestations of DTS and DTT are seen not only in big ways in the society or community but also in small ways in our everyday lives. People harbor grudges, hatred, jealousy, greed, anger, and all such negative emotions, and these emotions come out in several ways in their speech and actions. When they speak and do things, we notice the mismatch in their accents. It is interesting to see how many times we manifest our negativity and aggression in a given day—and this doesn't refer only to life-and-death issues. In our ordinary, everyday lives, we see our accents not matching with those of others in many ways. How often are we in conflict with God, others, and ourselves?

Our human history and everyday lives show us that we can survive and thrive both positively and negatively. While some people survive and thrive well and help others to do the same, others do just the opposite. While some people try to uphold the sanity of the world, others destroy it. Some find their harmony with God and others, while others alienate themselves from God and rip the world apart.

18

A Drive Turned into a Syndrome

A lot of people today have pets. And in many societies, these pets occupy an important place in people's lives. We hear people raving about their pets, giving us the impression that they are talking about one of their children or family members. They talk about the name of the pet, the qualities of the pet, the toys the pet has, and the fun things the pet does. They talk about their pets having a heart problem, thyroid problem, or some other health issue.

Pets vary in color and kind. Some have birds, others have animals, and still others have fish or reptiles. The most common pets are cats and dogs. In many ways, these pets are on par with human beings. They have sports. They have special hospitals. They have advanced technology developed for medical care. They have leisure time. They have special food manufactured for them. They have cemeteries designated for them. They have hotels and suites.

For many people, particularly for those with certain disabilities, pets are their best companions and security. For law enforcement agencies, dogs rival some of the most intelligent personnel on the unit in detecting dangers and protecting the public. As hunters and guards, dogs do a heck of a job in sniffing out prey or predators.

Theorists such as Sigmund Freud and Donald Winnicott have discussed the positive role of animals in human growth and development. Pets, according to Winnicott, take the role of transitional objects to which children get attached in their early development. Animals function as substitutes for emotionally absent parents for many children. Salman Akhtar, a psychoanalyst and author, suggested that since many animals are warm, soft, and available, children turn to them to make up for their physically or emotionally absent parents.

Pets particularly become great companions to people who are lonely and isolated. This is seen often in individualistic cultures, where excessive emphasis on independence and individualism has left many people lost and lonely. Maia Szalavitz and Bruce Perry, in their research, found that a quarter of Americans are pretty much disconnected from everyone else. They have no one they can call their family or relative. They are not orphans by the definition of the word; they do have family and relatives somewhere. However, they are totally disconnected from those relatives. They lose all contact and connection with them over the years. Just as children turn to animals and other objects to make up for their emotionally and physically absent parents, some of these adults who feel lonely turn to pets to fill the void.

Owning pets has positive effects on humans, but some of them need to be tutored first. Often when someone buys or adopts a dog or cat, one of the first things they do is take it to an obedience training class or they train it by themselves. The pet has to learn to obey the master or mistress. It has to be domesticated. The master or mistress tutors the pet in the way he or she wants. When the master says "Sit," it has to sit; when he says "Stand," it has to stand; when he says "Jump," it has to jump; when he says "Pick it up," it has to pick something up; when he says "Put it down," it has to put something down; and when he says "Lie down," it has to lie down. The master has the control button, and the pet has to follow the directions. The master may not be too happy if the pet does something contrary to what is expected of it. Punishments may be forthcoming if the pet does things that displease the master.

There is something to learn from this master–pet relationship. Sometimes our human relationships reflect something similar to our relationships with our pets. Many people suffer from what I would call "master syndrome" and "pet syndrome." Some people try to tutor and domesticate others, while others jump and dance according to the fantasies of their masters. Both master syndrome and pet syndrome are far removed from the ideal of our DTS and DTT. When we have master syndrome or pet syndrome, we are not surviving and thriving well; these are defective manifestations of our DTS and DTT.

We see master syndrome manifest itself in people's lives in different ways. Those with master syndrome try to use others to enhance their own lives. They want to survive and thrive at the expense of others. They channel their DTS and DTT in ways that are advantageous and profitable for them without any consideration for their negative impacts on others. They get a high by pushing others down. They become excessively aggressive, controlling, and dominating. They assume that they have a right to dictate and dominate. They become sadistic and take pleasure in inflicting pain on others. They become fanatic and dogmatic, holding on to ideals that are inherently flawed and distorted. They are set in their ways, and they are bent upon making others bow down before the idols they have created. They possess what Otto Kernberg and Sheldon Bach called a narcissistic personality—an inflated, aggressive, and grandiose self.

Those with a master syndrome feel entitled to every good thing in life. They might look sociable, but deep inside they are all about themselves. They seek all possible avenues to advertise themselves. When they speak, it's all about them. They seek adulation and adoration from others. When they don't find that, they feel bored, angry, and depleted. They act and speak as though they know everything about everything. They have an opinion about everything and everybody. They are afraid to admit that they know very little or nothing about many things.

Although they might look omnipotent and invincible, those with master syndrome might in fact be weak, vulnerable, and empty deep within themselves. They are often angry at and dissatisfied with themselves, and they turn that anger onto others. They become destructive and demanding in their relationships with others. Sheldon Bach would say that in the case of those with self-oriented and narcissistic personalities, all their actions could be construed as a defense against their own vulnerability and weakness. They appear to others and want others to think of them as strong and powerful, but in reality they are weak and vulnerable. They are like individuals who grow ferocious dogs to guard their houses. Deep inside they are weak and vulnerable, and afraid or suspicious of the enemy. But externally, through the barking dog, they appear to be strong and aggressive. Those with master syndrome may be weak and vulnerable inside, but externally they manifest an aggressive and sadistic personality.

Do these men and women know that they are operating with master syndrome or a flawed sense of survival and thriving? Most of them don't. For many of them, all these things appear to be normal and necessary for their survival and thriving. They don't think that they are doing anything bad to anybody. Their thoughts, feelings, and actions fit well with their character structure.

Those with pet syndrome, on the other hand, take pleasure in receiving pain. They take pleasure in being the victim. They allow others to walk all over them. They don't ask why they should jump and dance for everything and everybody. They have a masochistic personality—a deflated, dependent, and helpless self. They blindly support or silently approve individuals and systems that suffer from master syndrome. They are also responsible for the perpetuation of evil structures. They mistake domination for love and masochism for selflessness. They let the masters abuse and exploit them. They are afraid to stand on their own. They are afraid to stand up to those who want to survive and thrive selfishly. Some of such individuals might belong to the category of people that Sheldon Bach called "inactive sadists." All their victim-like behaviors might be, in fact, a defense against their dormant aggression and sadism. They are also often angry at and dissatisfied with themselves, but they turn this anger onto themselves. They become self-destructive and suicidal.

Do they know that they are operating with pet syndrome and a flawed sense of survival and thriving? Not really. They think they are doing the right thing. For some of them, that may be the best thing that they are able to do in their particular situation and according to their character structure. It takes a lot of effort and energy from within or outside to think and do otherwise.

Both the master syndrome and the pet syndrome are perversions of DTS and DTT. The master syndrome manifests the characteristics of homicide, and the pet syndrome manifests the characteristics of suicide. Sufferers of these syndromes may not kill others or themselves in the literal sense, but they do things that are equivalent to killing others or themselves. Both are bad and are perversions of our DTS and DTT.

Sheldon Bach conceptualized perversion as an "ego defect." A person with a master syndrome or pet syndrome thus can be considered an ego-defective person or a person with a defective DTS and DTT. Instead of leading the individual to a healthy development and harmonious living with others, they take him or her on the path of destruction and death, degeneration and decay.

We see master syndrome and pet syndrome playing out in different relationship settings.

Some marital relationships are riddled with conflicts because of one or both partners trying to dominate or domesticate the other. They become aggressive and sadistic or submissive and masochistic. They either stay in perpetual conflict or break up eventually. Parents and children engage in threats, control tactics, domination, withdrawal, and all such things in family relationships. They act either with master syndrome or pet syndrome. People find it hard to work in certain places because of the master syndrome or the pet syndrome of their colleagues or bosses. Communities and groups find it hard to keep their focus because of these syndromes playing out in their leaders or members. Proponents of certain ideologies and faiths do the same. They suffer from master syndrome or pet syndrome. Master syndrome and pet syndrome are manifested in relationships between nations, and it causes insurmountable conflicts in the world arena.

Force, intimidation, violence, and bloodshed—strategies and methods might differ, but those who are driven by master syndrome speak with wrong accents and create unhealthy environments wherever they are. They survive and thrive at the expense of others. Those with pet syndrome perpetuate such unhealthy environments by being blind supporters and adherents of such unhealthy practices. They survive and thrive to some extent, but their positive survival and thriving are at stake. According to Sheldon Bach, "Every sadist is a latent masochist, and every masochist a potential sadist." Those who act with master syndrome might gain control over everything and everyone for a while, but unfortunately it doesn't last long. They dig their own graves. Soon they might realize that their unquestionable power over their victims is not eternal and unbreakable. The irony is that the villain or the hero— however you may want to name the one with master syndrome—is often blind to the fact that those with pet syndrome also have DTS and DTT that could unleash themselves in an equal or more forceful negative manner someday.

In every victim there is a victor. In every slave there is a master. The roles may be reversed, and those with master syndrome might find themselves in the position of the victim. Those who act with pet syndrome might be waiting for an opportunity to strike at the master's heel and inflict pain on him or her. They may be keeping their aggression and anger dormant and hidden, waiting for an opportunity to strike back. Today's victim becomes tomorrow's victor; today's slave might be tomorrow's master.

Those who are driven by master syndrome and pet syndrome possess a defective DTS and DTT. They do not survive and thrive well, and they deny others the opportunity to do so as well. They cause great damage to themselves and others, and their accents do not match with those of others.

19

At the Systemic Level

The negative and sadomasochistic dimensions of DTS and DTT sometimes take a collective identity and create havoc not only for certain individuals and families but also for their societies. This happens when like-minded people with defective DTS and DTT join hands. This may occur in the form of one person taking the lead and others rallying behind him or her, or a group of people sticking together behind an idea or ideology. They form themselves into a system. They become organized and institutionalized. To start with, they may appear to be good and beneficial for everyone, but gradually they turn on their real color and manifest their master syndrome in devastating and destructive ways. They will begin to control and contaminate everyone. And they always find people who rally behind them. Those with master syndrome often survive and thrive because there are others with pet syndrome to support them. Obtaining uncontrolled power, they become answerable to none. They become a system by themselves. When something becomes systemic, it has an overarching influence and impact on a larger community of people.

We see the negative dimension of DTS and DTT taking a collective or systemic identity in many ways in our world. Political, social, religious, and economic—on all these fronts, people are subjected to systemic and systematic manipulation, intimidation, exploitation, subjugation, domination, and even annihilation.

We see political systems that suppress opposing voices, social systems that favor one group over the other, religious systems that are intolerant of different views or other religious faiths, and economic systems that favor one class over the other. One group threatens the other. They outsmart and annihilate, subjugate and humiliate, and assault and abuse others.

On the political front, defective DTS and DTT show up in several ways. There are political leaders who become dictatorial and suppressive. They don't tolerate dissenting voices. Their focus is their survival and thriving by all means, even if it means trampling others under their feet. Then there are others who grow fanatic about their political views and ideologies. They become nationalistic and fundamentalist. They get stuck in their ways, and do not find space for anyone else. The systems of such leaders have large-scale impacts on societies or world. They become a nuisance to everyone.

The most dangerous of all political systems are those that have power without any control or accountability. They are beyond reason or reproach. Power without control and accountability is dangerous even in the hands of a saint. Of course, we then don't call the person a saint! Nevertheless, some might act saintly and savior-like even though their hidden agenda is not any saving act but rather self-aggrandizement. They silence everyone who dares to question them.

Wrongly directed desires for survival and thriving result in nations and groups engaging in aggressive confrontations. In most of these aggressions and conflicts, the driving force is that of a select few who are driven by their defective DTS and DTT. Everyone else rallies behind them, either by force or by frenzy. Masters always find pets who follow their orders.

Sometimes the society as a whole might actively promote aggression among their members. The instinct of aggression is given a societal approval. They frivolously engage in building up their stockpiles of arms and ammunition. They procure weapons of mass destruction and of deadly effect. They don't inquire whether their citizens have food on their plates, but they ensure that their arms depots are stockpiled with weapons and ammunition. Instead of investing in the growth and development of their people, they invest in their weaponry.

There are industries that thrive on this philosophy of aggression. Although they take on an identity of their own, these industries are simply the institutionalized version of people's negative DTS and DTT. It is an institutionalized version of people's aggression and master syndrome. Many people become part of such large systems that perpetuate the negative manifestation of DTS and DTT. They cause death and destruction all over the world. They determine how much blood will be spilled all over the world. They determine how much death and destruction await our future. They thrive on others' suffering. Many of them become part of these systems without knowing that their bread is born out of the blood of several others. Sometimes we get ourselves into systems that we find it difficult to come out of.

A veteran of World War II whom I met recently told me how shattered he felt about the direction our world has taken since the end of the war. He said that there was much relief when the war ended, and he had hoped that there would not be any more war in human history. But his hopes and expectations were short-lived. He saw many more wars waged between nations and people.

Then there are other veterans who rave about the wars they fought. They glory in the power of their army and armaments.

If we don't contain our aggression and master syndrome and stop supporting those who negatively survive and thrive, we will see many more world wars and conflicts.

On the economic front, things have not changed much for the better. The divide between the rich and the poor has been growing steadily. Wealth gets pooled in a few hands and a few countries. Economic exploitations of the poor and the disenfranchised go unchecked in many societies. The commandment, "You shall not steal" (Ex 20:15) has been deliberately ignored by many people. Those with master syndrome and defective DTS and DTT continue to dictate the course of world affairs.

The social realm may be one area where unimaginable changes for good have occurred over the years. Although they are not completely wiped out, caste discrimination and slavery are largely relics of the past. Gender discrimination and the neglect and abuse of children, the disabled, and the elderly are taken note of and are getting rectified. Things have changed, but there are still many instances where the poor and the weak are neglected. People continue to unleash their vices and negative DTS and DTT onto hapless and helpless folks in the society. When the society itself or groups within the society condone such practices, it becomes difficult to contain the consequences.

The negative and destructive dimensions of DTS and DTT are manifested in the religious realm as well. Much blood has been spilled over religious beliefs and practices. Many religions call themselves a "way of life." But the way that they choose is one of hatred and intolerance, division and isolationism, and fanaticism and fundamentalism. It is not a way that leads to life, but rather to death and destruction. People try to control the realm of the holy, trying to domesticate God or the divine.

God might be the one concept that has been butchered and revered the most in our human history. Although trying to appease a bloodthirsty God is often thought to be a thing of the past, it continues even to this day. In the religious garb of pleasing or protecting God, people engage in unholy acts and alliances to advance their agendas of negative survival and thriving. They promote fundamentalism and fanaticism, and engage in vices and violence. They appear absolutely sure of everything, even God, and no one can question them. They threaten, silence, and kill those who oppose or deviate from their path. These may be only a select few, but they can rouse up passions and emotions in people. Fanned by a passion for their beliefs, like-minded people rally behind these select few and follow their path of violence, destruction, and death. Even if God were to tell them that he did not desire violence and bloodshed in his name, it is doubtful whether they would stop their violent devotion. They want to take care of God. They become passionate, like one of the disciples of Jesus, Simon Peter, who drew the sword and cut off the high priest's servant's ear (Mt 26:51). Peter wanted to take care of Jesus through a violent act, but Jesus told him, "Put your sword back into its place; for all who take the sword will perish by the sword" (Mt 26:52).

Religious fanatics and fundamentalists have always found the religious sentiments of people as the best tool to manipulate and arouse passions. It is not difficult to recruit sympathizers for religious causes, and religious extremists who are driven by the negative dimension of

DTS and DTT know this fact too well. Those with master syndrome always find people with pet syndrome to follow suit. We see such elements of negativity and destruction in almost every religion and sect. Violence and hatred are their paths. Their God must be too small to need them to take care of him. Jesus asked his violent disciple, "Do you think that I cannot appeal to my Father, and he will at once send me more than twelve legions of angels?" (Mt 26:53). But some don't realize that. They think God's existence depends on their ability to execute and eliminate his enemies. They are like roosters who think that the rising of the sun depends on their crowing. But when we look deep down into them, we realize that their violent devotion is not so much about God but rather about their own master syndrome. They have their way, and they want to make sure that everyone adheres to that.

In all of these instances, we see that it doesn't take too long or too many people to give a collective identity to the negative dimension of DTS and DTT. There are always people who want to negatively survive and thrive, and they always find sympathizers and supporters to help them accelerate their agenda. Standing alone is not the best choice in many situations. Elisabeth Noelle-Neumann, a political scientist who developed the spiral of silence theory, noted that people in general fear isolation from the majority, and if they find themselves in the minority, they are unlikely to voice their opinion. We are constantly observing the behaviors of those around us, and we look and see which behavior gets approval and which one doesn't. Most people tend to rally behind the behavior that gets the approval of the majority, even if it is evil or wrong. Based on this theory, there is no wonder why sometimes a whole nation or community takes the path of torture, violence, hatred, and destruction. Many of them may be afraid that if they oppose the opinion of the leader or the majority and stand alone, they themselves will be isolated and tortured. They know that if they align with the evil-minded leader or the majority, they participate in the negative manifestation of DTS and DTT, but if they oppose the leader or the majority and stand alone, they will be isolated and even annihilated. Being afraid for their own lives, they sometimes go with the leader or the majority.

Structures and systems are givens in our societal and communal lives. Whether they are political, social, economic, or religious in nature, systems and structures help us advance and develop as communities and groups. But when wrongly oriented, they also cause irreparable damage to our world. They not only scuttle our individual growth and development but also cause colossal damage to society. Instead of uniting us with God and one another, they tear us apart.

20

Indoctrination

Many people are familiar with the Auschwitz-Birkenau extermination camp, known as the death factory, in Poland. During the Nazi rule, people were herded onto trains by the thousands and brought to this camp to be tortured and killed. Those who were forcefully taken had no idea where those trains were headed for. They were told lies when they were taken away from their families. Sometimes whole families were taken. Many of them saw their siblings, spouses, and children for the last time. They were used for medical experiments. They were lied to and deceived before being pushed into gas chambers. Before they were murdered, they were stripped of everything in their life. Hundreds were executed daily, and several thousands of people perished in those camps. Today the camp houses loads of belongings left behind by the inmates. The heaps of sandals, shoes, eyeglasses, clothes, and human hair put on display there give a feeling of Auschwitz-Birkenau as a ghost town. The descriptions and graphic display of what happened there are heartbreaking. The smell of death and decay still persist in those camps even after half a century.

The Abraham Lincoln Presidential Library and Museum in Springfield, Illinois, is a state-of-the-art library and museum illustrating the life and legacy of Abraham Lincoln, the sixteenth president of the United States. It is a treasure trove of history and information, but walking through the halls of that museum, one cannot miss the darkness and death that enveloped that history. The museum gives a glimpse of the brutality of slavery and the senselessness of war. Unfathomable atrocities were unleashed on people kept in slavery, and innumerable lives were lost during the American Civil War.

The National September 11 Memorial at the World Trade Center site in New York is a tribute to those who lost their lives in the terrorist attacks of February 26, 1993, and September 11, 2001. The two beautifully designed memorial pools bearing the names of the deceased inscribed in bronze make those people impossible to erase from our memories and history. However, that does not stop us from feeling the sadness that surrounds those memorials.

I have been to these and a few other memorials and museums in different countries. Today those museums and memorials are open to visitors and tourists. I hate to call myself a tourist in such places. Those men, women, and children who perished there deserved something better. Whatever is left of them should not be on display. Their lives were not meant for museums and tours. However, if those displays did not exist, those people would be completely forgotten. So I am glad that I went and got to pay them my respects. I would call myself a pilgrim rather than a tourist; I went to pay my respects and ask for forgiveness for what was done to them.

Visiting these museums and memorials, one may ask whether human beings are evil, as they have unleashed such atrocities onto their fellow human beings. We are fortunate if we return from some of these places without being sick to our stomachs. Full-fledged wars, genocides, ethnic cleansings, terrorist attacks, and holocaust-like atrocities occur all across the world every day. Nobody is going to raise memorials or museums for those innocent people who are being killed or tortured in those wars and conflicts.

Human beings and human history have always been associated with wars and violence. I am not sure whether we were ever free from them. Cain slaying Abel (Ge 4:8) has been a recurring theme throughout our human history. If not everywhere, at least in some parts of the world, it happens all the time. How many thousands of lives are brought to a sad end by wars and violence? How many lives are lost in armed conflicts? How much bloodshed do these conflicts bring on the earth? Innocent lives are brought to a grueling and untimely halt. Who can atone for the rivers of blood that we have already spilled?

Some wage wars to safeguard their freedom, while others do it to attain freedom. "Freedom" is a big word that makes sense for both the victors and victims. Criminality is present in both. Criminals misuse and abuse their freedom and infringe on the freedom of others. Courts apprehend criminals and assuage assaults upon victims. But life is at stake in both crime and punishment. A criminal takes pleasure in inflicting pain on others, while the court takes pleasure in inflicting pain on the criminal. One is moved by an uncontrolled passion or emotion to harm or kill, while the other is moved by a similar passion for justice and punishment. One is branded as lawful, while the other is branded as unlawful. One is approved of by society, while the other is disapproved of by society. How often have you desired to see a criminal getting punished? How often have you wished that the criminal would experience the same or an equal amount of pain that he or she inflicted on the victim or your loved one? How many movies or shows have you watched where you waited to see the villain get punished or killed? Aggression and violence, revenge and hatred, run almost in everyone's blood. When taken over by passion and rage, our blood boils within.

It is worth noting how aggression gets inflamed in our psyche. The idea of the threat of the enemy grows in our head even without our own awareness. Sometimes we are socialized to fan our aggression into flames. A person who is in no way related to me or associated with me is my friend if he or she belongs to my community or country, or a friendly community or country. But another person can turn out to be my enemy because he or she happens to be on the other side of a border, belonging to a rogue nation or community. Has the former any better quality than the latter to be my friend? No, but that's how I am socialized. Indoctrination is a powerful tool to fan our aggression into flames.

Recently I had someone tell me how in his younger days he was taught to view some countries and communities as inimical and others as friendly. Patriotism and group membership were coupled with hateful feelings about those who were labeled as enemies. Even if he had no personal animosity toward anyone in the other country or group, the philosophy behind his patriotism and group membership had to be, "If the country or group is inimical, everyone in that country or group is inimical. If he or she is not one of our own, we treat that person with caution." He also believed that similar ideas were planted in the minds of those in the other countries or groups as well. He never asked whether people in the other countries felt and thought like his compatriots. When it comes to national, tribal, or group membership, allegiance is coupled with hatred for the enemy. Questions and opinions contrary to accepted beliefs are often not welcome. Members with differing opinion will be branded as unpatriotic or disloyal.

The hateful feelings may have some history going back to wars, confrontations, injustice, or exploitation in the past. But a group or tribal mentality is inculcated in us from early on. Maybe this has a history going back to our ancestors, when such a group or tribal mentality was necessary to stay safe. They had to stick together to remain safe from predatory animals or other tribal groups. But even with the passage of time and all the globalization, we seem not to have shed our tribal mentality. And no one dares to take a different path. Our so-called patriotism and tribalism keep perpetuating in us hateful feelings toward each other. We may wonder whether being civilized means only building cities, eating fancy food, and dressing in modern fashions.

The most effective tool that systems and groups use to expand their empires of negative survival and thriving is indoctrination. The adherents or sympathizers are made to believe that it is about them, their dignity, and their manliness. They are told that it is about those they care for, what they stand for, and their present and future. "Why?" is an unwelcome question. There is no question of asking how the other, even the innocent in another community or across the border, becomes an enemy. Someone whom I have never seen nor will ever see in my life is portrayed as my enemy. Since my safety and security require adherence to the nation's or group's philosophy and doctrine, I seldom express a dissenting or different opinion.

In today's environment, it is hard to find a nation or community that is free from narrow-minded and exclusivist feelings. We may connect with others on the Internet, but not in our hearts. There is large-scale mistrust between people. Nations and groups spy on each other. Even friendly nations and groups have hidden agendas behind their friendliness.

How are we going to be free from these inimical attitudes and ideas? It is not a malady with any one nation, leader, or army in particular, but it is a widespread malady all over the world, pervading the human race. But can wisdom prevail over such ideas and ideologies? Will our presidents, prime ministers, kings and queens, leaders of militant and military forces, leaders of religious and ethnic groups, men with racist and nationalistic mentality, and men and women with fanatic and fundamentalist mindsets come out of their own little worlds and see the larger world of the millions beaming with life? Will they lead their nations and people along the path of peace rather than hatred and enmity? Will we recognize how tribal and uncivilized we are in our thinking and relationships? Will we pay a little more attention to the new standard of life that Jesus offered?

> You have heard that it was said, "You shall love your neighbor and hate your enemy." But I say to you, Love your enemies and pray for those who persecute you, so that you may be children of your Father in heaven; for he makes his sun rise on the evil and on the good, and sends rain on the righteous and on the unrighteous. For if you love those who love you, what reward do you have? Do not even the tax collectors do the same? And if you greet only your brothers and sisters, what more are you doing than others? Do not even the Gentiles do the same? Be perfect, therefore, as your heavenly Father is perfect. (Mt 5:43–48)

We know we have the ability to do things differently. How great a world would we have if we had no more armed forces, no more borders between nations and states, and no more stockpiling of arms and ammunition! How great a world would it be if our children could wake up and see their parents and siblings alive, if they could have enough food to eat, and if they could play and dance without fear! Wouldn't our legends and dreams come true if the young and the old could understand each other's accents, if people of different religious beliefs, ideologies, and races could coexist peacefully, and if societies learned to value the dignity of each of their members?

PART IV

The Reason

21

Why the Negative Route?

We are often caught up in a philosophical conundrum about where the buck should stop or who should be blamed for all our problems, both personal and communal. Do we blame others, or do we blame ourselves? Do we blame the criminal for the crime, or do we blame the environment and the societal system that makes one a criminal? Do we blame our nature, or do we blame our nurture? Or do we blame both? Our judgments and system of justice are often flawed because we don't see the whole truth. Jesus knew why we should not judge—because we often tend to take the splinter out of others' eyes when we have a log in our own. (See Mt 7:1–5.) We don't see the whole truth. And however much we might try, we may still not know the whole truth, because we often carry our own accents and we look at things and people with partial information.

A person who commits a crime is often judged based on the crime that he or she committed. No one might ever ask how he or she ended up being a criminal. Was the person groomed to be a criminal by his or her parents or responsible guardians? Did the person grow up in an unhealthy environment? Did the person grow up with a view of the world as unjust and unworthy of compassion? Does the person view the crime itself as a virtue rather than a crime? Was the person taught to view the crime as a virtue? Does the person have psychological issues that are beyond his or her control?

These details are often not what determine the judgment. Judgment is often based on justice, vengeance, retribution, and punishment. If the judgment is made solely based on the crime and punishment, then it is based on partial truth. And if the judge is leaning more toward a fuller truth, considering both the crime and the reasons for the crime, justice and mercy have to be debated as different options. But if mercy rather than punishment becomes the choice, then there is the question of how much responsibility should be put on the individual for the crime. Does the criminal become not a criminal because he or she grew up in an unhealthy environment? Does one's unhealthy background absolve him or her from the crime that he or she committed? Could everybody commit crimes and blame it on his or her background, misguided education, and psychological issues? This is the conundrum that we are often caught up in. And in most cases, the principle of choosing the lesser evil becomes the parameter for judgment.

When it comes to understanding what makes a person take the wrong direction in life, we have to look at a fuller truth, considering several things. Negative survival and thriving or master syndrome and pet syndrome are not just one day in the making. They are products of a combination of many things. I see them as a result of things such as our distorted sense of self and vision of life, our immediate circumstances, our genetics and heredity, the material from the early stages of our lives, our temperamental differences, our character structures or personality styles, the overall environment in which we are born and raised, our education and formation, and the state of affairs in our culture and society. They all play a major role in leading us in the wrong direction. Spiritual guides and writers as well as authors and clinicians in the area of psychology and other disciplines have looked into and spoken at length about all of these factors influencing the routes that we take in our lives.

Some individuals are confused about who they are. They don't know why they do what they do. And they have little idea about where they are heading. When people are unclear about their self and do not have a clear vision of life, it can cause many problems in their life and relationships. If we don't know why we should survive and thrive well, we may not care how we survive and thrive. We might end up speaking with an accent that does not match with those of others.

In the discussion on the operations of DTS and DTT in the prenatal period, we saw that the new human organism is born out of the union of the male and female gametes. Once united, they have a unique DTS and DTT. But that does not rule out the acquisition of certain characteristics from the father and the mother or previous generations. The child is unique and is different from the father and the mother, but in many ways he or she is similar to the father and the mother. We hear people saying, "He behaves just like his father [or mother]." The father and the mother, in turn, acquired such traits from their parents. Looking closely at some of our character traits, we may recognize their connection with many generations in our ancestry. Some of these inherited characteristics may determine whether we take a positive or negative route with regard to the manifestation of DTS and DTT. We may not understand it fully, but the place of genetics and heredity cannot be ruled out in our survival and thriving. We may not have too many choices when it comes to influencing or altering traits that have been genetically passed on to us. We have to make the best out of what we have inherited. A better understanding of them will, however, help us to avoid situations and decisions that scuttle our growth and development, and our interpersonal relationships.

The influence of our early life experiences on our later life and development is a fact. Even though our genetics may have some influence on what and how we acquire, a lot of it depends on the environment in which we live and grow. We are not completely predetermined by and for something. Our environment and experiences play a vital role in shaping our personality and how we survive and thrive. A person with a consistently negative DTS and DTT may have a dark history that may have been hidden and brewing for many years. The seeds of negative survival and thriving may have been sown long before they began to germinate and show forth. These people survive and thrive, but they don't do it well.

It is generally accepted that children who are exposed to or not protected from excessive amounts of aggression, trauma, life-threatening and scary illnesses, chemicals and substances, shame and humiliation, disappointments and disapproval, and abuses of all kinds—physical, verbal, emotional, and sexual—are likely candidates for many mental health disorders and negatively oriented life. Their DTS and DTT might take a negative direction, creating conflicts and problems in their lives. Rejections, resentments, and negative experiences that a child receives in his or her early development, both prenatally and postnatally, leave a vacuum and a mark of injury for his or her later life. Children are not equipped to deal with challenging and trying situations in later life. Happy, healthy, and positively oriented adolescents and adults are thought to be products of strong and stable homes and environments.

We are also heavily influenced by what is going on in our societies. Many social and cultural elements, which will be discussed later, negatively influence our life and relationships.

Our individual differences in temperaments and character structures could be another reason for negative survival and thriving. It is a fact that temperamentally we are all different. Temperaments are, in fact, patterns of observable behavior that distinguish one person from another. Authors such as Stella Chess and Alexander Thomas have done extensive studies on temperamental differences in children. According to such studies, some children are found to be flexible or easy, others are feisty or difficult, and still others are fearful or slow to warm up.

Flexible or easy children are generally positive in their mood. They can be easily comforted, they eat and sleep on a regular schedule, and they readily adapt to new situations. Feisty or difficult children are more negative in their moods. They have a hard time tolerating discomfort, such as hunger. They are irregular in their eating and sleeping schedules. And they are very hard to comfort when upset. Fearful or slow-to-warm-up children are moody and slow to adapt to change. They show more negativity than other children. But they eventually warm up as parents or caregivers persist with attempts to comfort them. There is found to be some continuity and steadiness in these temperamental dispositions even when the children grow up. Thus there are adults who are flexible or easy, difficult or feisty, and fearful or slow to warm up. These differences in temperaments could contribute to the generation of negative DTS and DTT. A person with a feisty or difficult temperament, for example, may be very sensitive to provocative comments or actions, and this can create ill feelings and a mismatch of accents in relationships.

There are also differences in character structure or personality styles that could negatively influence one's survival and thriving. Psychoanalysts such as Nancy McWilliams talk about character structures or personality styles, such as narcissistic personality, depressive personality, paranoid personality, masochistic (self-defeating) personality, obsessive and compulsive personality, hysterical (histrionic) personality, dissociative personality, schizoid personality, and psychopathic (antisocial) personality. Some people may have a combination of two of these personality styles, such as paranoid-schizoid personalities. Some others may have features of several of these personality styles. Some of us may have certain features of some of these personality styles, but there are people in whom some of these character structures find some consistency and solidity, making them pathological. People with such clearly defined pathological character structures might be prone to negative DTS and DTT. Disordered personality styles could cause hurdles for a person's growth and development, and interpersonal relationships.

Certain immediate happenings or circumstances could generate the negative manifestation of DTS and DTT in our lives. The sudden death and loss of a loved one and an unexpected threat to one's safety and security are a couple of examples for immediate happenings that could arouse all kinds of emotional responses and reactions. Sometimes they evoke negative emotions and consequently wrong accents in relationships.

Thus there are several factors that contribute to the negative manifestation of our DTS and DTT. We are the product of our genetics and environment. We inherit certain traits, and we acquire certain traits. Some of them are inborn, and some of them are learned. Our nature and nurture play a vital role in our personality development. We absorb our experiences in different ways. Some of them we absorb partially, and some we absorb in their entirety. If some of those experiences are overwhelmingly negative and consistent, we may not have sufficient shock absorbers or capacity to handle them or process them. And that can have a negative impact on our DTS and DTT and the development of our accents.

We cannot divorce ourselves from the society and culture that we live in. And sometimes everything that we find in our culture and society may not be all that helpful for our growth and development. Some societal and cultural aspects may have a negative impact on our survival and our ability to thrive. We are not insulated from all the twists and turns of our lives. Hence, some of the unexpected and emergent happenings in our lives also may negatively impact our DTS and DTT. In the next few chapters, I shall elaborate on some of these factors that contribute to the negative manifestation of DTS and DTT, and the mismatches in our accents.

22

Distorted Sense of Self
and Vision of Life

The ancient Greek maxim "Know thyself" has a lot of wisdom enshrined in it. Knowing oneself is very important for one's growth and development. Lack of knowledge of oneself debilitates life and relationships. One of the reasons for our defective DTS and DTT, and the consequent debilitating accents, is our distorted sense of self and vision of life. Knowing ourselves and having a true vision of life, as I understand it, involves three things: knowing who we are, knowing why we do what we do, and knowing where we are going. Referring to these three dimensions of our life, people of all ages have asked, "Who am I," "Why am I doing what I am doing" or "What is the meaning of my life," and "Where am I going?" The first question refers to our identity; the second, to the purpose of our life; and the third, to our ultimate destiny.

These three questions about our identity, purpose, and destiny have always been topics of great interest in both science and religion. Philosophers, theologians, spiritual gurus, psychologists, and other thinkers have tried to find answers to these questions. The language they use might differ, but the questions are the same. Superficial answers do not satisfy them. They would like to get to the crux of the matter. They know that we can search for answers for all our problems on the surface level of our lives, but unless we get to the depths of our being and answer these fundamental questions, things are not going to change much. We need to know ourselves on these three levels. When answers to these three fundamental questions are confused and convoluted, or ignored and denied, we end up with problems. If we want to grow and develop well and bring the best out of ourselves, we have to know who we are, be clear about why we do what we do, and know where we are headed. Both scientists and religious leaders know this fact too well. And more often than not, they complement each other with their answers.

The first question is "Who am I?" If we do not know who we are, we may not know what true survival and thriving is. There are a lot of people in this world who do not know who they are. They are confused about their identity. I am not referring to people who have physical and mental disabilities, but rather those who are more or less healthy physically and mentally and yet confused about who they are. When they don't know who they are, they may not know what it means to survive and thrive well as human beings. They might just keep surviving like animals. But they may not consciously and conscientiously orient themselves to living and thriving well.

Secondly, if we do not know why we are doing what we are doing, we may not know how we should survive and thrive. We might survive and thrive as it pleases us. And that is also going to cause problems for our lives and relationships. What is the meaning of life? many people have asked. Most people would like to know why they live and why they do what they do. If we don't know why we live and why we do what we do, life becomes disoriented, meaningless, and burdensome. There are a lot of people in this world who do not know why they live and why they are doing what they are doing. That lack of clarity about their purpose in life causes many problems for them. They do a lot of things, but they find no joy or meaning in what they do, because they don't know why they are doing it. When they don't have a purpose in life or don't know why they are doing what they are doing, they can't live or thrive well.

And finally, if we do not know where we are headed, we may not know why we should survive and thrive well. And that is again going to cause many problems in our lives and relationships. We will become like a ship that has no clear direction. Having no clear direction and destination, the ship will be stranded on the waters and will be simply floating around. There are a lot of people in this world who are just floating around. They do not have any clear idea about their destiny.

It is anyone's speculation. And so they may not know why they should survive and thrive well.

Thus, these three dimensions of our lives are intimately connected with three questions about our survival and thriving. Our identity would clarify what it means to survive and thrive well as human beings; our purpose would clarify how we should survive and thrive well; and our destiny would clarify why we should survive and thrive well. To have a healthy sense of our self and vision of life, we need to know all these things.

We can look at our identity, purpose, and destiny from different perspectives, such as physical, psychological, and spiritual. All of them are important and make sense, but the most inclusive and meaningful of all, I believe, is the spiritual perspective. It includes the physical and psychological aspects as well. Hence, I am going to look at each of these fundamental questions about our lives from a spiritual point of view—specifically, from a Christian perspective. I assume that these answers will resonate with or share common ground with ideas and concepts offered by other cultures and traditions.

Our Identity

Perhaps the most important and yet intriguing question that we have asked in our life is "Who am I?" We want to find an answer to the profound mystery of our being. Jesus asked his disciples, "Who do you say that I am" (Mt 16:15). People had all kinds of ideas about who Jesus was. Some thought he was a prophet; others thought he was the reincarnation of one of the ancient prophets; and still others thought he was a great teacher and reformer. Being God himself, there is no reason for us to doubt whether or not Jesus knew who he was, but he wanted to know what his disciples and others thought about him. Simon Peter had the most accurate answer: "You are the Messiah, the Son of the living God" (Mt 16:16).

What about us—do we know who we are? The answer is not easy as there are many things that make us who we are. When we think of our identity, we can think of it as multi- dimensional or multi-layered. We have a role or functional identity (father, mother, daughter, son, etc.), a vocational identity (husband, wife, priest, religious, etc.), a professional or occupational identity (doctor, nurse, teacher, engineer, farmer, etc.), a religious identity (Christian, Hindu, Muslim, Jew, etc.), and a denominational identity (Catholic, Baptist, Lutheran, etc.). Then we have a national identity (American, Indian, Mexican, German, Chinese, etc.), a continental and intercontinental identity (European, Asian, African, Indo-American, Latin-American, etc.), a racial identity (Arian, African, African-American, Caucasian, Dravidian, etc.), and an ethnic identity (German, French, Italian, Malayali, Aymara, Kechua, etc.). In addition, we have a linguistic identity (English, Spanish, German, French, Malayalam, etc.), a color identity (black, brown, white, etc.), a gender identity (male, female, or transgender), a caste identity (Brahmin, Kshatriya, Vaisya, Sudra, etc.), and a class identity (upper, middle, or lower). Above all these, we have an animal identity (different from inanimate beings, plants, or fish), a human identity (different from other animals), and a divine identity (children of God).

All these are part of who we are. Among these, some of them are temporary and surface level identities while others are permanent and deeper level identities. Many things about us could change sooner or later. Our vocations, occupations, nationalities, religions, and classes can change over the course of time. Our races and ethnicities can change over centuries. Interracial marriages create biracial and multiracial individuals. There are individuals who do not identify with any race. Who knows what the race of our ancestors was a million years ago. And who knows what the race of our descendants would be a million years from now. Our roles, genders, and several other specificities also will disappear when death strikes us. But there are two things that would remain even after we die: our human and divine identity. We are both human and divine. We are human beings created in the image and likeness of God. (See Ge 1:26–27.) And these two identities, which are intertwined with one another, are permanent and will stay for all eternity.

There may be a question about whether or not after death our human identity is going to stay. I tend to think that it would. Everything else will disappear but our human identity, which is intertwined with the divine identity, will remain for all eternity, because that is who we are. We are not angels or seraphim. We are not God either. Angels, seraphim, and other heavenly beings remain as they are. And God remains as God. We are human beings, intertwined with the divine. We have a unique place in God's family, and we will continue to have that identity for all eternity.

This human and divine identity that we have is not be confused with the identity of Jesus. He was also both human and divine. But he is the creator and we are the creatures. Our divinity is derived or drawn from him, but his divinity is not derived or drawn from us.

Thus, at the core or the deepest level of our being we are both human and divine. Even if everything else disappears, these two dimensions of our identity remain. They are permanent and eternal. Although our humanity and divinity are two dimensions, they are inseparable. This is "who" we are. Every other dimension of our identity could be categorized under "what" we are. And when it comes to the core and essence of our being, who we are is more important than what we are.

This fact of our identity as human beings infused with the divine has many implications.

First, we are privileged and special. There is no other being that is so unique and special as we are. We are created in the image and likeness of God. (See Ge 1:26–27.) We share in his divine nature. (See Gal 4:6–7.) God has crowned us with glory and honor. (See Ps 8:5) Through Prophet Jeremiah, God tells us, "Before I formed you in the womb I knew you, and before you were born I consecrated you" (Jer 1:5). In the book of Isaiah, we hear God saying to us, "I have called you by name, you are mine" (Isa 43:1). Calling someone by name makes it very personal. Telling someone, "You are mine," points to intimacy and closeness. We are the precious sons and daughters of God. We are his. We hear the same message again in chapter 49 of the book of Isaiah, "Can a woman forget her nursing child, or show no compassion for the child of her womb? Even these may forget, yet I will not forget you. See, I have inscribed you on the palms of my hands (Isa 49:15–16). It is rare that a woman forgets her child, but even if that happens, God assures us that he would never forget us. Saint John, the apostle, tells us in unequivocal terms about our privileged position. He says, "See what love the Father has given us, that we should be called children of God; and that is what we are … Beloved, we are God's children now" (1Jn 3:1–2).

God loves his creation, but he has a special place for us. Other creatures or created things cannot take our place. It is like the difference between children and pets in a family. A family may have cats and dogs as pets, and everyone might love them. But the pets cannot take the place of children. Children are special. Parents don't give the same importance to their pets as they do to their children. Of course, in some families, parents might say that their pets behave better than their children. But even then, the pets cannot take the place of children. For God, we are special. We are not like other creatures and created beings. We are his children, created in his image and likeness. Just like some parents, God also could say that some of his creatures behave better than the human beings. But still, other creatures cannot take the privileged place that we possess. It doesn't matter how we look, what we do, and where we come from, we are special and precious to God. We may be hurting, poor, and unrecognized, but we are still God's special creation, deeply loved by him. Ignorance of this privileged position, will curtail our healthy survival and thriving.

Second, our privileged position in the creation is a gift and responsibility rather than a right. Everything in our life is simply a gift. God wills that we enjoy a unique and special position in the creation. But having a privileged position doesn't mean that only we are of any worth and all the rest of the creation is a trash. Everything in this universe has its own beauty and worth. We can only behold them with awe and wonder. Our privileged position does not accord us a right to dominate, exploit, or misuse the rest of the creation. In the past, there have been many such interpretations and mistaken ideas about the privileged position of human beings in the creation. The privileged position that a son or daughter has in the family does not accord him or her the right to kick and abuse the dog or cat. The dog or the cat needs to be cared for and treated well.

Being created as his sons and daughters, God wills that we care for the rest of the creation as he himself does. Our intelligence is not given for self-aggrandizement or exploitation but rather for making this world a wonderful place for everyone to live in. We become cocreators with God to add to the beauty and blessings of this world. We are to be good and responsible stewards. It is like enthroning someone as a king or queen or installing someone as a president or prime minister. It is a privileged position that is given to that person. If he or she begins to consider that position as a right and entitlement, we will be in great danger. The person might begin to subjugate and suppress the very people who put him or her in that privileged position. Ignorance or dismissal of our responsibility towards the rest of the creation could lead to domination, exploitation, and abuse of everyone and everything around us. Our survival and thriving might become the only focus of all our endeavors.

Third, our privileged positions in the community or society are for service. The privileged positions that we hold because of the roles, functions, and other surface level dimensions of our identity are for service rather than for domination. Realizing that they were arguing about something, Jesus asked his disciples, "'What were you arguing about on the way?' But they were silent, for on the way they had argued with one another who was the greatest. He sat down, called the twelve, and said to them, 'Whoever wants to be first must be last of all and servant of all'" (Mk 9:33–35).

Jesus reminded his disciples that being chosen as an apostle or disciple was not for superiority or domination but rather for service. Reiterating the same message, Saint Paul says, "God has appointed in the church first apostles, second prophets, third teachers; then deeds of power, then gifts of healing, forms of assistance, forms of leadership, various kinds of tongues. Are all apostles? Are all prophets? Are all teachers? Do all work miracles? Do all possess gifts of healing? Do all speak in tongues? Do all interpret? But strive for the greater gifts" (1Co 12:28–31). The greater gifts that Saint Paul refers to are all about love, which he elaborates on in chapter 13 of the same letter. Privileges and positions are given to us for love and service.

Going back to these basic ideals of Christian discipleship, Pope Francis in his apostolic exhortation, *Evangelii Gaudium*, reminds those in hierarchy that functions and roles in the Church are for service rather than for domination. Whether it is in the Church, family, or society, we are to remember that our privileged positions are for service and not for domination. Ignorance or denial of this fact can make us seek our own survival and thriving at the expense of others.

Fourth, as human beings and children of God, we are equal in dignity. If we believe that at the core of our being we are all human beings and children of God, we have to accept that all of us share the same dignity and honor. There is no one who is less human and less divine. All of us share in that same human and divine nature. In that equal status, there is no place for disparity or discrimination based on color, class, or creed. In essence, we are all equal. Our real beauty and worth consists in this truth about us. The external factors cannot take away that beauty.

Saint Paul tells us that this identity that we have as God's children unites us as one family, one body. We are like different parts of the body working together to keep the body healthy. He says, "For as in one body we have many members, and not all the members have the same function, so we, who are many, are one body in Christ, and individually we are members one of another" (Ro 12:4–5). Just as different parts of the body are held together, God holds us together as one family, as brothers and sisters. We belong to God, and we belong to one another. We are one body; we are one family. Saint Paul again tells us that when it comes to our identity as children of God, there is no distinction, " ... for in Christ Jesus you are all children of God through faith ... There is no longer Jew or Greek, there is no longer slave or free, there is no longer male and female; for all of you are one in Christ Jesus" (Gal 3:26, 28). He repeats the same in his letter to the Colossians, " ...there is no longer Greek and Jew, circumcised and uncircumcised, barbarian, Scythian, slave and free; but Christ is all and in all" (Col 3:11). Christ is beyond castes and classes, religions and regions, nationalities and races. He is all-inclusive, a Savior to all. In Him we find our true identity as children of God.

This truth about God being all-inclusive is powerfully present in the story of the magi in the infancy narrative of Saint Matthew in the Bible (Mt 2:1–12). According to the narrative, wise men, known as magi, came to pay homage to the child Jesus, who was born in Bethlehem. The magi were not Jewish people. They came from other nations. We don't know what country or race they came from. We don't know what they looked like. We don't know what language they spoke. They represented the non-Jewish people. Their presence at the birth of Jesus indicated that

Christ was born not just for one group of people, but rather for all. No one was to be excluded from the salvific plan of God.

No matter who we are, where we come from, or what we look like, we all have a place in God's heart. We are all human beings and children of God. But this is a great challenge for us in our interpersonal relationships. We have to have the heart of God by being all-inclusive and the heart of the magi by going beyond our territories and lands, and our barriers and boundaries. We have to see people beyond their caste, color, and creed. Faith affiliations, race, nationality, and gender become secondary to our common identity as human beings and God's children. These specificities disappear, but our essence remains. The challenge is to step out of our comfort zones and familiar surroundings, and accept and love others who are different. The challenge is to like those who are not like us externally.

Ignorance or denial of this truth about our equal dignity causes problems in our lives and relationships. When we deny or are unaware that we are all human beings and children of God, we begin to focus on the nonessentials, the externals. We see each other as black and white, Christian and Hindu, Muslim and Jew, rich and poor, and male and female. These are undeniable facts about us, but those things are not our essence. In essence, we are all human beings and children of God.

Fifth, our identity as human beings and God's children calls for a transition from exclusion to inclusion. Jesus prayed, "That they may all be one" (Jn 17:21). Jesus desired that we live as one family, united with God and one another. Our world is enormously divided and segregated. Socially, economically, culturally, politically, and religiously we have divided ourselves into groups and sects. In the story of the rich man and Lazarus in the gospel of Luke (Lk 16:19–31), we hear the rich man crying out to Abraham asking him to send Lazarus to dip the tip of his finger in water and cool his tongue because he was in agony in hell. Abraham replied that there was a great chasm between them that they could not cross from one side to the other. In fact, the rich man had created that chasm when he and Lazarus were alive on earth.

We see the culture of the rich man and Lazarus in many areas of our life. Socially, economically, religiously, and in many other ways, we create great chasms between us. The various surface-level dimensions of our identity keep us apart from each other. The great challenge for us is to recognize our core identity as human beings and children of God, and remove the chasms that we create between us. We have to transition from being exclusive to becoming more inclusive.

To survive and thrive well, we need to be clear about our true identity. Sometimes we get stuck with the surface level dimensions of our identity and fail to recognize who we truly are. In essence, we are human beings infused with the power and presence of God.

Our Purpose

The second fundamental question about our self and vision of life pertains to our purpose in life. What do we think is the reason for our life and actions? What is the purpose of our life?

Saint Francis de Sales, one of the great spiritual writers, in his spiritual classic, *Treatise on the Love of God*, says, "God in creating man in his image and likeness wills that just as in Himself so too in the human person everything must be regulated by love and for love" (De Sales, 2005). Essentially, the purpose of our life, according to the saint, is to manifest God in our life by loving and being loveable. Reiterating this point, Saint John says, "Beloved, let us love one another, because love is from God; everyone who loves is born of God and knows God. Whoever does not love does not know God, for God is love ... Those who say, 'I love God,' and hate their brothers or sisters, are liars; for those who do not love a brother or sister whom they have seen, cannot love God whom they have not seen. The commandment we have from him is this: those who love God must love their brothers and sisters also" (1Jn 4:7–8, 20–21).

The purpose of our life thus becomes the fulfillment of the two commandments of the love of God and the love of our neighbor (Mt 22:36–40). We build a community of love and become a witness to God, who is all love.

This clarity about the purpose of our lives has many implications for our daily lives and relationships. It behooves us to give our best to God and to one another. It implies that we love and serve one another as we would love and serve God himself. Jesus reminds us that this would be the yardstick that would be used to judge our lives, "Then the king will say to those at his right hand, 'Come, you that are blessed by my Father, inherit the kingdom prepared for you from the foundation of the world; for I was hungry and you gave me food, I was thirsty and you gave me something to drink, I was a stranger and you welcomed me, I was naked and you gave me clothing, I was sick and you took care of me, I was in prison and you visited me' ... Truly I tell you, just as you did it to one of the least of these who are members of my family, you did it to me" (Mt 25:34–40). Whatever we do, we do it with this one purpose of strengthening our bond with God and others.

Beginning with our own individual families and extending to the larger world, our goal thus becomes putting ourselves at the service of God and others. Whether we work as doctors, nurses, teachers, businessmen, social workers, engineers, politicians, or leaders in the community, the purpose of our life is the same. A doctor becomes a visible presence of God to his or her patients. A teacher does the same to his or her students. Political leaders or leaders in the community do the same to those whom they serve. Whatever may be the role that we play in the family or society, we are here to be witnesses to all that is good and godly. We do things that promote life and love. We find God in others and become a presence of God to others. We find the kingdom of God within us and among us (Lk 17:20–21).

To the Jewish leaders who asked him why he was baptizing if he was neither the Messiah, nor Elijah, nor the prophet, John the Baptist replied, "I am the voice" (Jn 1:23). Coming as the precursor to the Messiah, John the Baptist invited people to turn away from their sins and change their ways so that they could experience the new life and freedom that God was offering them. People from all walks of life flocked to him in huge numbers and asked him what they must do to experience salvation (Lk 3:10–14). He said they should stop extortion and intimidation and start living fraternally. Those who had more were asked to share what they had with those who had less. Those who cheated and exploited were asked to quit doing that. Those who had turned their hearts and minds to evil and themselves were asked to turn toward God and others.

John's way of manifesting God was by being a voice, the voice of God. He prepared his people to receive the Lord by calling them to a life of holiness, righteousness, justice, peace, and love. He invited them to build a new community with God and one another.

Like John, we are in this world to be a voice, the voice of God. This could mean many things. It could mean that we are here to manifest God by the way we live. It could mean that we are here to live with a sense that we are one family with God and others. And it could ultimately mean that we are here to build the kingdom of God as Jesus envisioned. (See Lk 17:20–21.) Saint Paul, in his letter to the Romans, tells us what it means to build the kingdom of God: "For the kingdom of God is not food and drink but righteousness and peace and joy in the Holy Spirit. The one who thus serves Christ is acceptable to God and has human approval. Let us then pursue what makes for peace and for mutual upbuilding" (Ro 14:17–19).

The purpose of our life thus is not to survive and thrive in isolation or as it pleases us, but rather to make a concerted effort at living a life in communion with God and others. Saint Paul, in his first letter to the Corinthians, uses the example of human body to tell us how we are called to survive and thrive in unison:

> Indeed, the body does not consist of one member but of many. If the foot would say, "Because I am not a hand, I do not belong to the body," that would not make it any less a part of the body. And if the ear would say, "Because I am not an eye, I do not belong to the body," that would not make it any less a part of the body … God arranged the members in the body, each one of them, as he chose … As it is, there are many members, yet one body. The eye cannot say to the hand, "I have no need of you," nor again the head to the feet, "I have no need of you." (1Co 12:14–21)

We are one body; we are one family. And the glue that strengthens this bond is love. Anything that deviates us from this union with God and others should be a red flag. That means that we denounce what is evil in us and in our world. We should have the courage to say that an evil is an evil, whether it is in us or in others. Following up on that denouncement, we have to abstain from being dominant, exploitative, unjust, fraudulent, dishonest, cruel, bossy, mean, unforgiving, vengeful, aggressive, abusive, angry, and selfish. We have to stop being fanatic, militant, hateful, divisive, racist, sexist, parochial, territorial, and tribal in our attitudes and actions. We have to stop being destructive toward ourselves, because we have to love our neighbor as we love ourselves. If we don't love ourselves, we may not know how to love others. We have to take care of ourselves to take care of others. If by mistake or ignorance we have fallen into any of the traps of unhealthy behaviors or attitudes, we need to immediately find ways to extricate ourselves from such evils and set our priorities right.

A lot of our problems, defective DTS and DTT, and mismatched accents are because of ignorance or negligence of our purpose in life. When our purpose is not clear, we might survive and thrive as it pleases us and that always may not be healthy for others and us.

There are many people who do things not because they have a clear purpose in life but because they feel obligated to do them. There are also people who do things because everybody else is doing them and they don't know what else to do. When we are not directed by a clear purpose in life, we could be sabotaging our own growth and development and becoming a problem for others. We may have many things in life but not be living and thriving well.

Our Destiny

The question about our ultimate destiny has been a point of contention and debate for all ages. Heaven, hell, and afterlife have been topics of great interest for a lot of people in every age. What is our ultimate destiny? Where are we heading? We know that our life in this world or on this earth is short. Death puts an end to the journey that we begin in our mother's womb. Although we have not experienced it ourselves, we know death is not going to escape us. It will be here before we know it. But what does death mean for us? What happens during and after death? Is that the end of everything? Is there anything after that?

There are a lot of people who do not believe in anything outside of this earthly life. For them this world is the end. They cannot see or imagine anything beyond the physical realities of this world. For them we are born one day, and we die one day. That's it. There is nothing more and nothing less. But for the vast majority of people, that is not a satisfactory answer. They speculate that there is something more, but they are not sure what it is. To know why we should survive and thrive well, we should have a more-or-less clear understanding of our destiny.

To find the answer to this question about our ultimate destiny, I turn to one of the discourses of Jesus. In fact, it is a prayer that Jesus made on behalf of his disciples and those who would come to believe in him. Addressing his heavenly Father, Jesus prayed:

> I ask not only on behalf of these, but also on behalf of those who will believe in me through their word, that they may all be one. As you, Father, are in me and I am in you, may they also be in us, so that the world may believe that you have sent me. The glory that you have given me I have given them, so that they may be one, as we are one, I in them and you in me, that they may become completely one. (Jn 17:20–23)

Jesus desires that we may be one—one in union with God and one another. Addressing his heavenly father, Jesus said, "And now I am no longer in the world, but they are in the world, and I am coming to you … Father, I desire that those also, whom you have given me, may be with me where I am, to see my glory, which you have given me because you loved me before the foundation of the world" (Jn 17:11, 24). Jesus wants us to be with him. And being with the Father, he wants us to be part of that union. Thus, united with God and one another, he wants us to form one family not only on this earth but also for all eternity. That is what he desires for us. That is our destiny. We are destined for eternity, and the life in eternity is one that is going to be in union with God and others. With that being our destiny, death does not put an end to our lives. It simply takes us to a state where we are no longer limited by the physical realities of this world. We become one with God and one another.

This understanding of our destiny as being in communion with God and others in eternity has many implications for our life. It reminds us that we have to be in communion with God and others not only in eternity but also while we are here on earth. God's ways are not our ways, but in our normal understanding of salvation and eternity, we have to admit that we cannot keep ourselves away from God and others while living in this world and then expect that union to occur after our death. If we look at life on this earth and eternal life as a continuum, we will recognize that our union with God and others after death becomes a continuation of what we begin on this earth. Jesus taught his disciples how to pray: "Our Father in heaven, hallowed be your name. Your kingdom come. Your will be done, on earth as it is in heaven" (Mt 6:9–10). Jesus taught us to pray that things may be on earth as they are in heaven. If heaven is conceived as a state of union with God and others, Jesus reminded us that it should begin here on earth. Heaven, eternal life, or resurrected life becomes a perfection and completion of that union with God and one another that we begin here on earth.

As children of God, our sole purpose in life while on this earth is to serve God and one another, to be a visible presence of God in this world, to be a witness to truth, life, and love. Eternal life becomes a continuation and perfection of the union that we build with God and one another on this earth. In eternal life, we experience life, light, and love in their fullness. We experience God in his fullness. We experience our union in its fullness. For that we have to come out of our little worlds and be connected with God and others. We have to let go of ourselves and be at the service of God and others. We have to seek to live the two commandments of loving God and loving our neighbor. Jesus said, "For those who want to save their life will lose it, and those who lose their life for my sake will find it" (Mt 16:25–26). We will find life when we die to ourselves.

Jesus said, "Very truly, I tell you, unless a grain of wheat falls into the earth and dies, it remains just a single grain; but if it dies, it bears much fruit. Those who love their life lose it, and those who hate their life in this world will keep it for eternal life" (Jn 12:24–25). A grain of wheat left to itself is dry, tight, and constricted. But if it falls to the ground and germinates, it will produce many more grains. Sometimes we might be living as dry grains, closed up in ourselves, living in darkness, and feeling tight and constricted. But if we are willing to come out of our shells and be in communion with God and others, we will experience a new light, come out of darkness, and become a blessing for others. Hating our life in this world means hating a self-only life or selfish life. What takes us to our destiny of communion with God and others is a selfless life. In other words, with reference to our relationship with God and others, our self becomes less. It is neither a self-inflation nor a self-negation; it is neither a denial of God nor a negligence of others; it is rather a self in communion with God and others. It is a union of God, others, and us.

Those who do not believe in this common destiny of being in communion with God and others might engage in behaviors and actions that keep them separated from God and others. They may not care much about any union or communion. They might not bother whether their accents are matching with those of others. They might survive and thrive as it pleases them. They might isolate themselves and live a life engrossed in themselves. As long as the disconnectedness with God and others exists, we will not survive and thrive well. We will continue to do things that separate us from God and others.

Our ultimate destiny of union with God and others is undeniably connected with our identity and purpose in life. We are born into this world as human beings and children of God. Directed by the Spirit of God, we live in this world with the clear purpose of building the kingdom of God by being in communion with God and others. And when our earthly life comes to an end, we move on to an experience of the fullness of our union with God and others. These triple dimensions of our lives cover our entire lives, from conception to eternity. A true sense of self and vision of life will always keep these basic facts about our lives in focus. Any deviation from these causes defective and negative survival and thriving, as well as consequent mismatches in our relationships.

These truths about our self and life or our identity, purpose, and destiny are not exclusive to Christianity alone. We find these in many other cultures and traditions across the globe. In many cultures and traditions, people share in this belief that we are all human beings and children of God. In many cultures and traditions, people believe that the purpose of our lives is to build a community of love by being in service to God and others. And in many cultures and traditions, people also believe that our ultimate destiny is to be united with God and others for all eternity. Our identity, purpose, and destiny, the three fundamental facts about our lives, are thus interconnected. But many people get these basic facts distorted and confused. If they don't care about God and others, they are bound to develop unhealthy relationship patterns and behaviors. They survive and thrive as it pleases them, and they are not able to bring the best out of themselves.

23

When the Past Becomes Present

Being clear about our identity, purpose, and destiny is important for our growth and development, but attaining clarity regarding all these is not easy for many people. There are things in our life that blur our understanding of all these facts. Since many of us are not insulated from the troubles and struggles of life, as we have seen in the discussion on the operations of DTS and DTT through the developmental stages, it is not surprising that we sometimes get our identity, purpose, and destiny distorted and confused. Many of us begin with or develop a wrong sense of self and vision of life. In many ways and on many levels, we experience the weaknesses and brokenness of our humanity, individually and communally.

As mentioned before, things such as our immediate circumstances, our genetics and heredity, the environment in which we grow, the material from the early stages of our lives, our temperamental differences, our personality styles, our education and formation, and the state of affairs in our culture and society have a great impact on how our lives and relationships turn out. In many ways we feel weak, broken, and stuck. Life is not pretty for many people. Many people struggle with their inability to live a healthy and happy life. They have sick personalities and character issues. They get disgusted with themselves, and they become a problem wherever they go. The truth that we are children of God, deeply loved by God and others, does not cancel out our own individual struggles that we face because of our humanity. We inherit some and develop or absorb others over the course of time.

When our lives are not begun well, we end up with many problems. A distorted sense of self and vision of life are already in the making as some begin their lives. They develop a confused and convoluted sense of identity, purpose, and destiny. Since our early life experiences have an indelible impact on our later life and development, it is appropriate here to discuss a little more in detail about them. Sometimes our past is brought into the present in many ways that we ourselves may not understand.

Many children begin their lives with many negative experiences in their mother's womb. They experience shocks and traumas of various kinds prenatally. They are to grow up with a sense of identity as God's children and being loved by others, but their first experiences themselves are not very loving and encouraging. They already get a sense of this world as an unloving and unsafe place for them to survive and thrive. Children who are conceived by mothers who resent their pregnancies, mothers who are exposed to traumatic experiences while they are pregnant, mothers who are incapable of normal physical and mental functioning, and mothers who engage in actions and behaviors that are detrimental to their health and the health of their babies experience a negative and unhealthy environment even before their birth. The negative messages from the unhealthy experiences or actions of the mother get passed on to the infant in the womb, and that has a debilitating impact on the developing child.

For many children, what begins in the womb continues after birth. They are neglected and unattended. They are subjected to emotional torture and isolation. They are shamed and humiliated. They are rejected and frowned upon. They are terrorized by their alcoholic or drug-addicted parents. They are compared with and contrasted against their siblings and peers. They are used and abused by parents who are compensating for faults or who have experienced narcissistic injury. They are treated as the narcissistic extensions of their parents rather than seen by their parents as separate individuals. They are blamed for all the ills in the family. The children themselves might feel that they are the cause for their parents' fights.

The violent and overemotional behavior of the parents puts them on high alert constantly. They may helplessly watch the parents physically and verbally attacking, humiliating, and berating each other. There is constant tension in some families, and children have to be on high alert always. Mothers and other caregivers who go through spells of depression or serious physical and mental illnesses cannot be as emotionally and physically available to their children as the children need. Some children who grow up in single-parent families do not have the privilege of experiencing a father's or mother's love and support. Many children develop a void in their psyche because of the unavailability and lack of emotional connection from their parents or significant others. There is nothing in their immediate environment that indicates that they are the beloved children of God or deeply loved by others.

Traumatized by illnesses, surgical procedures, and prolonged hospitalization, some children begin their lives terrified and shocked. Abandonment, corporal punishments, and sexual and emotional abuses mark the daily lives of many children. Starvation and malnourishment make many children beg and ragpick. Some children are burdened with heavy manual labor and parental responsibilities inappropriate to their age. They are meant to love others, but there is no indication that they can be loved too. Some children live in constant fear and threat of death. They are exposed to gruesome murders and other traumatic events. Some children are discriminated against because of the caste, class, or religion they belong to.

Children experience loss in several ways. Many of them lose their mothers, fathers, or siblings by death, abandonment, murder, forceful separation, or other reasons. Many of them lose significant relationships and familiar surroundings when they are removed or displaced from their homes and lands. When these things happen, they don't even have a chance to mourn and grieve, because their own survival may be at stake.

For many children, it is a long chain of trauma and negativity, abuses and abandonment, and an experience of being unloved and unlovable. They are exposed to negative experiences in different forms and measures, and some children absorb these negative experiences in their entirety. Such experiences cause irreparable damage to their sense

170

of self, worth, and lovability. They feel unwanted, unloved, unlovable, and helpless. They develop different and often negative images of the unfriendly and unpredictable world. They have no experience of a loving God or a loving world.

As children get older and move through the later stages of life, the environment gets more complex and the relationship involves multiple people. They try to fill the void created by the feeling of being unwanted, unloved, and unlovable by turning to peers, neighbors, teachers, employers, masters, and other non–family members. Some of them are again neglected, ignored, and abused by these people they turn to. If they get rejected and removed from positive emotional connections, they are again going to have long-lasting negative impacts on their DTS and DTT caused by subsequent negative experiences. They may not know how to survive and thrive well. Sometimes they are inhibited by these negative experiences. They will approach others with the conviction that they are going to be rejected because they are unlovable. So they already anticipate failure or disappointment and unconsciously set themselves up for it. They do things or speak with wrong accents that make others reject them.

Many children who have been exposed to excessive negative experiences are like a time bomb or a simmering volcano waiting for the opportune time to explode. Already in their adolescence and early adulthood we begin to see indications of the emerging volcano. Anyone—parents, siblings, peers, or teachers—can be subjected to the task of satisfying their need to feel wanted and loved, and recognized and reassured. For some of them, if love and reassurance are not given voluntarily, they try to get it by force. They act out, protest, resist, rebel, and become aggressive. They play control tactics, take on the victim role, become the aggressor, and even fake a nice-guy look. They become a constant nightmare for everyone, leaving them clueless as to how to handle the situations. Because this demand is often made in a forceful and violent way, people do not understand the motive, and they push them back even further into rejection and unwantedness. Not knowing how to address the situation, people might try to control, threaten, and reject these children even further. So they once again feel unloved, unlovable, empty, and helpless.

As they grow older, some of these individuals may turn to peculiar, self-destructive, and antisocial behaviors to make up for the emptiness they feel within. People do all kinds of things to get others' attention. Their unspoken message to others is "Look at me." Some individuals seek attention through destructive behaviors. They become destructive toward themselves or others. In either case, others will notice them. The loneliness and isolation they feel within is so intense that they have to do something to get a high. They may become suicidal to escape the pain and homicidal to avenge the pain. They might perceive suicide or suicide attempts as a good way to get others' immediate attention. They may not even worry whether they live or die. As long as they are noticed and get the attention, they feel the neglect has been avenged and emptiness filled.

They may turn to drugs and substances to numb the pain and feel a sort of high. Sometimes they become antisocial and do harm to others to fill that void and avenge that neglect. They may steal to fill the void. They may lie to protect themselves. They will do many things in protest against the unloving and uncaring world. But all these actions will keep them "safe" or make them feel filled only for a limited period of time. They will again be rejected and pushed back by others because of their attitudes and behaviors. Some persons may not explode but may become excessively self-focused and grandiose to make up for the low self-esteem and depletion felt within. Some may cling to others excessively and become overdependent to avoid the fear of abandonment. Some may move into deep depression and withdrawal. All these behaviors again make others uncomfortable, and they distance themselves from people exhibiting such behaviors.

Some individuals become psychosomatically ill. Their psychic conflicts and painful affects come out in the form of physical symptoms, and these symptoms serve as a defense mechanism. Physiology and psychology are inseparable. All the stress and negative experiences that they absorb and experience within often come out in the form of physical ailments. When looking for the etiology of some such illnesses, complaints, or problems, often no clear cause is found.

Some individuals who have been abused and exploited might do many unusual and unconventional things to avenge the pain and shame that they were made to bear. They might identify with or incorporate the characteristics of their aggressors or abusers. They might disown their real identity and take on the abuser's identity. They might become abusers and exploiters themselves or desire to be something other than who they are. They might do things to abuse and shame themselves, and they might think that they are doing the right thing. We may wonder why people would abuse and shame themselves, but they do. That has been their experience, and they don't think that they deserve anything better. But in many such cases, things happen unconsciously. Often their families and friends don't understand why they behave in such ways, and this leads to the further estrangement and isolation of such individuals.

As these individuals move into adulthood, the same dynamics play out in adult relationships. In the new scenario, spouses, colleagues, and superiors or bosses will replace the parents, siblings and peers. The individuals do many things that distance them still further from others. They engage in negative behaviors and employ defense mechanisms. These behaviors sometimes serve as a shield or defense against their painful affects. But those behaviors cause distress and difficulties for others, and it may result in further isolation, rejection, and abandonment.

In a marital or spousal relationship, for example, the negative experiences of one's early life could be carried into the relationship. Partners come into the marital relationship with different accents. They differ in their personal characteristics, family backgrounds, ideas and ideologies, beliefs and values, thoughts and feelings, networks of relationships, educational and professional backgrounds, and sometimes in religions, races, and ethnicities. These differences themselves make it a herculean task for two people to find a common path for survival and thriving. In addition to such differences, if either or both of them come into the relationship carrying the baggage of negative experiences or elements from their past, their spousal relationship will be a rough road. They may be expecting each other to fill the void they have been experiencing thus far. If they both come with a large void to be filled, they both may not have the required "material" to satisfy each other's need. They may feel depleted. Consequently, they may end up being disappointed with each other.

Couples with negative experiences from the past may also approach each other with the conviction that the other is going to reject him or her because he or she is unlovable. They fear being rejected because they feel unlovable or they regard themselves as unlovable. Thus they set themselves up for rejection and failure. Or they unconsciously wish the other person to reject them because that has been their experience thus far. They may not even allow the partner to enter into their world, because they may be afraid that ultimately the other is going to get disappointed and reject them or they are going to disappoint. So they may conclude unconsciously that it is better to keep the other at a distance rather than be rejected later. They were already hurt and rejected over and over again by their parents and significant others in their childhood or later, and they dread that happening again from their spouse.

Unconsciously, they may keep themselves away from their spouse emotionally or do things that would make their spouse reject them. They may engage in speaking with wrong accents. They may do things that would make the other person reject them. They may engage in bragging and nagging, accusations and contempt, neglect, violence, and abuse. Although rejection may look painful, they may enjoy being masochistic, deriving an unconscious pleasure from that rejection. There may be a hidden pleasure in being a victim.

They may also become verbally, emotionally, or physically sadistic, inflicting pain on their spouse to make up for the pain they feel within. The pain inflicted on the other gives them pleasure and fills the void or discharges the tension they feel within. Slavery to certain things is often a mixture of pain and pleasure.

The more the spouses feel dissonance in their accents, the longer it takes them to understand each other and make progress in their relationship. If they are not able to go beyond their accents or understand each other's accents, they will not be able to understand their children's accents when their family becomes threesome or foursome. Caught up in a complex negative relational system, they will all engage in destructive behavioral patterns with each other. These patterns and dances might continue for a while, but when it becomes unbearable and goes beyond proportion, they cause irreparable damage to the whole family system.

Although not all of the pathologies and negative developments in later life can be blamed on early life experiences and parents, it is important to note that our experiences and significant people in our early life play a vital role in our future. It is a fact that some parents and families fail to provide healthy environments for their children. They become unresponsive, unavailable, and abusive to their children. It is a fact that some children grow up in unhealthy environments. These negative experiences can have an impact on the future of those children in so many varied ways.

To find out the reason why these parents and caregivers turn out to be that way, we may have to look into their early life experiences. They could be deeply influenced by their own previous personal experiences in childhood. If the parents had a series of negative experiences in their childhood, they will not have the required capacity to provide a positive and loving experience to their children. As the saying goes, you cannot give what you don't have. The child who feels depleted, unloved, and unwanted by his or her parents today becomes a parent tomorrow (if he or she decides to become one). The dance might be repeated. He or she may not know how to be any different from what his or her parents were. If the household consists of three or more generations with similar experiences and dynamics, these relationship struggles will be more complicated. As Murray Bowen suggested, a multigenerational transmission of negative and unloving experiences characterizes certain families, and they exhibit many features of negative DTS and DTT. They engage in communicating with wrong accents and consequently create conflicts in their everyday lives and relationships.

Exploring one's past experiences, especially in the early years of one's life, is very significant in terms of understanding one's sense of self and vision of life. That would tell us why a person survives and thrives in the way he or she does. For many people, their earlier life becomes a persistent burden and negative influence on their later development. If they have not had an experience of being loved by God and others, how would they understand the necessity of finding communion with God and others? If they don't know how to survive and thrive well, how would they bring the best out of themselves? The positive or negative routes that our DTS and DTT take have a lot to do with where we come from and what we carry with us.

24

What Do the Theorists Say?

Although it is not possible to review all the theories about what causes all our problems in life, it may be useful to briefly review here some of the prominent theories on the working of our psyche, influence of past experiences, and the impact of the environment in which we live.

Sigmund Freud, the father of psychoanalysis, is one of the theorists who extensively studied and wrote about personality development and its influencing factors. I shall focus on two of Freud's central ideas that refer to our psychic processes in early and later stages of life.

Freud suggested that as we grow and develop, we pass though different psychosexual stages, each of which has a bodily preoccupation associated with it. In each of these stages, pleasure or instinctual gratification is centered on a particular part of the body. The five stages of psychosexual development that he mapped out are the oral stage (the first year of life), the anal stage (one to three years old), the phallic stage (three to six years old), the latency stage (six years of age to puberty), and the genital stage (from puberty onwards). Freud believed that we all go through these five psychosexual stages in the development of our personalities.

Each of these five stages has certain difficult tasks associated with it. To develop a healthy personality, the internal conflicts at each of these stages have to be handled and resolved appropriately. If some of these tasks are not successfully completed, or if certain issues of these stages are not resolved appropriately, we become fixated; we stay focused or get stuck on those issues without being able to move to the next stage of psychological development even though we may have moved to the next stage of physical development. A person's character in later life will show effects of this fixation.

In the oral stage, for example, the psychosexual energy or libido that drives the individual is centered on mouth. The child derives pleasure from oral stimulation gained through activities such as sucking, biting, and breast-feeding. Children at this stage put all sorts of things into their mouth because it is not only pleasurable to do so but also dissipates and discharges the tension that arises from frustrations. The mother's breast gives the child not only nourishment but also oral pleasure through sucking. But the mother may not be available always, and that can create tension or frustration for the child. The mother's unavailability could be the beginning of a series of unpredictable environments.

To make up for the emotionally and physically absent mothers or other caregivers, children sometimes turn to other things, such as their fingers, blankets, toys, and teddy bears, which are often referred to as "transitional objects" (Winnicott, 1953). They put these objects in their mouths and bite on them or chew them, deriving oral pleasure. That, in turn, dissipates their frustration and calms them down. If the need for gratification at this stage is too little or too much, children develop an oral fixation. This fixation will be manifested in later life through behaviors such as thumb sucking, nail biting, smoking, overeating, aggression, domination, etc. Character-wise, Nancy McWilliams said, if a person has a depressive personality in later life, it is construed as a result of either neglect or overindulgence at the oral phase of his or her development. The individual may have grown up physically, but psychologically he or she may be stuck at the oral stage.

Although trying to understand and interpret an individual's personality, character, and behaviors in later life solely from the instinctual fixations of early life was not totally acceptable to all the later theorists, Freud's theory has offered many insights into the working of our psyche. It tells us how some of our early life experiences influence our later life. We know that some children are deprived of and denied instinctual gratification and pleasures, while other children are overloaded or flooded with pleasures and instinctual gratification. Both of these are extremes, and they could have a negative impact on a child's future growth and development.

Children take in their experiences as they come without having much capacity to differentiate between the good and the bad. It is akin to infants putting all kinds of things into their mouths without being able to differentiate between the good and the bad. They grab things and bring them to their mouths. This tendency to absorb everything can happen mentally or psychologically as well. Every experience that they encounter, both good and bad, is absorbed. They take in everything just as a sponge would absorb any liquid—sweet or bitter, green or red. They don't have much capacity to filter those experiences adequately. They tend to retain almost everything that they absorb.

Adults also experience both good and bad in life, but they are better equipped to filter and keep what is good and healthy. In the case of children, that capacity to filter and keep what is good is very minimal. As they grow older, the capacity to filter and keep what is good increases. If the bad experiences outweigh the good, it can cause many problems in later life. I previously discussed children needing to have a stable love relationship with parents or caregivers to develop a good sense of self and vision of life. Otherwise their sense of identity, purpose in life, and destiny can be greatly compromised. Children who are consistently presented with experiences of rejection, neglect, and lack of love are candidates for a distorted sense of self, wrong vision of life, different sorts of fixations, and defective DTS and DTT.

The second central idea from Freud that I would like to focus on is the "unconscious mental processes." As human beings, we go through an array of experiences. We experience different kinds of thoughts, feelings, and wishes. And we also experience many conflicts, challenges, and frustrations. Sometimes we may not be able or may not have adequate help to process and handle all these experiences in a healthy way. Sometimes some of our wishes, feelings, and thoughts do not garner approval from our parents, others, or ourselves. They are unacceptable to all. The best way we find to handle such issues in the moment is to push them into the unconscious realm of the mind. We push them out of our conscious mind or awareness so that we don't need to experience the unpleasant feelings or emotions associated with them in the moment. They are repressed.

However, according to Freud, these experiences, wishes, feelings, thoughts, and memories do not disappear. They lie buried in the unconscious and continue to influence our actions, words, and thoughts. They are like a volcano bubbling in the belly of the earth. And since they are not easily available to the conscious mind and yet continue to have an influence on our being, we sometimes don't understand fully why we behave the way we do. Taking a cue from this idea of Freud, we can think of the thousands of experiences and their memories that we might have pushed down to our unconscious from our early life on. We can assume that in many ways they continue to influence our actions, thoughts, and words today.

Some later theorists such as Ronald Fairbairn, Melanie Klein, and Donald Winnicott distanced themselves from some of the concepts of Freud. In today's context of a better understanding of human psychology and relationships, not all of Freud's theories and ideas are proven. However, Freud offers us many valuable insights about some of our innate characteristics, our psychic functions, and the influence of our early life experiences on later life and development. Concepts like fixations and psychic conflicts give an idea of things in our lives that could lead to negative DTS and DTT, and the generation of mismatches in accents. Individuals who are psychically conflicted or fixated on certain issues will most likely not be able to bring the best out of themselves.

Erik Erikson, another psychoanalyst and developmental psychologist, reformulated Freud's psychosexual stages of development and proposed the theory of psychosocial development. Erikson saw development as a result of both the intrapsychic and interpersonal dynamics going on in a person. He categorized the human life and personality development into eight stages: infancy (0–1 year old), early childhood (1–3 years old), play/preschool age (3–6 years old), school age (6–11 years old), adolescence (12–18 years old), early adulthood (18–35 years old), adulthood (35–64 years old), and old age (65 and above). Each of these stages of development involves an emotional paradoxical conflict:

1. Infancy: trust versus mistrust
2. Early childhood: autonomy versus shame and doubt

3. Play/pre-school age: initiative versus guilt
4. School age: industry versus inferiority
5. Adolescence: identity versus identity diffusion
6. Early adulthood: intimacy versus self-absorption
7. Adulthood: generativity versus stagnation
8. Old age: integrity versus despair

A healthy personality, according to Erikson, requires the resolution of the paradoxical conflicts at each of the developmental stages. For example, in infancy, children have to confront and resolve the paradoxical conflict of trust and mistrust. When the parents or caregivers provide affection, love, care, and reliability, children develop a sense of trust. But if children are deprived of these experiences, they develop a sense of mistrust. Both these experiences are possible in a child's life, and to move on to the next stage and develop a healthy personality, children have to successfully confront and resolve the conflict that arises from this paradoxical experience. If these conflicts are not adequately addressed and resolved, they will have a negative impact on a child's later life and development.

In certain families and societies, children have no one they can trust. They live in the midst of extreme stress and fear. Their survival itself is at stake. If they manage to survive, they continue to grow physically. But psychologically, their issues remain unresolved. In later life, it is no surprise if they survive and thrive negatively. They will not be able to make an uninterrupted healthy development, which, in turn, will lead to a failure in bringing the best out of themselves.

Erikson also has contributed much to the understanding of the working of the human psyche. It may be appropriate to think that the failure to resolve conflicts at each of the developmental stages might give rise to the negative manifestation of DTS and DTT, and the subsequent mismatch of accents in later life. However, in today's context of advanced research and evidence-based theories in the mental health field, Erikson's ideas may not find many takers.

Jean Piaget, the author of the theory of cognitive development, is another developmental psychologist who mapped out significant and distinct stages in an individual's cognitive development. Piaget was interested in learning about the thinking and learning process in children. How do children understand or make sense of the world and themselves? He observed and studied children, including his own children. From these observations and studies, he concluded that a person goes through various stages of cognitive development before he or she reaches a state of intellectual maturity. Piaget discerned four key stages in this cognitive development: the sensorimotor stage (from birth to age two), the preoperational stage (from age two to age seven), the concrete operational stage (from age seven to age eleven), and the formal operational stage (from age eleven to adulthood).

Healthy individuals, according to Piaget, are those who progressively move through these four stages of cognitive development and ultimately reach a state of intellectual maturity. The failure to make that forward movement could result in the person getting stuck in his or her development. And getting stuck in one's development is not good news for the person's life and relationships. For various reasons, many people get stuck in their cognitive development and fail to reach a state of intellectual maturity. They don't make sense of the world or themselves appropriately. Such individuals might get stuck in their DTS and DTT. They may not survive and thrive well or bring the best out of themselves.

John Bowlby is another psychologist and psychoanalyst who looked into what helps the healthy development of an individual. He suggested that what a child needs most for a healthy development is a secure, safe, and positive attachment with his or her parents or parent figures. He laid out three patterns of attachment in a parent-child relationship: (1) a secure attachment pattern, meaning that the individual or child is confident that his or her parent or parent figure will be available, responsive, and helpful should he or she encounter adverse or frightening situations; (2) an anxious-resistant attachment pattern, meaning that the individual or child is uncertain whether his or her parent or parent figure will be available, responsive, or helpful when needed; and (3) an anxious-avoidant attachment pattern, meaning that the individual or child has no confidence that his or her parent or parent figure will be available, responsive, or helpful when called upon; rather, he or she expects to be rebuffed when asking for help.

A child who has a secure and positive attachment experience in childhood will be confident, self-reliant, empathic, resilient, emotionally stable, and dependable in adult life. An insecure and negative attachment experience in childhood leads to a negative development in later life where the person becomes negative, frightened, shy, withdrawn, and emotionally unstable. Mary Ainsworth and several other theorists later built their theories on this idea of secure attachment as a necessary component for healthy development.

The thoughts and theories of Bowlby and Ainsworth are similar to the findings of René Spitz, another psychoanalyst and researcher on child development, who suggested that a lack of human warmth and interactions, attachment, and emotional connection in the early stages of life, particularly in the first year, often causes enormous damage to children's subsequent physical, psychological, and social development. Children who are rejected or neglected by their mothers are sure candidates for severe developmental problems.

Children who are removed from emotional connections partially or for brief periods of time go through what Spitz called "anaclitic depression," a state of grief, anger, and failure to thrive. But they will be able to recover if the emotional connection is restored within three to five months. If the emotional deprivation and lack of human warmth is near total and continues for more than five months, children will develop what he called "hospitalism," a severe condition of deterioration in their growth and development. They often suffer from "marasmus," a failure to gain appropriate body weight and energy. Usually marasmus occurs as a result of severe malnutrition, but in the case of children with severe deprivation of emotional connections and attachment, marasmus can occur even if they are provided with adequate physical and medical care. Even if they are fed well, they will still fail to gain adequate body weight and energy as compared to normal expectations for their age. Many of them die or end up physically, mentally, and socially retarded.

These findings of Spitz were related to the thoughts and theories of Donald Winnicott, a psychoanalyst and object relations theorist, and Heinz Kohut, another psychoanalyst and the developer of self-psychology, who suggested that empathic, responsive, and emotionally available mothers or caregivers are essential for the healthy emotional development of a child. Mothers who mirror or reflect on their faces the positive and happy countenances of their children tremendously help the healthy emotional development of the children. Children who are deprived of such mirroring, children whose mothers look away or whose mothers are emotionally unavailable, will have a difficult time with their emotional development. Such findings were reconfirmed in the investigations of Edward Tronick and his colleagues, where they found (via what they termed the still-face experiment) that mothers who were emotionally and physically unresponsive, distant, and still-faced caused great distress to their children. Children made repeated attempts to regain the attention of their mothers, but when they failed, they gave up their hope of any reciprocity and withdrew from their mothers emotionally.

All these things mean that for children, when it comes to their emotional development and interpersonal relationships, their mothers or the first caregivers open the window to the rest of the world and the rest of their lives. They function as a link to the rest of the world and their future. Children learn from them what the rest of the world looks like and feels like. Children who are deprived of emotional connection and healthy interpersonal relationships often have serious problems in later life. They may have issues with trust, dependence, and emotional attachment. Based on these findings, it can be assumed that children with severe negative experiences in early stages of life will be more likely to manifest negative DTS and DTT in their adult lives.

It is not only the parents and the immediate family members that contribute to the health and well-being of a developing child, but also the overall environment. Looking into this aspect of the influence of the overall environment on human development, Urie Bronfenbrenner, a developmental psychologist, developed what is known as the ecological systems theory of human development. The theory focuses on what facilitates the growth and development of a person or dyad. The two major concepts of this theory are the environment and the dyadic relationship development. According to the theory, a healthy and supportive environment promotes the development of the person, while a disruptive environment interferes with or inhibits the development of the person.

The environment that supports or interferes with the person's development consists of different layers, which he called the microsystem, the mesosystem, the exosystem, and the macrosystem. The microsystem is the immediate environment of the developing person, consisting of family members, relatives, friends, peers, neighbors, schoolmates, his or her faith community, etc. The mesosystem consists of the interactions or interconnectedness between the various microsystems, such as home and school. The exosystem consists of the settings that the developing person may never enter or participate in, though events that occur in those settings affect the immediate environment of the developing person. And the macrosystem refers to the overarching patterns of values, ideologies, and norms of the society or culture or social institutions that influence and determine all other settings of the environment down the line and ultimately affect the person.

"Dyadic relationship development" refers to the necessity of a mutually affective and attuned relationship between the dyadic partners for their growth and development. Two partners—a mother and a child or a husband and a wife, for example—begin their relationship in a small way and then gradually build it up to a point where they develop affective and intimate feelings for each other and begin to influence each other's behaviors in substantial ways.

If we think of the growth and development of a child in terms of the ecological systems theory, his or her mother or primary caregiver becomes the immediate context and dyadic partner for his or her development. At the beginning of the relationship, it is highly imbalanced, as the child is totally dependent on the mother. If the mother is affectively attuned and available to the child, she becomes a supportive environment and helps the development of the child. If she is emotionally and physically absent or disruptive, it interferes with the development of the child. However, the capacity of the mother or caregiver to serve as an effective context and attuned presence for the child depends on the presence and participation of others, such as, relatives, friends, neighbors, and the faith community.

The capacity of these constituents to function as an effective context for the mother and the child depends on the interconnectedness between them and other settings, systems, organizations, and institutions in their environment. For example, if a mother is a working woman, the environment at her workplace will have a great impact on the growth and development of her child even though the child is not directly connected with the mother's workplace. If the mother has a stressful job or unhealthy work environment, she might carry home the stress and struggles of her work, and that, in turn, might be reflected in her emotional and physical interactions with her child. The environment that supports or disrupts the child's development extends far beyond these settings and systems. It includes the customs, traditions, ideas, ideologies, values, and norms that affect the child directly or indirectly. If the culture or society has ideologies, values, and norms that are not supportive to the growth and development of the child or the parents, it is not a healthy environment for the latter.

A perfect environment and a perfect mother are too idealistic. But if a child receives what Winnicott called a "good-enough" mother and environment, he or she will survive and thrive to a satisfactory extent. The good-enough concept—in which the mother is satisfactorily attuned and attentive to the child, or the environment is more or less healthy—is a minimum requirement for one's growth and development. It is not that we would not survive and thrive without that, but the absence of such an environment and attuned relationship with the mother or caregiver could cause some damage to our normal and healthy growth and development. Such deprivations could sow the seeds for a distorted sense of self, negative DTS and DTT, and wrong accents in later life.

A healthy and supportive environment and mutually affective and attuned relationships are necessary not only for a child but also for all people. In every stage of our lives, we need affective and attuned relationships with those with whom we live and interact. We also need a healthy and supportive environment to bring the best out of ourselves. These are especially critical and important in the early stages of life, as we are pretty much dependent on others for everything at that point.

The few theories reviewed above show us how our personal experiences—especially those of the early stages of our lives, and our environment—are important considerations when we think of our growth and development. The people and the environment we interact with have a tremendous impact on how we develop a sense of our self and the world, and what direction we take in our survival and thriving. Positive and supportive experiences and environments will enhance positive survival and thriving, while the negative and debilitating experiences and environment will give rise to negative survival and thriving. Given the context of being the recipients of many disordered hereditary characteristics and being exposed to deficient and debilitating environments of living, it is no surprise that many people in our world develop a distorted sense of self and vision of life, and end up with defective DTS and DTT.

25

Unequal Avenues

When we look at the environment in which we live and grow, one of the things that we notice as a reason for people's negative survival and thriving is the inequality in our thriving avenues and chances for survival. Although DTS and DTT are universal, the available avenues and opportunities for survival and thriving are not the same for all people. In other words, everyone wants to survive and thrive, but not everyone has the same measure of thriving avenues and chances for survival. One's physical status, for example, can determine how long and how well one will survive and thrive. A physically healthy person has better chances for survival and more possibilities for thriving than a physically unhealthy person. An individual from a developed and strife-free country or region has better opportunities to survive and thrive than someone from a poverty-stricken and violence-ridden country or region.

Similarly, the chances of survival and the availability of thriving avenues for a child born healthy are not the same as those of a child born with physical and mental deficiencies. The survival possibilities and thriving avenues of a child conceived by an alcoholic and drug-addicted mother are different from the survival possibilities and thriving avenues of a child conceived by a healthy mother. Families stricken with poverty and families living in luxury have different survival and thriving possibilities. The chances of survival and thriving avenues are not the same for a child born in a war-torn area and a child born in a free and peaceful town. We see these differences in the survival and thriving avenues for children who are orphaned and children who have both parents, for a rich man and a poor man, for a free man and a slave, and for a president of a nation and an ordinary citizen. There is never equality when it comes to the possibilities for survival and availability of thriving avenues—not even in the same household. A person's possibilities for survival and thriving can shrink if he or she becomes a victim of someone's abuse, violence, threat, or manipulations.

The systems and environments in which we are born and raised contribute to this inequality in a major way. Some are born free, but some are not. Some are born into healthy environments, but some are not. Some are born in wealth, but some are not. Some are born with both parents, but some are not. Some are born in peace, but some are not. And some are born with opportunities, but some are not. We are not equal in our available resources and the way we are supported. There is no equality in the castes and classes we belong to. Our races and groups are not placed on an equal footing when it comes to survival and thriving. As long as we have these inequalities in all these realms of our lives, we will have unequal thriving avenues and possibilities for survival.

We saw that as human beings and children of God we all have the same identity and are all equal. Every one of us possesses an inalienable inherent worth and dignity as one of God's children. There is no one who is less human or less divine. The United States Declaration of Independence reechoes this truth through the famous line "All men are created equal." Thomas Jefferson, one of the founding fathers and the third president of the United States, found it necessary to give this truth its worthy place in the foundational principles of his nation. This line has been used also in many speeches and vision statements of communities and groups down through the centuries. However, if we look at our world, look at everyone around us, we realize that this equality that God endows us with is not translated into our real-life situations. The actual and the ideal are far apart from each other. If we are all equal as human beings and children of God, every one of us deserves an equal opportunity to live and thrive. But what we experience in the real world is a different story. When it comes to our survival and thriving, we don't see that equality anywhere.

It is from here that we all begin to operate. We are all equal, and we all have the drive to survive and thrive, but we don't all have the same possibilities and chances for development and growth. This inequality has a possibility to generate negative survival and thriving in us, and that, in turn, leads to mismatches in our accents.

Because of the differences in the chances of survival, one might stay alive and the other might not. Because of the differences in the available thriving avenues, one might thrive more than the other in quality and quantity. Sometimes one's chance for survival and domain for thriving are already large when he or she is born into this world.

In spite of the inequalities, some might stay alive, but that doesn't mean that they are going to thrive like everyone else. They may have to expend most of their energy to fight the odds in their lives to stay alive. As mentioned earlier, for some people, DTT is not and cannot be on their radar, because their primary need is to stay alive. Children and others in war-torn zones have only one focus, and that is to stay alive. They just want to stay safe from the bombs, rockets, and gunshots. They just want some food on their plates. They just want to find some water to drink and use for bathing. They don't have much time or energy to focus on thriving or bringing the best out of themselves. People involved in serious automobile accidents, natural calamities, or some unexpected crises face sudden interruptions in their normal rhythm of life, and they are also in a survival mode. Their whole energy is spent on surviving the shock and tragedy. DTT, in its true sense, is not on their radar. Their survival is foremost among their needs.

People who are engaged in negative survival and thriving because of inequalities may not even know that they are negatively oriented. Kennedy Odede, in his article, "Terrorism's fertile ground," spoke of his own experience of growing up in a slum in Nairobi, Kenya, and described how violence and terrorism becomes alluring and attractive to many. For people who live in abject poverty, a sense of hopelessness and helplessness dominates their psyche. They have no reason to believe or hope that the next day will be a better day than the last. They are treated as disposable and undeserving of any value. Their lives are ridden with violence and threat. They helplessly watch the brutal killing or deaths of their family members and peers. They have to be resigned to the idea that their fate is not going to be any different. Living in such circumstances, Odede said, "Violence becomes a vehicle for survival." Since they are regarded as people of no value, they begin to seek some voice and recognition by showing themselves as people with some power—the power to destroy and kill.

Deprived of chances for survival and opportunities for thriving, many people unconsciously operationalize the negative dimension of their DTS and DTT, and that gives rise to mismatches in accents. They may not know it, but others can feel it. These mismatches may come in the form of extreme individualism and narcissism, perversions and destructive behaviors, suicidal and homicidal tendencies, violent confrontations and hostility, lust for power and pleasure, hatred and contempt, anger and rage, sarcasm and humiliation, greed and envy, and so on and so forth. A large-scale extension of these behaviors manifests in riots, wars, terrorism, and militancy. The vicious circle never stops; one leads to the other, and many are caught up in this madness.

26

Group Differences

It is not only the individuals but also groups and communities that want to survive and thrive. The inequality in the thriving avenues and chances for survival is prevalent among groups and communities as well. These can be political, social, economic, religious, or ideological in nature. The systemic extension of DTS and DTT can also be seen in groups based on race, ethnicity, gender, language, culture, and nationality. Every group wants to survive and thrive.

As the inequality in chances for survival and avenues for thriving creates mismatches in accents and conflictual relationships between individuals, it creates conflicts between groups as well. Just as with individuals, when it comes to survival and thriving, some groups have better chances and avenues than others.

Revolutions, proletarian struggles, and freedom movements speak for these group differences and conflicts in the political realm. Forms of government have come and gone one after another. The inequality in the thriving avenues has often made the ruled rise against the rulers. If they succeeded in toppling the government, the ruled became the rulers. But the new occupants sometimes proved to be no better than the incumbents. The representatives of the proletariat or the revolutionaries become the new power holders, and power is often concentrated in a few hands. They sometimes become worse than those whom they overthrow. Even the proletariat and revolutionaries themselves resent their leaders, because when given power, they become dictatorial like their predecessors and the resentment starts all over again. Additionally, the former rulers become the ruled, and they resent the state they have been forced into.

On the social front, the exploited and discriminated groups in society resent the wide gap in the survival and thriving avenues, and they fight to bridge the gap and bring about much-needed social changes. Individuals and groups have struggled hard to create a class-free and caste-free society. Castes, classes, races, and genders have been at loggerheads over inequality and discrimination meted out to one group over the other. There have been many conflicts and mismatches in accents between them. Slavery, caste systems, and colonialism have been some of the worst evils that human beings ever inflicted upon their fellow human beings. Those with a master syndrome and defective DTS and DTT used and abused people without any regard for human values. The abusers and the abused could not understand each other's accents. Much blood has been spilled in the process of rectifying this inequality and developing a mutually understandable language. The work of bridging the gap is left undone, and the struggle continues.

The uneven thriving avenues get very prominently highlighted between genders, especially between men and women. Sexual and gender discrimination and exploitation is an age-old problem that human beings have been dealing with, although it came to high prominence only in the past few decades. The feminist movement is an example of women trying to reduce the gap in the survival and thriving avenues between men and women. Under the patriarchal system, it was unthinkable to have men consider the opinions of women in the family or community. Men were the decision makers and the sole masters of their households and communities. Many people in the United States are familiar with the radio and television comedy series titled *Father Knows Best*. The show gives a glimpse of the male-dominated family system in the US in the mid-1900s. Over the years, things have changed—at least in some communities and cultures. Now women and children are recognized or are starting to be recognized, and their opinions count in many communities and cultures. Family and community decisions are more of a collective endeavor than a one-man show. But it took centuries to come to that state. There is still a lot of disparity in the survival and thriving avenues between different genders in many societies. Women are treated as objects and deemed unworthy of the dignity and respect offered to men. The struggle continues.

The differences in the thriving avenues and chances for survival within and between religions have been a cause for mismatch in accents and many conflicts over the centuries. Every religion and sect wants to have a monopoly over the realm of the holy and the divine. A respectful and peaceful coexistence has been too hard for all religious groups and sects. Vowing to annihilate everyone who does not adhere to their beliefs, many religious groups and sects unleash their master syndrome and defective DTS and DTT on to the rest of humanity. Their accents do not match with those of others. They speak a language that is totally incomprehensible to the rest of the world.

Intolerance and religious persecutions have often been a part of our world history. When one religion comes to its senses and realizes its mistakes, another one goes weird and crazy. Communities in the same village and town tear each other apart in the name of their beliefs and practices. They don't understand each other's language. They don't see the other's humanity as sharing in their own humanity. They can't see others as human beings and children of God. There is a battle between "them" versus "us." And often "they" are made out to be or looked at as nonhuman or enemies of God rather than children of God. Therefore "they" can be killed without the killers feeling any guilt or remorse.

Mismatch of accents due to the inequality in the survival and thriving avenues is prevalent not only between religions but also within many religions and sects. The mismatch in accents manifests itself through open revolts and splits. Sometimes the split occurs in the form of the founding of a new religion or sect by one person or a group of persons who claim to have had an enlightenment or special call. At other times, it is an open revolt that does not cause a split. For some, the enlightenment becomes "necessary" because the parent religion or group stops showing the light. Thus enlightenment sometimes becomes a protest against the stagnant parent system or a revolt against those who survive and thrive negatively within the community. Sometimes the split-away group itself is a collection of individuals driven by defective DTS and DTT, and master syndrome. They are also in a situation as vulnerable as that of the parent religion, as they might start facing similar resentments within its rank and file over the years or over a period of time. Every established system is prone to stagnation and rigidity, and defective DTS and DTT, which ultimately result in much disenchantment among its rank and file.

Human history is a chain of such struggles. Struggles and resentments arise as some realize that their growth and development get highly compromised and limited because of the inequality in the survival and thriving avenues between groups. Today this inequality and struggle may be based on the political, economic, or gender issues. Tomorrow it might be based on something else. In the past it was based on race, caste, nationality, religion, and many other issues.

Maybe we belong to a gender, family, community, race, or nationality that possessed a large domain of thriving avenues and survival possibilities and exploited the less fortunate folks through gender discrimination, slavery, a caste system, colonialism, or religious, political, or economic hegemony. Maybe we belong to a gender, family, community, race, or nationality of the less fortunate folks who had smaller domains and were exploited. Maybe we belong to a family, race, or nation who occupied and confiscated other people's land and property. Maybe we belong to a family, race, or nationality that was expelled or displaced from its land and forced to seek asylum in another land. Whatever may be the history of our family, community, race, and nation, we are all connecting dots in a long chain of this struggle. We have inherited much of what we have today, and we sometimes continue to contribute to its perpetuation.

Ill feelings and resentments between groups still pop up every now and then, but things have changed on many fronts. Many things have become history now. Things may have become better on certain counts. We might see many other things changing for better on many such issues in the struggle to equalize the thriving avenues and survival possibilities. It is an ongoing struggle. The past was a present and a future at one time. History is constantly in the making. The human history is a chain of inequality, resentment, mismatches in accents, and conflicts. When Pharaoh's cruelty toward the Israelites reached its zenith, God sent Moses to Pharaoh with the words "Let my people go" (Ex 9:1). This command of God continues to be heard in many communities and nations today. Cruelty and inhumanity continue to raise their heads in many places. Adequate survival possibilities and decent thriving avenues are denied to many. To all those who patronize and promote unjust structures and systems, God continues to say, "Let my people go."

27

Busy Lives and Endless Choices

Whether or not our environment helps us to survive and thrive well depends also on the culture and society in which we live. The rapid change in our culture and lifestyle today could be another reason for the negative DTS and DTT, and the consequent wrong accents in our lives. A commercial that I heard some time back on the radio called the attention of the listeners to the busyness of our lives and how the company had adjusted its services for shopping to fit with the needs of the customers. The commercial started by explaining how the day starts for a typical busy person: "We brush our teeth while driving our car, drink our coffee while making a phone call, eat our lunch while having a meeting …" And then the advertising company nudges in its catch phrase: "We know how pressed you are for time; you can shop at our store in your pajamas."

Has our present-day culture of busy lives and endless choices contributed to the escalation of the negative DTS and DTT, and mismatch in accents in our lives? I believe it has. Many of us are busy, and we look for a society and culture that cater to that busy mode. Responding to this need, our world is becoming more and more a 24-7 enterprise.

There was an age when people used to think that there was a set time for everything: a time to wake up, a time to work, a time to eat, a time to relax and rest, a time to pray, a time to spend time with the family, a time to sleep, etc. This stipulation of time applied to every aspect of life. People worked only up until certain hours. Television and radio stations transmitted programs only up to certain hours. Stores and shopping malls remained open only up until certain hours. Vehicles and transportation facilities were still after certain hours. But this concept of "up to certain hours" has disappeared, and now it is the concept of twenty-four hours, seven days a week. It's a 24-7 world. Go out to the street at any time of the day or night, and you will see stores open and vehicles moving back and forth. Turn on the television or radio at any time of the day or night; programs are aplenty on different channels and frequencies. News channels bombard us with information twenty-four hours a day. Look for jobs for any time slot during the day or night; they are available. It is a world of busy lives, unending stimuli, and unlimited choices.

It is not only a 24-7 enterprise but also an enterprise of instant satisfaction. We don't need to wait for weeks and months to hear from or see our relatives or friends across the country or overseas. We have instant messaging and e-mail facilities to connect with them. We can use Skype and FaceTime to view them live. We don't need to take the trouble of going to the store to buy things; we can sit at home and buy them online, and they will be delivered to our door. We don't need to go to the store to buy books or wait for them to arrive by mail; we can buy their electronic versions and read them instantly on our computer, iPad, Kindle, or Nook. We don't need to order a car and wait for weeks to see what it looks like; the dealer next door has it ready for us. The concept of community now is in terms of real-time, virtual, and Internet-based interactions.

Our busy mode of life has brought us a culture of endless choices. Barry Schwartz, the author of the book *The Paradox of Choice*, discusses how we are overloaded with choices today. He went to a GAP store to buy a pair of jeans. He asked for 32×28 size jeans. The sales girl asked, "Do you want them slim fit, easy fit, relaxed fit, baggy, or extra baggy? Do you want them stonewashed, acid-washed, or distressed? Do you want them button-fly or zipper-fly? Do you want them faded or regular?" He was stunned. He just wanted regular jeans. The girl didn't know what "regular jeans" meant. He had too many choices, and now he himself was not sure what he wanted. In the past, he says, he would have bought his jeans in five or ten minutes, but now with all these choices available, he had to try out all of them, and it took hours to do the shopping. He was introduced not only to distressed jeans, but also to a distressed lifestyle.

Schwartz takes the readers' attention to the endless choices that consumers are provided with today. Go to a supermarket, he says, and you will see two hundred plus varieties of cookies, crackers, soups, sauces, oils, vinegars, cereals, tea bags, coffee, rice, spices, and all such things. They come in all sizes and forms—fat-free, sugar-free, big boxes, small boxes, etc. Enter a store selling electronic goods, and you will see varieties of TVs, stereo systems, computers, iPads, etc. Sign up for a cable network, and you will be provided with two hundred plus channels. Go to a car dealer, and you will find varieties of cars available. We can shop for things online or by mail, and they will be delivered to our doors. We can shop for and complete degrees and courses online. People have more choices today about how they want to love and live. With family, without family, with children, without children, married, living together—choices are plenty in love relationships. People have choices about what religion or community they want to belong to; choices are plenty. Schwartz comments that when we are denied of choices, life becomes difficult, and when overloaded with choices, life again becomes difficult.

The 24-7 mode of life and endless choices have brought about a sea change in the way we perceive everything. This new lifestyle has changed the rules and expectations of our lives. Many people are in a customer satisfaction frenzy and a use-and-throw-away culture. The phenomenon of around-the-clock activity and instant attentiveness has affected every aspect of our lives. Family life, marriage, interpersonal relationships, business relationships, international relationships, religion and spirituality—everything is influenced by this busy mode, instant satisfaction, and customer-friendly interactions. Many people are out there car shopping, doctor shopping, insurance shopping, relationship shopping, entertainment shopping, God shopping, religion shopping, and so on and so forth. The instant availability of things and services has created high expectations in people. There are not many takers for the old systems and traditions, where roles and responsibilities were assigned and people were expected to resign to those expectations. People who live with the old time frame and mindset will find themselves out of date. Anyone lagging behind or failing to meet these expectations will feel the heat of the customer's displeasure and will eventually lose out in the bargain.

There was a time when people had to wait in line for several hours and hope and pray that the service provider would be kind and merciful in considering their applications or petitions. Those equations have changed, and expectations have been reversed. Now the service providers have to wait in line and hope and pray that the customer will be kind and considerate in accepting their services. If they don't provide people with services that meet their expectations, there are others waiting for them next door with more incentives and better quality. Within no time they will discard the first and move to the other. Governments, political parties, business enterprises, the entertainment industry, religious and spiritual institutions, and all such people-oriented service entities feel the heat emanating from the new culture of busy lives and endless choices.

Life has become complex and complicated. However, oftentimes, our expectations are beyond the expertise of the service provider, so we discard one and turn to the other. After a while no one seems to be satisfying. Some people end up as totally dissatisfied wrecks.

Then there are some of us who have become great "multitaskers." Blaming it on lack of time, people do two or more things at the same time. They talk over the phone or text while driving. People read books or watch TV while they eat. Students listen to music while doing their homework or reading their books. Men and women listen to music while working out or doing some work. People play videogames or do other things while talking to others. It is a world of multitasking. Of course, this kind of lifestyle has not come into every society or culture, but sooner or later those lagging behind will follow suit.

Although we can say that our lives have become better in many ways, our busy mode of life and endless choices have also taken us into a way of being that may not be helpful at all times. The good thing is that with all the new developments, we have been forced to come out of our narrow little worlds and connect with the larger world out there.

We cannot live anymore with our parochial, patriarchal, and narrow-minded outlook. We don't have to be at the mercy of people who tend to act bigger than who they are. There is a new culture that demands we all live and relate with mutual respect. But the bad thing is that the new developments have led to a surge in extreme individualism and narcissism in certain societies. Pleasure by all means and individual survival and thriving at all costs become the focal points of many people's personal endeavors. The value of community life has been de-emphasized. And the traditional values and institutions of the society have been greatly disregarded.

There is narcissism in all of us. We all seek to please ourselves in some way. We all become self-focused in some way. We all want to be "seen" in some way. But unhealthy narcissism takes us to the extreme of all these. Although not everything can be blamed on the culture and new developments in society, the market and the media have their fair share in the increase of unhealthy narcissism in certain societies. They "feed" the consumers. Products are presented as a need, and people fall for this. Those who are driven by extreme narcissism make use of everything they can find to inflate themselves. But the irony is that the market, the media, and everything else that takes us to the culture of narcissistic survival and thriving are our own making.

The unlimited choices and the freedom to do whatever one wants create a group that we may call "control freaks." They develop a highly inflated desire to control their lives and get the best deals available in the world. They see others as threats or as tools for their survival and thriving. They see everything with a consumerist and use-and-throw-away attitude. Their interactions and relationships become businesslike and superficial. They become less respectful of others' presence and needs. Their ability to tolerate frustration and pain diminishes. Any slight disappointment or provocation causes them great distress. They feel angry and agitated. But the irony is that the more they try to control life, the less controllable it becomes. The more they seek pleasure and satisfaction, the more frustrated they become, because nothing satisfies them. It takes them back to where they started, and the cycle starts all over again. A lack of control and dissatisfaction with everything create nervousness and fear. They feel empty, powerless, sad, and lonely.

That nervousness and fear, emptiness and powerlessness, sadness and loneliness makes them attempt controlling life yet again and seek more pleasure. This attempt of trying to control yet not being in control, seeking pleasure and not feeling satisfied, and demanding endless choices but not being satisfied with anything, continues in a vicious circle unendingly.

Our busy lives and endless choices have also made us less attentive and present to each other. Our attention is divided, and our relationships become superficial. One example is our culture of multitasking. When we multitask, we cannot give full attention to any one thing. Our attention is divided. As a result we are neither here nor there. We cannot fully be present to any one thing or person.

The busyness of our lives makes us move from one thing to the other. We often float. We don't stay still. Life simply is an unending chain of hectic schedules with things to do and appointments to keep. There is no rest and restoration for our body, mind, and spirit. We don't have time to be in touch with our emotions and feelings. We don't ask ourselves what is going on with us. We have no time to ask how we are doing with our lives. For many of us, our busyness may be our way of avoiding being in touch with our humanity, our limitations, and our emotions and feelings.

The culture of busy lives and endless choices may have added some spice to our lives, but the changed environment has also escalated the negative survival and thriving of many people.

28

Our Protective Turf

Another reason for our negative survival and thriving is our territorial sensitiveness. Many of us are very protective of our territories. As countries don't easily open their borders to anybody, we don't open ourselves up to others easily. It takes time for people to win our trust. Generally, people find it too hard to become vulnerable before others. Since we differ in our personalities, beliefs and values, likes and dislikes, temperaments and characteristics, interests and talents, and many other features, we are often cautious about who we are dealing with. And sometimes some of us might place ourselves at a level higher than others to protect our territory. And that makes our borders harder to cross. Because of this sensitivity about crossing into each other's territories, we see people reacting in a variety of ways when they encounter others who are different from them. This difficulty can be seen in family relationships, communities, and intercultural and international relationships.

We can think of three main reactions from people when they encounter others who are different. Some people are intrigued by others who are different, and they want to learn more about them. Some others notice the difference but remain indifferent. They go about as before, remaining largely uninfluenced by the newcomers. And some others fret and fume over others who are different. The presence of the other agitates them. They might assign a superior quality to themselves and their kind. Some of these reactions can take us in the wrong direction of survival and thriving and interpersonal relationships.

Those who are intrigued by others who are different might show some interest in connecting with that person or group. They may or may not have to engage in a sustained relationship with the other, but they choose to engage in the relationship out of curiosity, genuine interest, or both. It may stay at the curiosity and feel-good level or evolve into a lasting relationship and mutual growth. For example, as a newcomer in the US, if I take the route of connecting with the new place and people, I will begin to show interest in learning more about the American culture and people. An American who wants to do the same will engage in a sustained relationship with me and learn more about me. The same thing happens with people who are different with regard to race, religion, language, or other specifics. They will begin to learn about each other rather than seeing each other as threats. They will show a willingness to expand their sense of community and relationship and become more inclusive. They will see others also as human beings and children of God rather than considering them as individuals or groups to be hated and kept at a distance. They will help build up a community of love and the kingdom of God.

Those who notice the difference but remain indifferent are often uninvolved with the other. They don't feel the need to engage the other person in a sustained relationship. Hence they show neither interest nor dismay. The presence of the other doesn't have much of an impact on them whatsoever. They are often in their own world. There is hardly any room for good or bad feelings between the two parties, as their relationship is very minimal or nil. There may be some minimal impact made by the other person or group, but there may not be any substantial impact.

I can be in America but live like I am in India, bothered little about getting connected with the new culture and people. I can live or work with an American, but the American can remain aloof and largely uninfluenced by my presence. The same thing can happen in other relationship settings. In marital or family relationships, for example, the partners or members of the family might live like islands, having minimum impact on each other. Everyone lives in his or her own way, and there is nothing much in common that solidifies their relationship. In neighborhoods and societies where people of different races and faiths live side by side, such indifference and disconnectedness can exist. They might live as islands without much interaction with or interest in each other. They remain exclusive and protective of their territories. They don't have a sense of community outside of their particular group. They may not see others as children of God and as human beings with equal dignity. They may be loyal members of their group, and pious and devout adherents of their faith or ideology. They may not hate or harm others who are different, but their exclusivist attitudes and actions do not help to build up a community of love or the kingdom of God.

Those who fret and fume over others who are different often enter into a combative mode. Although they might like to keep away, they may have very limited options in avoiding another person or group from a sustained relationship. Since the encounter occurs out of a lack of choices, the new situation or the presence of others may be just tolerated rather than welcomed. Since the others are tolerated, the relationship is often not cordial. Others might be looked down upon or treated as undesirable. They may not be viewed as children of God and human beings with equal dignity. There is at play not only exclusivism but also hateful feelings. They may not only hate but also harm each other. Such relationships are open to conflicts and difficult interactions. This can happen in places and situations where people with different cultural backgrounds have no other choice but have to work or live alongside each other. The racial, religious, and ethnic differences can create a lot of tension and ill feeling when people or groups are just tolerating each other.

And this conflict doesn't have to be just between two racial or religious groups; it can happen in our own families and communities. When we are protective of our territories and just tolerating each other rather than accepting and loving each other, there is a possibility for conflict and tension. Such families and communities are like brewing kettles. The lid can come off anytime, and boiling liquid may be spilled, burning everyone around. People with such hateful and exclusive feelings and attitudes not only fail to build up a community of love and the kingdom of God but also do harm to it. Such relationships can be open to repair and reconstruction, but it may take a lot of hard work to melt the ice between the different parties.

Why do we become very protective of our territories and react in negative ways when we are confronted with individuals or groups that are different? Following are some possible reasons.

First, my negative reactions could be caused by my difficulty in understanding you because of your accent, meaning you have characteristics that are not conducive for a lasting relationship. Some people have behaviors, personalities, attitudes, beliefs, and values that we often find difficult to put up with. Even tolerating them becomes difficult. They may not know that they have such characteristics, and so they may be surprised by our reactions. If they don't rectify their ways at least to some extent, our difficulty in relating with them in a healthy way might continue.

Second, the difficulty could be because I am used only to my accent or my ways and I have difficulty in absorbing anything new. Embracing something or someone that is unfamiliar or foreign is a hard task for people in general. Our minds are used to the familiar. Anything new takes time to digest and absorb. Since I am used only to my ways and my perspectives, I treat anything new and unfamiliar with caution. I may have a very limited knowledge of other perspectives or ways existing everywhere else. My limited circumstances make me think that my world is "the world," or make me think that the rest of the world is like mine. If others are not like my world, I might think that they are all wrong. When I operate with that mode of thinking, I perceive everyone who has a different perspective as wrong. Many are accustomed only to their accents or ways, and when they see or hear anything different, they are totally startled. They may perceive the other accent as wrong rather than considering it as different.

I remember the story of the frog in the well told by Swami Vivekananda, an Indian spiritual guru. He said that many of us are like the frog that lived in a well, thinking that the waters of the well were the largest of waters in the world. When a frog from the ocean came to the frog in the well one day and tried to explain to him that the waters of the ocean were much larger than the waters of the well and that there were many wells and oceans out there, the frog in the well was not very amused. His world was the well, and in his mind, there was nothing larger than that. He was angry and chased away the frog from the ocean. Vivekananda said that people of different religions do the same, and that problems between religions arise because of our frog-in-the-well mentality. This is true not only of our religions but also of many other aspects of our lives. We are caught up in our own little wells and fail to see other wells and oceans around us. We fail to see the God of all wells and oceans. And we fail to see all of us as children of that one God. Our world becomes the world. When we are used only to our accents and ways, we may have great difficulty in understanding and accepting others who are different from us.

Third, the discomfort could be because of our attachment to our accent. Most of us have a special bond with our home. That bond is in our blood and in our psyche. Unless the experience has been traumatic, no one usually disowns that special bond. The different aspects of our home have been ingrained and inculcated into our personality over the years. I might disown many aspects of my home, but disowning my home in its entirety would be to disown myself in some sense. It is like criticizing our president or prime minister at home but extolling him or her when we are abroad. We may not like certain aspects of our home, but we don't disown it completely.

Maia Szalavitz and Bruce Perry said that we are not genetically wired to connect fast with people who are not our family members. We tend to be more kind and loving toward our family members, especially our parents and siblings, than others because we share our genes with them. Their survival is important for our survival. So we become protective of our territories and keep ourselves close to our homes. This attachment to our home is often coupled with our fears and biases about people from other homes. Hence, we may be cautious when we deal with them.

This "home attachment" extends to other realms of our life in gradation. On an extended level, this attachment could be with our culture, language, religion, race, nationality, etc. We may be attached to many of these specificities of our lives, and it might be coupled with fears and biases about others who are different. It doesn't matter whether we are living in our home country or not; that special bond continues even when we are away or even when we are uprooted and planted in another culture.

When it comes to culture and ethnicity, every now and then I hear people in the US, particularly those of the older generation, talking about their family heritage. Many of them trace back their families to some ethnicity in Europe or elsewhere in the world. Although they themselves were born in the US, they have a glow in their eyes when they speak of their families' roots. Even if their parents or grandparents were driven out of their country or were forced to leave their country for various reasons, they still esteem the culture of their ancestors with pride. They may not even ever visit the country of their ancestors, but they take pride in that link that they are part of. This is not because they despise the country of their current nationality or domicile, but there is something in their psyche that connects them with their roots. The intensity of that link may fade after a few generations. However, it takes a very long time for it to disappear completely.

The same thing happens with our religions, races, languages, and nationalities. Most people have a bond with these specificities of their lives. The problem is not with our bond with our culture, race, religion, language, or nationality, but sometimes our attachment to these is coupled with biases and fears about others who have a different background. Even if we are curious about someone else's backgrounds, we might assign a place of pride and superiority to our own. We may sound chauvinistic or nationalistic, and we may despise others who are different. When we do that, we carry a God who is too small, a culture that is too exclusive, a race that is too superior, and a language that is too difficult to understand. We sometimes give more importance to the surface-level dimensions of our identity than our core identity as human beings and children of God. Change is hard with such people, but it is not impossible.

Remember the conversation between Jesus and the Samaritan woman in the gospel of John. Referring to the woman's question about whether one should worship on the mountain in Samaria as the Samaritans did or in Jerusalem as the Jews did, Jesus said, "Woman, believe me, the hour is coming when you will worship the Father neither on this mountain nor in Jerusalem. You worship what you do not know;

we worship what we know, for salvation is from the Jews. But the hour is coming, and is now here, when the true worshipers will worship the Father in spirit and truth, for the Father seeks such as these to worship him" (Jn 4:21–23).

True religion and spirituality, according to Jesus, go beyond religions and regions, lands and territories. True worship of God should go beyond Jerusalem and Samaria. True humanity should see others beyond their caste and color, religion and region. Often our world is too small, and we have very little understanding of other worlds out there. When we are too attached to our world, we may have great difficulty in understanding and accepting others who are different. If we understand others as "different," it might lead to reflection and change. But if we consider them as "wrong," it leads to devaluation and avoidance. Loving relationships become possible only when we are able and willing to go beyond our territories, beyond our biases and fears, and embrace all others as human beings and God's children.

Fourth, our tendency to become protective of our territories and react in negative ways to those who are different could be because of the way the presence of others impacts our life. If someone is only a tourist or visitor just passing by, we may be most hospitable. We might make every effort to make the person feel at home and comfortable, because it is part of proper etiquette. It is part of the rulebook that we have integrated into our system: we have to be hospitable and good to people. It is also part of giving a good impression of our home, our culture, and ourselves. That's how hospitality for visitors works. We try to be as welcoming and helpful as possible. So if you are a visitor, I may make an extra effort to be hospitable to you. Even if you have some peculiarities that I cannot agree with, I may not worry too much about them, because today you are with me and tomorrow you will be gone. But my whole demeanor might change if I realize that you are not a visitor but rather you have come to stay.

If you are only a visitor, my association with you is very brief and I don't have to engage in frequent and sustained interactions and relationship with you. On the other hand, if you are going to stay, the nature of our relationship changes. I may have to engage in a frequent and sustained relationship with you, and that means a whole lot of new things. If you are going to stay, I might be challenged to revisit many of my assumptions, attitudes, beliefs, and thoughts. You bring to me a new and different world, and I may be forced to take note of that. I might become more conscious of your presence and person. And a new picture of you begins to unfold before me. In that picture, I become more conscious about your personality, your color, your looks, your customs and traditions, your family and friends, your affiliations and associations, your job and social status, your beliefs and values, and so on and so forth. I might discover things in you and about you that do not match with my style and interests. I might be challenged to come out of my small world and comfort zone.

Sometimes the challenge may be too overwhelming and my mind might tell me that it is too much to engage you in a sustained relationship. My mind might tell me that all these new facts that I am discovering about you are strange and even unacceptable, and that the best option might be to disengage. There may be a real difficulty in accommodating you, but the more difficult thing may be to engage you in a sustained relationship; to leave my comfort zone. I might dread the prospect of letting you into my territory.

If you are only a visitor, I may not even mention anything about your peculiarities, because today you are with me, and tomorrow you are gone. But if you are staying, I become a little more conscious about who I am dealing with. It is almost like the differences we see in the relationship dynamics and family interactions in a couple's life between the time of their courtship and marriage. In many cases, during the courtship, the relationship between the fiancé and fiancée and between their extended families is very cordial and loving. As part of being nice and creating good impressions, all parties may bring out the best of their etiquette to make the other feel comfortable. But once the wedding is over, the relationship changes its nature. Both parties will have to be engaged in a sustained relationship and interact frequently. They have to leave their comfort zones and build up a new family. They have to open up their borders and let others enter into their territory. In that process, they get to know each other better; they learn about themselves and their in-laws more personally, and they discover new things about their families. Along with the good things, skeletons might come out of the closet. The best of their etiquette may be replaced by the worst of their demons. It doesn't take much time for the engaged to become disengaged and the in-laws to become outlaws.

The true worth of a culture or community lies in its ability to embrace people who are different. Entertaining a visitor who is different from us is not very hard, but engaging someone who is different in a sustained relationship is the real test of humanity and godliness. Being able to go beyond our caste, creed, class, and color and accept and love others as God's children and part of our human community is the true sign of the people of God's kingdom. Exclusivism and narrow-mindedness leads to the destruction and demise of the community and culture. It harms God's vision for our lives.

As I mentioned regarding the ideal encapsulated in the story of Mahābali, cultures and communities are always in the making. God constantly renews our world. The real test of our humanity consists in our ability to open our doors and borders to those who come knocking. We have to make space for others, and the old and the new have to blend. We have to learn to go beyond our differences and difficulties. We have to build a new community—a community of love, the kingdom of God—where everyone is welcome and where everyone has a place.

Certain animals are thought to be very protective of their territory. It is an instinctual defense mechanism to ensure their survival. In many ways, human beings are not any different. Many of us are protective of our territories. Many of us maintain a clannish mentality. However global or international we might become, we still might maintain a clannish mentality in some corner of our psyche. We don't easily let anyone come into our territory, be it a member of our family, our community, our country, or another culture. This protectiveness may be our instinctual defense mechanism to ensure our survival. This protectiveness may be unconscious, and the threat to our survival may be largely imaginary. But we are not just like other animals. We are intelligent and conscious beings with the ability to make decisions for a better life.

To go beyond our protective boundaries or let others enter our territories takes tremendous courage and openness. To leave our comfort zones is a hard task. Most of us like to stay with the familiar. When we go someplace, we take the most familiar route. When we do that, we are almost sure that we will get to where we want without much hassle or heartache. Taking a different route also might get us to our destination, but that route may be unknown and more difficult. And it might create nervousness and fear in us. So we often try to avoid the unknown and untested paths. When it comes to our human relationships, it is not much different. Going beyond our familiar circle of friends or familiar ways is perceived as risky and dangerous. Our survival instinct will tell us to keep to our territory. But that creates a thick wall between others and us. Human relationships become very difficult when everybody creates such walls. Being excessively protective of our territories may not augur well for a healthy manifestation of our DTS and DTT, and building healthy relationships.

29

The Nature's Fork

"A fork in the road" literally means a point at which a road branches into two. When we think of our lives, we have to understand how our human nature has placed us. We are placed in a forked position with two prongs. We are given independence on the one hand, but we remain incomplete on the other. We relish our autonomy, independence, and individuality, but autonomy and independence come with a terrible price. We feel disconnected and incomplete. On the one hand, we couldn't ask for anything better from our nature; our independence is a prized treasure. But on the other hand, our human nature puts us at a terrible disadvantage. The more independence we seek, the more disconnected we become. We seek more freedom and space to survive and thrive, but that move comes with a heavy price. Our lives remain incomplete without other human beings. This paradoxical or two-pronged position in which our natures places us has a great potential for giving rise to negative survival and thriving, and mismatched accents in our lives and relationships. Let me explain what I mean by this.

Birth, as we discussed earlier, is the beginning of one's independence and separation from the mother. The child wants to free itself from the constraining amniotic sac and thrive in a larger world of space and freedom. There is a desire for independence, separation, and individuation. Only by separating and individuating does one develop his or her own individuality and independence. The separation from the mother brings greater autonomy and freedom of movement. The child can grow and develop further.

This longing for independence and autonomy can be seen throughout one's life. No individual wants to be constrained or limited beyond a certain limit. People try to free themselves from all relationships that are excessively constraining or restricting. Some theorists would say that this desire to separate and disconnect is because of a fear of engulfment. If people become too close to someone, they fear that they might be swallowed up by that person. It may be misplaced and irrational thinking, but that is how they feel. It is a fear of annihilation.

The autonomy and independence that come with our birth, however, are not without a price. Our birth marks the beginning of a long, lonely life. This is an unavoidable trauma that every individual goes through because of the law of nature. When one is born into this world, he or she is no longer enveloped by a cozy amniotic sac. The individual is no longer connected to the mother in the way he or she was in the womb. The feeling of disconnectedness is scary. For the rest of his or her life, it is going to be that way. And for the rest of his or her life, that person makes a relentless effort to find that connection, to go back to the womb, to escape the scary feeling of being alone. The cry that the baby makes when coming out of the womb is the cry that is going to last until the end of his or her life. That cry is the protest against the disconnectedness. The cry is the pleading to go back to the womb, to find the connection again.

Authors such as Sigmund Freud and Harry Guntrip have spoken about the "womb fantasy," a desire to go back to the womb. Freud's idea of a person's desire to go back to the womb is an oedipal or incestuous wish to possess the mother. Gungrip, on the other hand, saw it as a flight from life and all object relationships. A person's desire to go back to the womb, in other words, is to withdraw from all connections and relationships. Within the womb, a person doesn't have to be connected to anyone else, except, of course, to the mother. But I depart from these two positions of Freud and Guntrip and see the womb fantasy as something very different. I see it as a desire for connection. I don't see it as an incestuous desire for the mother or a desire for disconnectedness. I see it as a longing to regain the lost connection.

At one point, the child and the mother were one. But with birth that oneness is lost. During and after birth, they are two. Left to themselves, they are incomplete. Left to themselves, they feel disconnected. Both the mother and the child may feel this incompleteness and separation in their own unique ways. But it is impossible to go back to the womb. And it is impossible to have a totally uninterrupted connection with others in the extrauterine world. The child clings on to the mother as tightly as possible and hangs on to her breasts as often as possible. But interruptions in this connection occur every now and then. The mother also feels the disconnectedness. With her child in the womb, she feels filled. With her child gone, she feels empty.

Feeling filled and feeling empty here need to be understood both in the physical and psychological sense. Feeling empty, the mother tries to keep her child to herself as much as possible. But this clinging and holding are not going to last forever either. A time will come to wean the child, and the mother and the child will be disconnected in a greater way. It is not because the mother is bad or the child is bad, but that is the law of nature. The child needs to be weaned for his or her own good. The mother needs to wean the child for her own growth and development. For the rest of his or her life, the child will try to make up for this disconnectedness by finding connections in all possible ways. First, it starts with the father, the siblings, and other extended family members. And then this cry for connection extends to peers and teachers, colleagues and companions, friends and spouses, community and culture, nature and the universe, God and divine spirit, so on and so forth. Without these connections, life becomes miserable and unlivable. So our nature places us at a disadvantage of feeling incomplete and disconnected. And relationships are sought as the antivenom for this terrible feeling of loneliness and disconnectedness.

It may sound strange, but I see this longing for connectedness and union very concretely in sexual and genital relationships. In a sexual or genital relationship, two individuals give a concrete expression to their desire for union and connectedness. Without disregarding the elements of love, intimacy, and passion, sex can be also seen as an attempt to get away from the pain of separateness and enjoy the pleasure of becoming one with the other. This effort can be understood in two different ways.

First, the partners experience extreme pleasure in becoming one with each other, as it takes away the pain of separation. In that union, they forget about themselves and become one with the other. Second, sex and conception are efforts on the part of the man and the woman to regain the lost connection, to go back home, to go back to the womb.

Separating from the mother is painful for the child. It brings a sense of disconnectedness, loneliness, and incompleteness. But the child cannot go back to the womb. The child has to live with this loss of the womb or loss of the mother. However, when the child grows up, he or she compensates for this loss of the womb or the mother by his or her own sexual activity. A woman compensates for the loss of her mother by becoming a new mother, who will in fact keep a baby in her womb. She conceives and keeps her baby in her womb. She becomes the good mother who keeps the baby. By doing that, she compensates for the pain of separation she felt when she was pushed out of her mother's womb.

A man does more or less the same thing to make up for the loss of his mother or the womb. Since the mother is not available to him anymore, and since he cannot go back into his mother's womb, he finds a new mother in his wife or partner. He cannot go into her womb completely, and so he plants his seed in her womb. That seed helps him to feel that connection. He becomes one with the new mother. Through the child growing in the womb of his wife or partner, he accomplishes his dream of returning to the womb of his mother in a limited way. He compensates for the pain of separation he suffered at the hands of his mother. His wife or partner becomes the new good mother who keeps him in the womb.

The sad truth is that these sexual unions and "wombings" are not going to last forever. The woman will give birth to her child, and the separation will occur again. The couple may reenact the drama again with the conception of another child. They may do it a fourth or fifth or sixth time, but they will have to go through the same experience again. A complete and uninterrupted union and wholeness in the physical sense is a fantasy rather than a reality.

This longing for connectedness doesn't have to be seen only in terms of sexual or genital union. We can see it in friendships, associations, and all other networks of relationships. People long to be connected with others. Interruptions occur, pain is caused, the loss is grieved, and they attempt to connect again. People who sell their houses and move to another state or country grieve the loss of their connections with their neighbors, friends, and familiar surroundings. People who leave a company or place of work after many years of service grieve the loss of their connections with their company and colleagues. Patients who have been in therapy or analysis for many years dread the time of termination and grieve the loss of their connection with the therapist or analyst. Young men and women who go off to college or get married grieve the loss of connection with their parents and other family members. Feeling disconnected is a painful experience. Even those who claim to love disconnectedness and isolation might be angry that nobody connects with them, and their aloofness may be a silent and yet powerful way to attract others' attention.

To some extent, people try to make up for their unavoidable physical disconnectedness by mental and spiritual conceptions. They conceive in their mind the person of their desire. A lover, for example, cannot keep his beloved all the time to himself. She has other places to go to, other people to meet, and other things to attend to. He will be disconnected from her physically in many ways. But he tries to keep her to himself by conceiving her in his mind. He creates images and memories of her that keep him constantly connected to her mentally. He derives pleasure in connecting with her mentally, through his thoughts and imaginings. In that way, he has her inside of him (in his mind) rather than her being separate from him. And having her inside of him, he can never lose her. However, she needs to return to him physically every now and then to keep the connection strong. A long physical absence can weaken the connection and fade the memories.

Children often experience disconnectedness from their mothers whenever mothers move out of their sight and engage in other things. The child cannot keep the mother to himself or herself all the time. The mother may be gone for many hours. But children find a way to make up for this loss and yet keep the connection with their mothers through the development of what Jean Piaget called the "object permanence." Children develop a mental representation of their mothers during their mothers' physical absence. The mental representation helps them to stay connected with their mothers mentally. When this mental picture is present, the mother is inside of the child (in his or her mind), and thus she cannot be lost easily. However, mothers need to return to their children physically every now and then to reestablish that connection. It is something like recharging a battery. If a mother is gone for a long period of time, perhaps several months, the child's connection with her could grow weaker. The child might become frustrated and distressed, and the fragile mental representation might fade over time.

Similar things happen during the deaths and the losses of loved ones. The death of a loved one is very painful for people. The pain stems from disconnectedness and loss of union. However, the bereaved keep images and memories of the dead person in their minds to keep the connection alive. They perform rites or rituals to honor the memory of the deceased. But the dead person is not going to return. So after some years, the images and memories begin to fade gradually, and the feeling of connection becomes sporadic. The person learns to live with the loss, and the pain becomes less.

The pain of disconnectedness is something like being homesick. It is difficult to explain what homesickness is or how it feels. Homesickness comes about not because people dislike the others in their current place, but because the bond with their home brings out pain and anxiety when they are disconnected from it. It is like the cry of the baby when it is born; it is the cry arising out of the first feeling of being disconnected from the mother, the baby's home. But that cry does not last too long. Either the mother keeps the baby close to her and gives the baby that feeling of home, or the baby learns to adjust to the new reality of being disconnected from the mother. When someone feels homesick, he or she feels a longing to return home, return to the mother, and regain the lost connections. In the usual sense of the word, homesickness may not last too long for most people. Either they go back to where they came from and feel at home again, or their body and mind learn to adjust to the new environment. But that feeling comes back again when he or she feels disconnected at another time. Homesickness might occur even if one lives in his or her own home. It is the anxiety that arises out of feeling disconnected.

In a more psychological sense, we experience homesickness throughout our lives, from birth to death. We are all in a constant search to find our connections, to find our mother, to go back to the womb. But it is not just a longing for the womb or the mother; it is rather an unquenchable thirst for an uninterrupted connection. We are looking for a true feeling of being home, where we are comfortable. We may look for that connection in our partner, friend, community, and colleague. Sometimes we succeed, but sometimes we fail. Sometimes others push us away. The reason could be that we are overwhelmingly demanding or overly uninteresting. We may be speaking with the wrong accent, keeping the other party at a distance. We may have a sick personality or character issues. The other party may not feel aroused or interested to create a union or connection. And sometimes the other party may not have the capacity to connect with us. He or she may have a wrong accent. He or she may have a sick personality or character issues. But even if we all have the best of interests for each other, no one can assure anyone a perfect, uninterrupted connection in this world, because everyone is limited. Everyone has a limit to what and how much he or she can give. As much as we seek the connection, so much more we seek independence and freedom.

Frustrated with several failures in finding connections, some people give up. They don't express any interest in connecting with anybody anymore. They anticipate a failure, and they dread the shame, anger, and embarrassment that would arise from such failures, so they don't even try to connect. Moving into such indifference and lack of interest doesn't have to occur after a certain age. Even certain children can move into this state if they have been frustrated with failures in connecting with their parents or others over and over again. Some theorists would call this a fear of abandonment. In any case, it is not that they don't long for connectedness but that they are either convinced of being rejected or tired of trying to connect.

Being distressed about not finding this uninterrupted connection, many people turn to things that promise to be good substitutes. Objects of different kinds, drugs, alcohol, pleasurable activities, and many such things are sought by people to fill the emptiness they feel within because of the disconnectedness. But these things cannot provide them that connection either. They may love these things, but these things cannot love them in return. They in fact end up destroying them rather than helping them.

The most fulfilling and true relationship that brings us that connection is the one we have with God. That is where we find the true connection. But the irony is that even with God, we find it difficult to connect, because the forked position of independence and interconnectedness that our nature places us in plays out even in our relationship with God. As much as we want the connection, so much more we seek independence from God. In many ways and on many occasions we get separated from God. We come to realize that with all the limitations and problems we face in our lives, most of us find only an imperfect and partial union with God in this world. It is not because God does not love us, but because we separate ourselves from God because of our desire to live and do things as pleases us. God never stops loving us. We hear that over and over again in Scripture. God said to his people through Prophet Jeremiah, "I have loved you with an everlasting love" (Jer 31:3). The departing words of Jesus to his disciples were "And remember, I am with you always, to the end of the age (Mt 28:20). God's love is never denied to us, but we deny God in many ways and separate ourselves from him.

Thus, a perfect union with either God or others in this world is impossible. The perfect union occurs only in eternity, in our lives beyond space and time. All the connections that we find in this world are limited. We will never be fully at home in this world. Saint Augustine of Hippo, an early Christian theologian, is known for this famous saying that captures this thinking: "Our heart is restless [O God], until it rests in you." It is in God that everyone comes to rest and find the perfect home, the perfect connection. God is the one who holds everyone together. When we rest in God, we are united with others as well.

This is the paradox of life in this world: we want to be independent, but we want to be connected as well. Just as there is a need to be connected and a longing to go back to the womb, there is an equally forceful need and longing to be disconnected and be freed from the womb. As much as a child wants to be united with the mother, so much more does he or she want to separate and individuate from the latter. As much as a man wants to be with his wife or girlfriend, so much more does he desire to separate from her. As much as two friends want to be together, so much more do they desire to have their own independence. As much as we want to remain close to God, so much more we want to be on our own. The difficulty in handling this paradox can cause ruptures in relationships and make people speak with mismatched accents.

Parents and children want to be together, but they drive each other apart. Teenagers want to be together, but they engage in rivalries and separate from each other. Lovers and spouses want to be together, but they end up in conflicts and drive each other apart. Members of a community or group want to be together, but they drive each other apart. The young and the old want to be together, but they disagree and distance themselves from each other. People want to be united with God, but they often find their will in conflict with God's will. People want to be part of the community, but they also want to create their own little worlds. Nations want to build a global village, but they fight over their borders and territories. People want to be related, people want the other, people want to be interdependent, but the same people drive each other apart.

A sense of incompleteness, disconnectedness, and abandonment is the price that one pays for the autonomy and independence that he or she longs for. The fear of enmeshment, engulfment, the loss of self, and the loss of individuality is the price that one pays for desiring to stay connected. In either case, there is an inherent danger and a price to pay. It is something similar to what Margaret Mahler calls our "eternal struggle against both fusion and isolation." As the attempts to connect with others do not find success all the time, the attempts to declare one's autonomy also may not find success all the time. Relationships can become turbulent when one or both parties try to become too autonomous or too disconnected. They may be like two rails that never meet. They may not understand each other's accents. The feeling of connectedness may fade, and the parties may part ways. Relationships can become turbulent when one or both parties try to become too clingy and dependent as well. Refusing to leave the womb endangers the mother and the child.

Nature's fork is a given, and the inability in finding a balance in this paradoxical experience of independence and incompleteness has a great potential to give rise to negative survival and thriving, and mismatched accents.

PART V

Transcending the Accent

30

Leave Your Country
and Kindred

If we ask people what they desire most in their lives, the majority might say that they would like to have a happy, healthy, loving, and peaceful life. They would like to have a life free from tensions and worries, striving and fighting. The stories and legends that I have mentioned have shown these ideals and dreams that people carry. If we look at fairy tales, they too are often a projection of these wishes and dreams. Fairy tales often end with the line "And they lived happily ever after." But living happily ever after is not very easy for many people. We experience enormous amounts of problems in our lives. We find mismatches in our accents on multiple levels. We see people surviving and thriving negatively. Many of us find it hard to bring the best out of ourselves. We get stuck in our growth and development, and sometimes we become a problem for others.

Often when these things happen, many of us seek guidance and help from spiritual guides or mental health professionals. Our problems may be emotional, spiritual, social, or economic in nature. And we present these problems in different shapes and forms. Sometimes they are presented as personal; at other times they are interpersonal. Sometimes they are marital problems; at other times they are work-related. Sometimes they are in the family; at other times they are in the community. Sometimes they are in the present; at other times they are from our past. Sometimes we see them as our problems; at other times we see them as the problems of others.

In the language of psychology, some of these problems might be seen as behavioral problems, personality disorders, cognitive impairments, ego defects, self-alienation, character flaws, genetic imbalances, relationship issues, or environmental deficiencies. In the language of religion and spirituality, they may be labeled as sins or sinful inclinations, weaknesses, limitations, brokenness, imperfections, and fallen nature. The problems are more or less the same, but the way they get branded and examined in each field is different. What is often considered as extreme narcissism in psychology, for example, is the sin of selfishness in the language of religion and spirituality. What is branded as grandiosity and self-inflation in psychology is called the sin of pride, haughtiness, and vainglory in religion and spirituality. Those things understood as aggression, hostility, and rage in psychology often amount to the sins of anger, hatred, and lack of forgiveness in religion and spirituality.

Sometimes the responsibility for these problems is placed on the person who commits the act. At other times, the responsibility may be more collective. That is, it may be looked at as the result of many factors, such as personal flaws, familial drawbacks, and environmental deficiencies. Nature, nurture, and culture share the responsibility for the problem. Whether it is labeled as a sin or psychological issue, shame, guilt, and fear are often associated with it.

Whatever may be the nature of the problem, we experience mismatch in our accents. Our lives are disrupted, our growth and development are compromised, and our relationships are affected. To move on with our lives and to bring the best out of ourselves, we need to transcend these accents. We might call it a change, conversion, or transformation. But we need to move from where we find ourselves. To help this process of change or conversion, psychology and spirituality offer different ways and methods. People can use counseling or therapy and medication. If they are religious or spiritual, they can make use of prayer, confessions or reconciliation, and spiritual guidance.

These fields brand those who have problems and those who treat the problems in different ways. In psychology, those who have problems may be branded as patients or clients. In spirituality and religion, they get branded as penitents and confessants. In psychology, those who treat the problems are called doctors, psychologists, therapists, and counselors. In spirituality and religion, they are called pastors, priests, confessors, and spiritual guides. Both categories of people are instruments of change and healing. Psychologists or therapists help the healing process by the power vested in them by society and the mental health community. Priests, pastors, and other spiritual guides help the healing process by the power vested in them by society, God, and the religious community. Some people seek help only from one—either psychology or religion and spirituality—while others use both.

In my opinion, a combination of both psychology and spirituality would be the best to bring about the change we need in our lives. Psychology could be useful in helping with the healing process, but keeping God out of it is going to deprive us of the desired effect. It will be almost like siblings trying to keep the family together without involving the father and mother. A family is not a family when one member is kept away. Our human family will never be whole as long as God is kept away from us, because our origin itself is in and from him (see Ge 1:26–27). Our goal is to change or transcend our accents so that we can make progress in our lives and build up the kingdom of God, where we are united with God and others. A combination of seeking a better understanding of ourselves and the grace and wisdom of God would be the best approach for transcending our accents and building up healthy and happy lives.

In the Judeo-Christian-Islamic tradition, one of the persons who transcended his accents and brought about a change in the direction of his life is Abraham. He is believed to have moved from where he was, literally and figuratively, and his life was no more the same. He survived and thrived well, and he became a blessing for others as well. Abraham's story is repeated in the lives of his descendants too. Their stories reveal fascinating things about our lives as human beings. All the themes that we discussed so far in this book could be seen neatly interwoven in their stories. Although Abraham and his descendants are important figures of faith primarily for the Jews, Christians, and Muslims, they could be seen as representatives of all human beings. Let's take a brief look at their stories.

The story of Abraham in the Bible is described in the book of Genesis, starting from chapter 12. In chapter 12 we read, "Now the Lord said to Abram, 'Go from your country and your kindred and your father's house to the land that I will show you. I will make of you a great nation, and I will bless you, and make your name great, so that you will be a blessing'" (Ge 12:1–2). God called Abraham for something totally new. He was asked to leave his country and kindred and embark on a journey to a new horizon. Abraham, known then as Abram, took the call of God seriously, left his own land of Ur, which is considered to be in present-day Iraq, and set out for the land of Canaan, which supposedly includes present-day Israel, Palestinian territories, and parts of Jordan, Syria, and Lebanon. The land of Canaan, the land of God's promises, was an unknown and uncertain territory, but trusting in God, Abraham left his familiar surroundings and set out on this journey.

After wandering through various lands and territories, Abraham finally arrived in the land of Canaan. He and his wife, Sarai, began to settle down there. But before they could really settle down, the land was struck with a famine. They were forced to leave the place. Abraham and Sarai went to Egypt and pitched their tent there for a while. But that stay didn't last too long. Abraham's wife, Sarai, was a beautiful woman, and Abraham feared that if the Egyptians came to know her as his wife, they would kill him to take possession of her. Hence, before entering Egypt, he instructed Sarai to tell the Egyptians that she was his sister. So to save his own life, he lied to the Egyptians and made Sarai do the same. As feared, the news about Sarai's beauty became the talk of the town, and it reached the ears of Pharaoh, the ruler of Egypt. Being the ruler of the land and needing no consent from anyone, he took her in as his mistress. But God inflicted plagues on Pharaoh for taking Abraham's wife as his mistress. Upon learning about the real identity of Sarai, Pharaoh was upset with Abraham and expelled him from Egypt.

Abraham once again wandered through different lands and returned to the land of Canaan. He and Sarai once again began to settle down in the land of God's promises. However, one thing continued to bother Abraham: there was no indication of God's promise coming true. God had promised Abraham that he would make him a great nation, but there was no such thing happening. Abraham was advanced in age, eighty-six years old, and Sarai was thought to be barren. He could not have even one child, so he wondered how he could become the father of a great nation.

While wrestling with this problem, Sarai, his wife, came up with a new idea. Giving up the hope of bearing a child herself, Sarai asked Abraham to have relations with her Egyptian slave, Hagar, and produce children for her. Since slaves were treated as personal property, the children born of the slave would automatically belong to Sarai and become like her children. It was not uncommon in those days for men in various tribes to have relations with their slaves. Abraham took the advice of his wife, Sarai, and had relations with Hagar. Hagar conceived and gave birth to a son. They named him Ishmael.

The childless couple had a child now through the slave girl, but events surrounding the birth of Ishmael would not be all that happy. The relationship between Sarai and Hagar turned sour. It is not clear when exactly their relationship started going bad. It could be that Sarai became jealous of Hagar on account of her privilege of having a son, or Hagar started looking down upon Sarai on account of her childless status. Anyway, things were not happy between the two women, and Abraham was caught in the middle. As the uneasiness in the family relationship was unfolding, Abraham and Sarai had a surprise. The old and barren Sarai had a miraculous intervention from God, and she conceived and gave birth to a son, whom they named Isaac. It is possible that the fight between Sarai and Hagar actually started after both Ishmael and Isaac were born. Sarai might have seen Ishmael as a hurdle in her son's future prospects and asked Abraham to expel the slave girl and her son. Whatever may be the circumstance, the fight between Sarai and Hagar ended in the expulsion of Hagar and Ishmael from the household.

When they were expelled, God did not turn his back on Hagar and Ishmael. God had promised Hagar that her son too would become a great nation. (See Ge 16:10.) Ishmael moved through different lands, including Egypt, and his descendants grew in number (Ge 25:12–18).

After Ishmael and Hagar left the household, the greatest test of his life came when God asked Abraham to sacrifice his only son, Isaac. (See Ge 22:1–19.) The question before Abraham was about how much he was willing to make sacrifices for the sake of his love for God. We can assume that Abraham was devastated and heart-broken. But even in that most trying and difficult situation we see Abraham putting God above everything else. Although God spared him from what would have been the greatest pain of his life, Abraham proved to be a true friend of God who was willing to make any sacrifice for the sake of his love for him. Abraham's testimony to love, of course, was a prefiguration of what God was going to do for the whole human race through his son, Jesus. We read in the gospel of John, "For God so loved the world that he gave his only Son, so that everyone who believes in him may not perish but may have eternal life" (Jn 3:16).

After the test had passed, Abraham, Sarai, and Isaac continued their life in the land of Canaan. Many years passed by, and Abraham and Sarai died at a ripe old age, the former at 175 and the latter at 127. Their son, Isaac, carried on the promise of God, and the story of God's chosen family continued with many twists and turns. After Isaac's death, his son Jacob became the patriarch of the family, which by then had grown large. However, a famine struck the land of Canaan again, and they were forced to leave for Egypt and settle down there. Over the years they came to be known as the Israelites in Egypt. They flourished for some time, but their fortunes turned into misfortune as they were forced into slavery in Egypt. They struggled hard for many years. God eventually intervened in their lives, and under the leadership of Moses, they marched out of slavery in Egypt. They returned to Canaan and began their life there all over again. However, the subsequent generations faced similar kinds of hardships and problems. They were harshly ruled, occupied, and exiled. They found it difficult to become a great nation. God's promise to their forefather, Abraham, continued to remain an unfulfilled dream.

Thus we find in Abraham and his descendants a great struggle in making their dream come true. They found it difficult to become a great and lasting nation. They were driven out of the land of Canaan over and over again. We have Abraham leaving the land of Canaan because of famine and settling down in Egypt, Ishmael leaving the land of Canaan because of Sarai's displeasure and settling down in Egypt, the Israelites under Jacob leaving the land of Canaan because of famine and settling down in Egypt, and all the subsequent generations of the Israelites leaving Canaan because of exile or foreign occupations. They were all forced out of the land of Canaan at different times for different reasons.

But Egypt and other places were only temporary asylums for Abraham and his descendants. They all returned to Canaan after their sojourns abroad. Abraham returned to Canaan when Pharaoh expelled him. The Israelites returned to Canaan after they were fed up with the slavery and hardships in Egypt and God intervened in their lives. We don't know whether Ishmael ever returned to Canaan. But the future generations of the Israelites returned back to Canaan after being exiled or scattered all over the world. But then the story starts all over again. They would be driven out of the land of Canaan again at different periods of time. Their dream of becoming a great nation continued to remain unfulfilled.

Thus, beginning with Abraham and continuing through his descendants, we find a constant struggle in making the promise of God come true. Becoming a great nation was a dream that was so near and yet so far. Every time they came close to it, they faced new hurdles, and they were dispersed and scattered again.

What does this story tell us? What did God's command to leave his country and kindred mean for Abraham? What did it mean to go to the land that God was going to show him? What does the land of Canaan stand for? What did it mean when God said to Abraham that he would make him a great nation? What does becoming a great nation mean? Why was it difficult for Abraham and his descendants to become a great nation? This is where I find it useful to read between the lines. As we talked about the story of Mahābali and others, the stories of Abraham and his descendants need to be seen on two levels—the physical and the spiritual, and the actual and the symbolic. They have a surface-level meaning and a deeper meaning. They contain manifest content and latent content. Their stories tell us fascinating things about what happened in their lives. But they also tell us what God is trying to say to us on a deeper level. If we really want to transcend our accents and march toward a rejuvenating and fulfilling life, we have to understand both these levels of meaning.

The manifest and physical meaning of God's call and promise to Abraham and his descendants consisted in finding a land or territory, settling down in the new place, and building up a happy and prosperous life. It consisted in ensuring material, physical, and psychological well-being. It meant a secure life, free from external threats. But this is only the surface-level meaning. They had to go beyond that and find the deeper meaning of God's call and promise. The real and deeper meaning, or the latent, spiritual, and symbolic meaning, consisted in developing and following a new vision of life. It consisted in building a new community or family centered on God's will. It was a call to a new way of life. It was a call to leave the life of sin and idolatry, lies and dishonesty. It was a call to go beyond their usual ways and begin a new life with a new vision. And it was a call to transcend their accents and develop a language that was understandable for all.

For Abraham, leaving his country and kindred meant a multi-dimensional movement in his life. First, it meant a spiritual transformation. Abraham and his family were supposedly nature worshippers. They were called to move from the worship of false gods and goddesses to the worship of true God. But it could also be seen as a call to beware of things that had taken the place of God in their life. Like Abraham and his family, there may be many things in our life that take the place of God. It could be money, material possessions, sinful pleasures, and many other things. We may recognize that sometimes we become like the rich fool who relied on his wealth (Lk 12:13–21). Leaving the country and kindred could mean leaving everything that has taken the place of God in our life.

Second, leaving the country and kindred meant a psychological transformation. To begin a new life, Abraham had to leave behind everything that was holding him back, including the negativity and debilitating elements that he had inherited from his family and past generations. To embark on a new vision of life, we have to leave our hurt feelings, negative memories, bad attitudes, and unhealthy habits and behaviors. We have to leave behind or get healed from the emotional and psychological baggage we carry.

Third, leaving the country and kindred also meant a social and cultural transformation. Abraham had to come out of his comfort zone and familiar surroundings. He had to go to a new land and learn to live among people who were different from him. To experience the fullness of life that God offers us, we have to transcend our social and cultural barriers. We have to learn to live among people who are different from us. We have to go beyond the surface level dimensions of our identity and recognize that we are all human beings and children of God.

The land of Canaan, or the Promised Land, represented a new horizon, a new life of growth and development. It was not so much about lands and territories, but rather about building a new community—a community united with God and others, a community based on truth and justice, love and peace. To do that, they had to shed their ungodly and unhealthy characteristics. They had to stop fighting among themselves. They had to recognize who they were at the deepest level of their being. They had to realize that they were human beings and children of God and that their mission in this world was to give witness to God. That is how they were going to become a great nation. We read in the book of Jeremiah this vision of life that God had for them: "They shall be my people, and I will be their God" (Jer 32:38). The material prosperity and happiness were to be a result of this loving relationship with God and others. Governments and states were to be built on this principle of lasting bond with God and others. When united with God and others in love and peace, truth and justice, they could truly prosper and flourish and become a great nation. But the most important factor was the recognition of the deeper meaning of God's call.

Very often, this deeper meaning was either not recognized or forgotten. People focused on the surface-level meaning of God's promise to Abraham, and they were busy occupying lands and territories or seeking material prosperity. They were caught up in power and position, and prosperity and pleasure. Their lack of understanding of the deeper message of God's call was reflected in their personal and social lives. Sinful behaviors and unjust practices prevailed in their personal dealings and social interactions. God was often not in the picture, and the good of the community was not the focus. They fought among themselves. The oppression and exploitation of the poor and the weak went unchecked.

People were caught up in their own little worlds. People were divided into classes and groups. They were divided as the rich and the poor, the righteous and the sinful, and the Jews and the gentiles. It was often "them" versus "us." This was not the vision of life that God had called them to follow. This was not the way to become a great nation.

We find Prophets like Isaiah and Jeremiah strongly condemning the evil systems and structures in the society, and chastising people for deviating from the path that God had set for them. We read in the book of Isaiah, "Announce to my people their rebellion, to the house of Jacob their sins ... Look, you serve your own interest on your fast day, and oppress all your workers ... Is not this the fast that I choose: to loose the bonds of injustice, to undo the thongs of the yoke, to let the oppressed go free, and to break every yoke? Is it not to share your bread with the hungry, and bring the homeless poor into your house; when you see the naked, to cover them, and not to hide yourself from your own kin?" (Isa 58).

Even as they were marching toward the Promised Land, the people of Israel ignored God and began to do things that pleased them. They created a golden calf and started worshipping it (Ex 32:1–6). The golden calf represented the life of corruption and sin that they had moved into. We hear God saying to Moses, "Go down at once! Your people, whom you brought up out of the land of Egypt, have acted perversely; they have been quick to turn aside from the way that I commanded them (Ex 32:7–8). It was not just once, but several times in their history, that the people of Israel moved away from God's ways. The golden calf appeared and reappeared in many forms and shapes in their lives. They created their own gods and goddesses. They got stuck with their accents and ways. They oppressed and suppressed the poor and the weak. Seeing this corruption and sin in their life, God intervened every now and then in their history to tear down their false ideas and assumptions and bring them back on track. We see this attempt at the renewal and reorientation of the community in the words of God addressed to prophet Jeremiah: "See, today I appoint you over nations and over kingdoms, to pluck up and to pull down, to destroy and to overthrow, to build and to plant" (Jer 1:10).

People heeded the voice of God coming through the prophets for some time, and then they went back to their old ways. They returned to their own accents, sinful lives, and the usual ways of doing things. They mistook God's call for a call to occupy lands and territories and build up strong and powerful earthly empires or kingdoms. They continued their pursuit of material prosperity and happiness without any regard for God or community. They stayed with the superficial meaning of God's call and failed to go deeper to understand what God actually desired of them. They were stuck with the manifest content and did not seek the latent content of the call and promise that Abraham, their forefather, received.

Finally, God himself had to incarnate in Jesus to tell them that becoming a great nation or entering the Promised Land was not about a land or territory but a new way of life. In the letter to the Hebrews, we read, "For it is clear that he did not come to help angels, but the descendants of Abraham. Therefore he had to become like his brothers and sisters in every respect, so that he might be a merciful and faithful high priest in the service of God, to make a sacrifice of atonement for the sins of the people" (Heb 2:16–17). Jesus came to tell them that God was not leading them to a particular land or territory but to a new vision of life and faith. It was a call to a life of freedom—freedom from slavery to sin and selfishness. It was a call to build a community of love, the family of God. Jesus came to show them how they could transcend their accents and develop a new language that was understandable by all. He came to show them how to truly live as human beings. And imagine how many people were shocked, surprised, and disappointed when Jesus said that his focus was not the overthrow of governments or occupation of lands and territories. Seeing how popular, powerful, and miraculous he was, they thought they finally had someone who could become their king, overthrow their opponents, and bring them happiness and material prosperity.

In the gospel of John we read, "When Jesus realized that they were about to come and take him by force to make him king, he withdrew again to the mountain by himself" (Jn 6:15). They were disappointed. They needed an earthly king with power and glory, who would occupy lands and territories and defeat their enemies. But that was not his vision and mission. That was not what God had intended for his people. That was not the way to become a great nation. It was a different kind of nation or kingdom that Jesus envisioned. Jesus said to Pontius Pilate—the governor of Judea, who condemned him to crucifixion and death—"My kingdom is not from this world. If my kingdom were from this world, my followers would be fighting to keep me from being handed over to the Jews. But as it is, my kingdom is not from here" (Jn 18:36).

The kingdom that Jesus envisioned was a kingdom of human hearts united with God and one another. It was a vision of one nation under God, the universal family of God. It was a kingdom built on love. It was a kingdom beyond lands and territories. It was a kingdom where there was no division between "them" and "us." It was a kingdom of justice and truth, peace and joy, love and brotherhood/sisterhood, and forgiveness and mercy. Jesus mingled with saints and sinners, Pharisees and publicans, and the rich and the poor. Everyone had a place in his company. He touched the lepers whom no one ever dared to come close to; he visited the Samaritan towns, which no Jew ever dared to enter; and he recruited as his disciples men from all walks of life, which shocked almost every Rabbi living in his time. Jesus had a place for all. Even Judas Iscariot, the one who was going to betray him, had a place at his table (Jn 13:21–30). He forgave even his executioners (Lk 23:34).

Jesus did not reject anyone. He did not recognize a division between "them" and "us." Everyone was precious to him, and everyone was in need of grace and mercy. He came to heal the divisions and establish a new world order. The craze for power and wealth had to give way to hearts filled with love. The concept of worldly kingdoms had to give way to God's kingdom. But first, this spirit of God's kingdom had to be established in human hearts, not in terms of physical realities. Unless hearts were changed, the world was not going to change. The physical realities of states and governments had to be built on this internal reality of the universal family of God. They had to be built on this vision of God's kingdom, where justice, truth, peace, and love prevailed.

Jesus came to give the world this vision of life, and in this vision, everyone was included. Seeing Jesus, the holy man, Simeon exclaimed, "... for my eyes have seen your salvation, which you have prepared in the presence of all peoples, a light for revelation to the Gentiles and for glory to your people Israel" (Lk 2:32). Jesus came for the Jews and the gentiles, the saints and the sinners. Fulfilling his Father's will and bringing everyone together as God's family were his utmost priorities. In fulfilling this mission, he gave his best, and he gave it to the end. He did not bow to threats, suffering, sin, or death. He bowed rather to his heavenly Father, who sent him on that mission. When his mission was completed, he said, "Father, into your hands I commend my spirit" (Lk 23:46).

Thus, reading between the lines, we see many captivating things about this concept of leaving one's country and kindred and becoming a great nation that was promised to Abraham and his descendants. They teach us some rich and profound truths about our lives. Marching toward or staying put in the Promised Land was a call to a new life, a new ideal. It was not so much about the land or territory of Canaan. It was, in fact, about going beyond their territories. It was about pursuing a higher goal in life—a goal God had set for them. It was a call to transcend their accents. It was a call to transcend their territorial and tribal mentality. It was a call to step out of their usual ways and embrace a new vision of life. It was a call to a new faith. It was a call to see God and one another from a new perspective. And it was never easy for them to get to that ideal. It was never easy for them to leave their usual ways or transcend their accents. They often got stuck in their ways. They failed to understand the broader vision that God had for their lives. And they faced many hurdles and problems when they came close to their ideals.

Each of them experienced these difficulties in his own unique way. Abraham had to leave the land of Ur. He had to leave his familiar surroundings, his comfort zone. He had to come out of his protective turf, and he had to embrace a new faith and vision of life. On that journey, he encountered several hurdles and problems, both big and small, natural and human. He had to leave Canaan because of famine. He lied to the Egyptians for fear of losing his life. After returning to the Promised Land, the family dynamics grew more complicated with Hagar and Ishmael coming into the picture. Presumably, there were a lot of fights in the family. The family was divided, and Hagar and Ishmael were expelled or cut off. Following God's vision of life was never easy for Abraham.

Although we don't hear much of Ishmael after he left Abraham's household, we can assume that his descendants also struggled hard to become a great nation or people.

Jacob, Abraham's grandson, and his family, who came to be known as the Israelites, were struck with a famine and were forced to seek asylum in Egypt. They flourished in Egypt for some time, but their fortunes turned into misfortunes. They were forced into slavery there. But after they were liberated from slavery, they wandered through the desert and different lands for forty years before they set their foot in Canaan. Wandering through the desert could mean going through many difficulties in staying put with God's vision and mission. During their sojourn and later, it was never easy for them to stay put, because of the vision of life that God had for them. Sometimes they got disoriented, and at other times they got stuck in their ways.

The struggle of realizing God's vision of life and becoming a great nation was felt by all the other descendants of Abraham in subsequent generations, and it is narrated throughout the Bible.

Even Jesus himself experienced many trials and tribulations in bringing this vision of life to his people. To begin with, his birth itself startled and disturbed many, and they tried to get rid of him. Although he is God himself, in his incarnated humanity, he was linked to the lineage of Abraham. He was born in Bethlehem of Judea, in the Promised Land of Canaan, as a descendant of David, one of the acclaimed kings of Israel, whose lineage goes back to Abraham (Mt 1:1–17). But when Herod, the king of Judea, heard that a new king, Jesus, had been born for Israel, he feared that he would be toppled from his throne. Hence, to get rid of Jesus, he ordered that all the male children in Bethlehem and the surrounding regions who were two years old or under be killed. But after being warned of the threat of Herod by an angel, Joseph, the foster father of Jesus, took Jesus and his mother, Mary, and fled to Egypt. They stayed there until Herod died (Mt 2:13–23).

So we see history being repeated. Like Abraham and others, Jesus was also driven out of the land of Canaan to seek shelter in Egypt. Upon the death of Herod, Jesus and his parents returned to the land of Canaan. But even after he returned to Canaan and began his mission and ministry, it was never easy for Jesus to convince his people about the real vision that God had for them. They thought that God's plan for them was to build an ever-strong earthly kingdom. They envisioned material prosperity and freedom from the threat of their enemies. But when he said that God's vision for them was different, they were disappointed and upset. They criticized him, condemned him, and finally crucified him. But nothing prevailed over him. He was victorious over suffering, sin, and death (1Co 15:55–57).

The story of Abraham and his descendants often gets repeated in our own lives. Like them, many people tend to think that God's vision of life for us is all about lands and territories, kingdoms and empires, and material prosperity and happiness. If we think of our lives in that manner, then we miss the point. Then we are looking only at the manifest content or surface-level meaning of our lives, and not going deeper. God's vision of life for us is more about building a new community than building a kingdom in the political sense of the term. It is about a renewal and revival of our lives. It is about leaving our debilitating accents and developing a language that is understandable for all. It is about freeing ourselves from our slavery to sin and evils. It is about shedding our dead skins and resurrecting into a new life.

We are called to go beyond our physical selves and biology, and recognize who we are at the deepest level of our being. We are called to recognize our true mission in this world. We are children of God, and the purpose of our life is to give testimony to God, to be a visible presence of God in this world. Abraham and his descendants are pointers to a new way of life rather than a particular land or territory. Jesus tells us very clearly that this new way of life is not about lands and territories; it is about our hearts and minds, which need a renewal and reorientation.

The conversation between Jesus and the Samaritan woman (Jn 4:21–23) speaks about the need to go beyond Jerusalem and Samaria, beyond lands and territories. It is about freeing ourselves from our sins and selfishness. It is about transcending our accents. The systems and structures that we build up have to be based on this new vision of life. Our prosperity and happiness on this earth have to emanate from this vision of life where we are united with God and others. All other kingdoms and structures that we build up are going to crumble and fall. But even after two thousand years of Jesus saying it, we still don't get it. We still fight over lands and territories, and build kingdoms and empires as pleases us. We find Herods and Pharaohs in us, trying to kill or enslave others. We think it is all about building a safe and secure kingdom on this earth. We miss the real message. Even many Christians themselves, the followers of Jesus, do not get it. They too think that it is all about lands and territories and building an earthly kingdom.

What happened to Abraham and his descendants happens to all of us. We often find it hard to transcend or leave our debilitating accents completely and embrace the new vision of life. We face many hurdles and get stuck in our ways. We bounce back and forth between the healthy and unhealthy realms in our lives and relationships. We fight over lands and territories rather than evils and sins in our lives. We face several distractions and temptations on the way.

In the psychoanalytic field, theorists talk about people regressing into earlier stages of their lives to cope with stressful situations. They revert back to patterns of behaviors they had in the past. Such regressions that function as great defense mechanisms can be physical, psychological, emotional, or behavioral in nature. Regression and defense mechanisms give a temporary relief to the person. They defend the person against the stressor. But the person has to constantly confront and resolve those stressors and defenses to move to a healthy and fulfilling life. The regressive state is like one's own accent. The person may have made great effort to leave the usual ways, transcend his or her accent, and begin a new life. However, some stressors might make the person leave those ideals and revert back to his or her old ways or accent.

We might see this back-and-forth journey that we make between our healthy and unhealthy sides in many areas of our lives. The interplay of progression and regression happens in several ways in our lives. We may have decided to be positive and optimistic, but some misfortune or trouble may dishearten us and take us back to where we were before—depressed or discouraged. We may have come a long way in becoming altruistic and generous, but deep down in us, we may find some selfishness and unhealthy narcissism popping up every now and then. We may have worked hard to become forgiving and gentle, but some irritants might stir up some anger and aggression in us. We may have made much effort in being satisfied with what we have, but sometimes we might find ourselves desiring more and accumulating more than what we need. We may have made strenuous efforts in becoming global and international in our thinking and attitude, but occasionally we may find ourselves entertaining some tribalism, linguicism, and nationalism. We may have become very accommodating and accepting in our approach to people, but deep down in us we may find some racism, sexism, and casteism.

Because many of these "isms" carry loaded meanings and garner social disapproval, many might be even afraid to utter those terms and admit their presence in their lives. But that doesn't mean that they don't exist. Some stressors in our lives might make them resurrect again, and we might notice their presence in our words, attitudes, thoughts, and actions. The moment someone walks through our door, we might notice how our mind already makes conclusions and judgments about that person, and how these isms kick in even without our own volition. We revert back to our earlier patterns of behavior. We go back to our accents more often than we realize.

When we are faced with stressors in our lives, we might run back to our old accents or defense mechanisms. We might want to stay isolated and cut off from others. We might want to build up our own kingdoms and be protective of our territories. We might want to nurse the past wounds and pay back those who injured us. We might want to live in the slavery of hurtful memories, traumatic experiences, and deadly fear. But if we do that, we cannot live a full and free life and become a blessing for others.

Even while they were marching toward the land of Canaan, some of the Israelites desired to go back to Egypt. They said to Moses and Aaron, "If only we had died by the hand of the Lord in the land of Egypt, when we sat by the fleshpots and ate our fill of bread; for you have brought us out into this wilderness to kill this whole assembly with hunger" (Ex 16:3). Even though they had been enslaved in Egypt, they wanted to go back there. They were too stressed out about journeying to the Promised Land. Leaving the slavery is not easy sometimes. Even slavery becomes pleasurable in some ways. Thinking of the hardships involved in getting to the ideal, they preferred slavery to freedom.

Sometimes it may not be easy to let go of our past memories and experiences, our accents and defenses, our bad habits and attitudes, and embrace a new vision of life. We may get so used to our unhealthy ways that we begin to think that those ways are best. We might also get used to our ways so much that any thought of change might feel as difficult as climbing a steep mountain. Transcending our accents and embracing a new vision of life might demand sacrifices, discipline, forgiveness, accommodation, acceptance, frustration tolerance, regulation of emotions, denial of pleasures, and several other things. Transcending our accents and embracing a new vision of life are necessary to get to our ideals and dreams. Without these, we will not be able to grow and develop, and we will not be able to become a blessing for others.

To do something different, to break the cycle of negative DTS and DTT and mismatches in accents, and to bring the best out of ourselves and become a blessing for others, we have to transcend our debilitating accents. We may have become what we are for various reasons. We have to seek healing and restoration. We have to leave our country and kindred, our debilitating and destructive accents, and embrace the new vision of life that God offers us.

Just as leaving the womb is both scary and thrilling for a child, leaving or transcending our accents can be both scary and thrilling for us. Remaining in the womb might be comfortable, but if a child wants to thrive and grow, it has to leave the womb. The child has to leave the womb also for the sake of the mother. If the child continues to remain in the womb, it can threaten both the child and the mother.

To become a great nation and a blessing for others, Abraham had to leave his country and kindred. He had to live with hope and determination. He had to embrace a new faith and vision of life. He had to face famines and deprivations with faith and courage. He had to make great sacrifices. He had to come clean with his lies and hidden life and leave his temporary asylums. He had to seek reconciliation and peace among his family members who were fighting. He had to keep his eyes focused on the land of promises. Similar things had to happen with his descendants as well. Many times, for many reasons, Abraham and his descendants were forced or tempted to leave their ideals or mission. But God always called them back. Jesus sets a beautiful example of pursuing our vision of life with determination and courage. Not bowing to threats, fears, suffering, discouragement, or even death, but rather to God alone, who sets that vision for us, we can build a community of love—the kingdom of God.

Transcending our accents or changing the debilitating or degenerative elements of our lives and personalities may not always be too easy. We may occasionally experience uncertainties, famines, and fights (stressors). We may occasionally be forced or tempted to leave our ideals and dreams and return to our old ways. We may be asked to make great sacrifices. But in spite of all these setbacks and temptations, we are always encouraged to bounce back and move toward our ideals and dreams.

Individuals, families, communities, and nations get stuck in their lives and relationships because they find it hard to go beyond their accents or change the unhealthy elements of their lives and relationships. They stay with the surface-level meaning of God's call rather than going deeper. Our human history points to our perennial problem of getting stuck on our own accents. The materialization of the goals and dreams contained in our legends and stories calls us to revisit our accents, revisit our negative DTS and DTT, revisit our biases and prejudices, and revisit our attitudes and beliefs that make us distanced and disconnected. It calls us to have a new vision of life. We can either hold on to our accents and get stuck, or we can make an extra effort to transcend them and develop an understandable language. We may not get it all squared away, but we will be at a better place in our lives and relationships. We will not only excel in what and who we are but also become a support system for others who long to get there. As Abraham was promised, we will become not only a great community of nations but also a blessing for the future generations.

We can walk, swim, fly, or take a car, bus, or train, but to get to our destination, we need to make the first step. If we are not able to do it by ourselves, we can seek someone else's help to hold our hand or carry us to our destination. But we need to move. We need to move from where we find ourselves—not so much in the physical sense, but in the psychological and spiritual sense. To make that movement toward living to the best of our ability the vision of life that God has for us, and experiencing a healthy and rejuvenating life, I suggest a few things in the following chapters for our consideration.

31

Increased Awareness

To transcend our accents and move toward a healthy and joyful life, the first task for all of us is to gain a greater awareness of all that we have discussed so far. First, we need to be aware that God has a vision of life for us, and that is to build a community of love in union with him and others. Then we have to recognize that we all have an accent. We all differ in multiple ways. We need also to be aware that we all have a drive to survive (DTS) and a drive to thrive (DTT), and these drives can generate in us both positive and negative thoughts, feelings, and actions. Depending on whether they are positive or negative, we will find progress or regress in our lives and relationships. In addition, we need to be aware of the impact of our genetics and environment, our temperamental differences, our past experiences, our debilitating character structures, our distorted sense of self, the inequality in our thriving avenues and survival possibilities, the unhealthy elements of our present-day culture and society, our sensitiveness about letting others into our territory, and our paradoxical experience of independence and incompleteness in our daily lives and relationships.

The time and the manner of becoming conscious of all these things differ from person to person. Some might become conscious of them early in life, and others might do the same later in life. Some might become aware of these things mostly by themselves, and others might need some help to do it. In general, the awareness of these things is very minimal in the preadulthood stages of our life. As the conventional belief goes, "Wisdom comes with age." The earlier one becomes conscious of these things, the better it is for his or her life and for the rest of the world. A better and earlier awareness will help the person to steer his or her life in positive and constructive ways. And that in turn will help everyone else around that person.

We don't know how old Abraham was when he heard the call of God. Maybe he was already in his late adulthood. It didn't come when he was a boy or an adolescent. It took many years for him to realize that he had to take a different path and follow a new vision of life. But in the case of another Biblical figure, Samuel, this call came much earlier. He was only a boy when God called him (1Sa 3). For Saint Paul, the call of God came when he was still breathing threats against the followers of Jesus (Ac 9). He was probably in his twenties or thirties.

The manner in which we gain a greater awareness about our lives and the new path is also different depending on the person and circumstances. It could happen by intuition, enlightenment, or inducement. All these bring the concerned individuals a deeper insight or vision about their lives and relationships, and the need for a new path. It can occur through praying and meditating, reading a book, interacting with someone, or engaging in the therapeutic process with a psychotherapist.

We can gain greater awareness in miraculous and extraordinary ways as well. It can occur when someone searches for a deeper meaning about life or gets stuck in life with no apparent forward movement. It can happen when people are faced with certain crises in life or when they become the most hated or feared object in the community or society; something comes to them like a thunderbolt from the sky, and they have a dramatic change. It can happen because of personal or social situations.

For many prophets, such as Isaiah and Jeremiah, the call of God came as a response to what was going on in the society and community. For Moses, the call to take a new path in life came in response to the slavery of the Israelites in Egypt. For Abraham Lincoln, the call of God came as a response to the brutal system of slavery and senseless killing and hatred between people of his land. For Mahatma Gandhi, it was a response to the subjugation of his people by the colonialists. For B. R.

Ambedkar, it was a response to the subjugation of his people by the high caste community. For Nelson Mandela, it was a response to the subjugation of his people by the white minority. For Mother Teresa of Calcutta, the call to a new path in life came in response to the sufferings of the destitute in Calcutta.

Thus, the time and manner in which we gain greater awareness about our lives and the call to a new way of life differ from individual to individual. Whatever may be the case, when we gain this awareness, we are moved to do something different. We become a little more alive to who we are and what is going on with us. We become a little more present to ourselves and present to the world. Becoming a little more aware of our life and relationships, we can redefine our vision of life and apply our conscious mind to reach the true goals of DTS and DTT. That would mean that we strive to bring the best out of ourselves and disengage from actions and choices that threaten our own survival and growth. We can threaten our own survival and growth in so many ways and yet remain unaware of it. This also means that we strive hard to build a community in union with God and others, and stay away from everything that could sabotage our relationships. Thus, in becoming aware of our true focus of life, we become a little more watchful about the choices that we make.

The more and earlier we become conscious of all these things, especially the operations of DTS and DTT, the better able we are to steer our lives in ways that are healthy and constructive. It might be useful for us to have a checklist to gain this greater awareness and understand where we are in our lives and relationships.

The awareness could be brought about by a series self-scrutinizing thoughts and reflections, or a thorough examination of our lives. It could start with a reflection on our vision of life—how we see it, and where we find ourselves in the journey of life. Then we could move on to our accents, focusing on how much we differ from others and how many times in a given day we find our accents mismatched with those of others. We could ask whether we are a threat to others or ourselves. Are we surviving and thriving well and letting others to do the same? How often do we find ourselves positively or negatively oriented? How often do we lose patience, get irritated, get upset, and get stuck in our relationships? How often do we say things that we later think we should not have said? How often do we do things that we regret later, and that we wish we had never done or could undo? It is important to think about how many such things happen in our everyday lives. We could ask how many times we have ended up hurting others or getting hurt. Maybe we never regret any of our destructive behaviors. Why is this so?

We could ask how we feel about ourselves—whether we are content and satisfied with ourselves or dissatisfied and distressed. Do we love ourselves or hate ourselves? Are we easy or difficult to please? Are we easily forgiving or loaded with hatred and rage? It might help to find out the areas in us that we love and hate. We could ask how people feel in our presence, whether they feel a positive energy or negative energy emanating from us. We could ask whether we are negative and destructive, controlling and contemptuous, mean and humiliating, fanatic and dogmatic, or nationalistic and narrow-minded. We could examine whether we are too attached and fanatic about our race, religion, language, nationality, and all such specifics.

In reference to our survival and thriving, we can ask whether we are oriented toward bringing the best out of ourselves or whether we are heading in the wrong direction. Are we caught up in building kingdoms and structures that are not based on God's vision of life? Are we people with a frog-in-the-well mentality? Are our endeavors all about us? We should ask whether we are an advocate of life, goodness, grace, and growth in the world or a promoter of sin, evil, destruction, and death in the world. Are we people of peace or people of war?

An increased awareness of our lives includes a deeper understanding of our early life experiences and their impact on our present lives. Do we have a lot of baggage and negativity that we carry from our past? Likewise, we need to have a good sense of the survival and thriving avenues we had in the past, and what they are like in the present. It is important to think about how they affect the way we see others, the world, and ourselves. The culture and the society that we live in is another important component. Do we have a good sense of the culture and society that we come from and currently live in? How about our values and beliefs? Have they been helpful or detrimental to our life and growth? Are they divisive and destructive? It will also be helpful for our lives and relationships if we can find out what kind of character structure or personality style we have.

It is important to ask whether we have a good sense of our true identity, purpose in life, and ultimate destiny. Do we have a sense that we are human beings and God's children? Do we have a sense that our purpose in life is to build a community of love and be a presence of God to others? And do we have a sense that our ultimate destiny is to be united with God and others in eternity? Do we make an effort to stay united with God and others, or do we often follow our ways and get separated from God and others?

A greater awareness regarding all of these is to our advantage when it comes to living our lives to the best of our ability, and giving our best to God and others. It will help us to stay away from actions and choices that threaten our survival and growth. That will also turn out to be advantageous for others, as we will disengage from actions and choices that threaten others' survival and growth.

However, the paradox in all of this is that it is the same mind that makes us aware of the need to survive and thrive well and at the same time makes us do things that threaten our own survival and growth, and our relationship with God and others. We need to be aware of these twin operations of our mind as well. That will help us to make better choices. In other words, knowing that we are capable of both good and bad, we have to keep focusing on choosing the good. Of course, even there we are not assured that we will always make the right and healthy choices. Even after knowing that our mind can lead us to make choices that help our survival and growth as well as choices that threaten them, we might choose the latter. Even after knowing that something is going to kill me or sabotage my growth and development, I might still choose that. Even after knowing that something is bad, we might choose that.

We see this struggle in Saint Paul: "I do not understand my own actions … For I do not do the good I want, but the evil I do not want is what I do" (Ro 7:15, 19). In his second letter to the Corinthians, Paul refers to something specific in his life that was a constant irritant. He says, "Therefore, to keep me from being too elated, a thorn was given me in the flesh, a messenger of Satan to torment me, to keep me from being too elated" (2Co 12:7). Paul doesn't say what this problem was, but obviously it was something that he hated in himself, something that he was not able to get rid of.

There may be many things in us that we hate and do not desire. What do we do when we struggle with such internal conflicts, when we end up doing what we do not desire to do? That is when we turn to God and his grace more than ever. Healing requires personal effort and God's grace. Following the new vision of life is not a lonely trek; it is a journey with God. An awareness of our self and personal efforts alone is not enough. An abundance of God's grace is also needed. God has to walk with us. God walked with Abraham and his descendants. Without God's grace they would not have been able to do even what they did. With God's grace they did the best they could, and they accepted what they were not able to change. This is what we hear from Saint Paul. He put his faith in God to help him overcome this struggle or accept his weaknesses. "Wretched man that I am! Who will rescue me from this body of death? Thanks be to God through Jesus Christ our Lord" (Ro 7:24–25). He prayed to Jesus to free him from what was tormenting him, and what he heard from Jesus was "My grace is sufficient for you, for power is made perfect in weakness" (2Co 12:9). Paul found his strength in God and was able to accept the weaknesses that he was not able to change: "So, I will boast all the more gladly of my weaknesses, so that the power of Christ may dwell in me. Therefore I am content with weaknesses, insults, hardships, persecutions, and calamities for the sake of Christ; for whenever I am weak, then I am strong" (2Co 12:9–10).

There are many things that we are able to change in our lives; and with better awareness, personal effort, professional help, and God's grace, we can change them. But there may be some things that we are not able to change, and the reasons for this may be totally unknown to us. As Saint Paul and others did, we turn to God for strength to accept such things, and we pray that in spite of those limitations, we are still able to give our best to God and others.

32

Self, Community, and God

In many societies today, we experience a rapid growth in two extreme forms of thinking and life. One form is found in those who advocate a sterile philosophy of life, in which they do not see any relevance for God, and the other is found in those who advocate a removed spirituality, in which they do not see any relevance for community. The sterile philosophy of life is largely contributed by the extreme secularism and individualism that is growing in many societies today. The removed spirituality is largely caused by an out-of-touch theology and religion, which are also finding many adherents in many communities and societies. In both these, the focus is self. Personal gratification or individual survival and thriving become the focus of their decisions and actions. Both these are dangerous for our lives and relationships. When the self or individual survival and thriving becomes one's only focus, that person's life is bereft of real life. A life that has no place for God and others is not life-giving. It simply becomes self-focused. It is nothing better than a black hole, a region that absorbs everything into itself with a point of no return. Such a life is doomed to destruction and decay. And a world that is moving more and more in this direction of self-focused survival and thriving is not going to look very pretty after some time.

Extreme individualism and secularism make many people take the path of self-focused survival and thriving that exclude God and others from their lives. They find God unnecessary and others an inconvenience. Their focus is this world, and this world only. They don't ascribe anything in their lives to God or a higher power. And they don't feel that they owe anything to anybody or need to be connected to anybody. Either they consider everything in their lives as their right or they ascribe things to their own ingenuity and power. They live, but they are not life-giving. They survive, but they are lonesome. They undermine our interconnectedness with God and one another. Directly or indirectly, they help the growth of extreme narcissism in our society. Their vision of life is very limited and superficial. They get stuck with their accents, and they live like the frog in the well. They become extremely individualistic and isolated.

An out-of-touch theology and religion make people follow a removed spirituality. For those who take this route, God is a priority, but building a community in union with God and others is not their goal. It is more a spirituality of "me" and "my God." And the image of God they have is often distorted. They have theological ideas and religious beliefs that make them something like extraterrestrial beings. They are often out of touch with the reality and the daily lives of people. They are pious and devout, but they are rigidly set in their ways. They become painfully dogmatic and ultraorthodox.

Extreme scrupulosity and obsessive behaviors may not be uncommon for many such individuals. Rituals and rubrics might be extremely important for them. They might be very austere and rigorous in their religious practices. Although they may look totally focused on the "other world," they may not be too shy about receiving the pomp and glory of this world. They might glory in their titles, trophies, and ornamental trappings. It is no surprise if they develop a feeling that they are better than others. They don't see the need for any change in themselves. In their eyes, everyone else is sinful and in need of conversion. They might also entertain a false belief that they have answers for everything in the universe. They may not hesitate to claim monopoly over God and his ways. Extremism and fanaticism thrive well in their circles, and they might be very intolerant of those who have different views and beliefs. They might see it as a virtue to get rid of or inflict pain on those who oppose their views and beliefs.

This kind of spirituality is also bereft of real life, because such individuals are often closed in on themselves. They remain closed to any self-scrutiny or external intervention. Any alteration from their usual ways makes them extremely agitated. Although externally all their doings are intended to please God, ultimately it is all about pleasing themselves. They create a God according to their own image and likeness, and worshipping that God gives them tremendous pleasure and satisfaction.

Any change in that structure of life and lifestyle is very stressful for them. Any talk of change or correction might be taken as a personal attack and as blasphemous. Their spirituality often fits well with their personality or character structure. Most such individuals have a narcissistic personality and an obsessive and compulsive behavioral pattern. Their religious vehemence simply becomes a cover or carrier of their negative survival and thriving. They may even be willing to be subjected to torments and tortures for the sake of God; but in reality, it may not be God, but rather the glory and honor that arise from such sacrifices, that becomes their driving force. People driven by a removed spirituality are often out of touch with the rest of the community. Others will find it difficult to understand their language.

Saint Francis de Sales, in his spiritual classic, *Introduction to the Devout Life*, cautions about such distorted and removed spiritualty and devotions. Speaking about how devotion is often misunderstood, he says,

> Each one represents devotion according to his liking and imagination. He who is in the habit of fasting will think that because he fasts he is very devout, even though his heart is filled with hatred. He will not take a sip of wine, or even of water, anxious about sobriety but he has no scruples to sip the blood of his neighbor by speaking ill or by false statements. Another considers himself devout because of the very great number of prayers he recites every day, even though soon after this he speaks words that are annoying, full of pride and hurtful to those in his house and to his neighbors. Another very gladly opens his purse

to give alms to the poor but cannot take any gentleness from his heart to forgive his enemies. Yet another will forgive his enemies but will not pay what he owes unless he is legally forced to do so. All such persons are generally looked upon as devout whereas in fact they are not. (De Sales 2005)

Although they are distorted and defective in many ways, men and women with a removed spirituality will find others who are like-minded, and it will be no surprise if they manage to have a great following. Many of them are not aware how removed they are from God and others. They often live with the feeling that only they have it right. In their minds, they are the gem of the community and society and all others are mere mortals. They embarrass themselves with their words and actions. But the paradox is that they take even the ridicule and torment as trophies for their militant devotion, and they bear those pains for the sake of a fitting reward in heaven.

Jesus vehemently chastised both these categories of people—those who lived by a sterile philosophy of life and those who followed a removed spirituality. In the parable of the rich man who built up a world around himself without any regard for God and others (Lk 12:16–21), and the parable of the judge who neither feared God nor respected anyone else (Lk 18:1–5), Jesus points to the lifelessness and danger of following a philosophy of life that has no place for God and community.

In his indictment of the scribes and Pharisees (Mt 23), Jesus comes down very hard on those who follow a spirituality that is out of touch with the real-life situations of people. All their doings, according to Jesus, were neither for God nor for others, but for themselves. In Jesus' time, the Roman emperor and Herod were representatives of those who followed a sterile philosophy of life. They lived for themselves. Rome was sensuous and worldly. There was no place for God in their life or governance. They declared themselves as God and demanded adulation and adoration. Jerusalem was another extreme. It was representative of those who followed a removed spirituality. The priests, scribes, Pharisees, and other religious leaders and establishments followed a spirituality that was out of touch with the life of the community. They were not concerned about God, but themselves. Seeing its deviation from the right path, Jesus wept over Jerusalem (Lk 19:41–44).

A sterile philosophy of life or a removed spirituality is not what we need. They both emanate from a distorted sense of self and vision of life. And they both are dangerous and unhelpful if we want to build the kingdom of God and move toward a healthy and rejuvenating life.

What we need for transcending our accents and moving toward a healthy life is a reclamation of our true sense of self and vision of life. We need to reclaim our true identity, purpose, and destiny. We need to have a new vision of life that has its due place for God, community, and ourselves. We need to recognize that we are children of God, are called to build the kingdom of God, and are destined for an eternal union with God and others. We can search for answers for all our problems on the surface level of our lives, but unless we get to the depth of our being and understand these basic facts, things are not going to change much.

If we want to grow and develop well and bring the best out of ourselves, we have to know that we are human beings and children of God. We may belong to a particular family or community, but first and foremost we are human being and we belong to God. God says to each one of us the same thing that he said to his people through the Prophet Isaiah: "You are mine (Isa 43:1). The onus of making us aware of this identity falls first on our families and communities. It has to begin right from the beginning of our lives.

We saw earlier that a healthy life begins from our conception. Ordinarily, we cannot expect miracles to happen when someone turns into an adolescent or adult. Every parent and every community needs to communicate to the child that he or she is a child of God and that God loves him or her unconditionally and without any reserve. And this truth about God's love has to become experiential through their love for the child.

When parents, families, and communities fail to communicate this message to the child and fail to give to the child a sense that he or she is deeply loved, they are already causing damage to the child's sense of identity. When children or people in general have a feeling that they are loved neither by God nor by anyone else, their identity is fractured and blurred. They don't know who they are and they don't know whether anyone cares about them. Such fractured identity can cause enormous problems in their personal, social, and spiritual lives.

There are a lot of children and individuals who are just numbers in the eyes of the world. They don't really matter to the vast majority. They are treated not as human beings and children of God but as the scum of society. It doesn't take too long for such individuals to develop a negative sense of self and the world. They feel unwanted and unlovable.

Families and communities also have to raise their children with the awareness that as human beings and children of God we all share a common heritage and dignity. They have to teach their children that our physical or mental ability, race, nationality, religion, gender, caste, class, or color is not what determines and defines who we are. Our real identity goes beyond all these externals and specifics. More than anything else, we are God's children, and we all share in that dignity. When families and communities teach their children that we are black and white, Christians and Muslims, Americans and Indians, and all sorts of such things rather than as human beings and children of God, they are already sowing the seeds of division and discrimination in young minds.

When we forget that we are all human beings and children of God and begin to focus on the externals, we end up having problems in our lives and relationships. We tend to stay on the surface level of who we are and forget to get to the deepest level of our being. We fail to go below skin level. On the surface level we differ. But at the core of our being, we are all the same. There is a beauty in all of us that God sees. And that beauty goes deeper than our skin. Our physical eyes see only the surface, the externals. And if we are biased and stuck in our accents, we might see only the externals.

To see the core of our being, we have to look with the eyes of our hearts and minds. We have to go beyond what our physical eyes show us. Jesus told us to be cautious about the use of our eyes. They can bring light as well as darkness to our bodies. Warning us about its dark side, he said, "The eye is the lamp of the body. So, if your eye is healthy, your whole body will be full of light; but if your eye is unhealthy, your whole body will be full of darkness" (Mt 6:22–23). When we are prejudiced about others and do not see everyone as human beings and children of God, we allow our actions and behaviors to be determined by what our physical eyes capture. If we are all children of God, and if we are all equal before God, we cannot continue to pretend that others don't matter. We cannot continue to make our physical eyes determine our attitudes, actions, and behaviors. We cannot continue to look at others as objects for our use and abuse. We cannot continue to discriminate and harm others and keep ourselves on a pedestal. We cannot continue to think that everything is fine when our world is being torn apart by our obsession with our racial, class, caste, religious, and national identities. These are not our real identities. We have to transcend these identities and accents, go beyond our externals and specifics, and appreciate our commonality and equality as human beings and children of God. Claiming our true identity as human beings and children of God and admitting our equality are very essential to move past our defective DTS and DTT, and debilitating accents.

If we want to transcend our accents and bring the best out of ourselves, we have to be clear about the purpose of our lives too. Seeing two of the disciples of John the Baptist following him, Jesus turned toward them and asked, "What are you looking for?" (Jn 1:35–39). Jesus wanted those men to be clear about what they were looking for. If we don't know what we are looking for or what the purpose of our following is, we become disoriented and disillusioned. Blind or directionless following doesn't take us anywhere. When it comes to our life and activities, we should know what our purpose is. Otherwise, we will neither survive and thrive well nor allow others to do the same.

Presented with all the struggles and troubles of life, our first inclination may be to seek our own survival and thriving. We may do that, but gradually we have to move from that self-focused life to a God-centered and other-centered life. We can and we should seek and ensure our survival and thriving. We have to love and care for ourselves. Our goal is to bring the best out of ourselves. But that is not to be done in isolation from God and others. The real purpose of our lives, as we saw before, is to build a community of love in which everyone can survive and thrive well. The purpose is to build the kingdom of God, which essentially means to build a community in which we are united with

God and others. It is to keep the two commandments of the love of God and love of neighbor (Mt 22:36–39) always on our mind.

Loving ourselves is important, but it is equally important to love God and others. We are not to live in isolation or in a self-only world. We have to be united with God and the community. We are also not meant to make it a God-and-me-only life. It is not a private spirituality or personal-only salvation that we are seeking. It is both personal and communal. Our spirituality and salvation are undeniably connected with our communion with others. The prayer of Jesus was "they may all be one" (Jn 17:21). Whatever we do, it should be oriented toward this one purpose—to build a community of love with God and others. A sterile philosophy of life and a removed spirituality do not see this connection.

Speaking of how he will evaluate our lives, Jesus said, "Truly I tell you, just as you did it to one of the least of these who are members of my family, you did it to me" (Mt 25:40). Any spirituality or way of life that deviates from this path is a selfish or self-focused spirituality. A true spirituality is one that is selfless. Jesus said, "If any want to become my followers, let them deny themselves and take up their cross daily and follow me" (Lk 9:23). Renouncing ourselves, we know, is not easy. Our tendency is to show off and stand out. And we might also want to look for easy paths. But Jesus does not offer any easy way. We have to carry our crosses daily. We have to work hard. When building up the kingdom of God, there is no place for laziness or sloth. And we have to renounce our ways and embrace God's ways.

In Indian philosophy and spirituality, there is a concept called *nishkaama karma*, which means "selfless service or action." One who is moved by nishkaama karma has only one focus—to love and serve God and others. In such a life and spirituality, there is no place for selfishness. In such a life, there is no place for exploitation, meanness, revenge, aggression, dishonesty, abuse, fraud, racism, sexism, nationalism, extremism, or any kind of godlessness. When building a community with God and others becomes our focus, we cannot look at others as objects for our pleasure. Respect and love for one another are requirements for building God's kingdom. This task requires us to leave aside our petty self-seeking goals and desires. The joy of life is found in a selfless life, a life in communion with God and others. The only focus is to give our best in love of God and others.

The onus of raising us with the awareness of the true purpose of our lives falls on our families and communities. Every family and community has to constantly communicate to its members that they are not isolated individuals, but rather members of a larger family that includes God and others. If a child grows up with the idea that the purpose of his or her life is individual survival and thriving without any regard for God or the rest of the world, it is going to create in him or her defective DTS and DTT, and mismatched accents.

To transcend our accents and live healthy lives, we have to also be clear about our ultimate destiny. We are reminded that our life is not just destined for a short stint on this earth, but rather for one that is permanent. We are destined for eternal life. And the road that leads to eternal life is a life of holiness and grace, and a life in union with God and others. Jesus said to Nicodemus, one of the Pharisees, "Very truly, I tell you, no one can see the kingdom of God without being born from above … without being born of water and Spirit" (Jn 3:3–5). We have to constantly renew ourselves, be washed clean, and be anointed by God's Spirit. We have to remain united with God and others. If eternal life is going to be a continuation of the union with God and others that we begin here, our hearts and minds should be always focused on that goal. If that is our ultimate goal, we cannot afford to live without God and others while we are here on earth. We have to live our earthly lives with our eyes set on heaven.

Once again, the onus of bringing this awareness to us falls on our families and communities. Every family and community has to keep reminding its members that they are destined for eternal life and that this world is not the end. Being unaware of the real destiny, some live as if this world is everything. And when this world is taken as the be-all and end-all of one's life, the person might live without any regard for God or others. If we ignore or are confused about our real destiny, we are going to be very limited in our vision of life. If we don't see anything beyond this earthly life, our decisions and desires are going to be influenced by that. If this world is the only thing that matters to us, we might be concerned only about the immediate and the here and now. We need both the immediate and the distant, the here and now and the eternal. Our life is intertwined with both today and tomorrow, the immediate and the distant, the temporal and the eternal.

Most people start well with these three dimensions of our lives. Most families and communities raise their members with the awareness that they are human beings and children of God, their purpose in life is to build a community of love, and their destiny is to be united with God and others. But as time goes by, this awareness fades for many. Either they distance themselves from God and others or they are pushed away by families and communities. They take the route of not needing God or others in their life, or they place themselves above God and others.

When people deny or move away from God, they tend to become self-focused. When people move away from the community, they again tend to become self-focused. Both these are extremes. To transcend our accents and to move past our defective survival and thriving, we need to reclaim our real identities as children of God, refocus on the real purpose of our lives as building a community of love, and reaffirm our ultimate destiny as union with God and others eternally. Getting these three facts wrong or confused can cause enormous problems in our lives. As mentioned before, we can try to find solutions to all our problems on the surface level, but unless we get to the bottom of these three dimensions of our lives, things will not change much. The same problems will keep repeating over and over again. The only difference will be that they take new shapes and forms.

Instead of a self-focused and sterile philosophy of life, what we need is a God-centered and love-abundant philosophy of life. Instead of a self-driven and removed spirituality, what we need is a community-oriented and God-driven spirituality. When our lives and spirituality have a place for God and others, all of us can survive and thrive well. To make progress in our lives and transcend our accents, either we need to recognize these things by ourselves or someone has to help us to come to this awareness.

33

Returning Home

Another necessary step to address our negative DTS and DTT and transcend our accents is to go back home. Many of the debilitating elements in our lives may need more than a lifetime to be repaired. The only way to repair them may be to embrace them as part of who we are and make the best out of what we have. There may be many things that happened in our past that we might like to undo. But many of them are a done deal. They are irreversible. However, there may be things that are still changeable. And we might do better if we give ourselves a chance to do that. And one of the ways to do that is to go back to those memories and experiences that have made our DTS and DTT become defective. We have to go back home and find healing or repair wherever they are needed.

Returning home can be either pleasant or traumatic. Some people look forward to the moment of returning home to be reunited with their family. They can't wait to meet their loved ones and again experience their familiar surroundings. They gleefully remember their past experiences and memories. Other people dread the prospect of returning home. Memories of home bring them pain, trauma, and shame. They stay as far away from home as possible. They hate to go back to the old memories and experiences. But their homes still exist. They may have buried the memories of their homes, and they may have chosen to stay far away from home; but even while they are away, those memories haunt them. Those memories make them see everything through tinted glasses.

The orientation of their DTS and DTT may be heavily influenced by those memories. If they are able and if they are helped to revisit their homes or revisit those memories and find ways to process the pain, grief, anger, disappointment, and all such things connected with those memories, they may be on the path of reorienting their DTS and DTT, and transcending their accents.

Even as we make an attempt to go back home, the first thing we must do is admit that we don't remember everything that happened at home. We all have our own unique experiences of growing up. Unfortunately, much of the data about our early experiences remains inaccessible to us. How many of us know how things happened to us when we were in our mothers' wombs? Our mothers can tell us what happened to them when they were carrying us, but they can never tell us what happened to us when we were in the womb. They can never tell us how we experienced what we experienced.

How many of us remember everything that happened after we were born—particularly in the first two or three years of life? Again, our parents can tell us a few things in bits and pieces, but they can't tell us everything that happened to us moment by moment. Did we cry or laugh, breathe or suffocate, and feel cold or feel warm? Were we sick or were we healthy? Were we fed and hydrated, or were we malnourished? Did our mothers soothe us or look away when we cried or were excited? Were we protected or were we neglected? Were we washed and cleaned, or were we left in our poop and pee? How did we feel when our mother left us with somebody else? How did we feel when our mothers were sick and could not be near us? How did we feel if and when our mothers left us forever, either by death or abandonment?

How did our dads come into our picture? Were they in our picture at all, or did we grow up without a dad? What did we feel about them? How about our siblings? How did we feel about them taking our parents' attention away from us? What did we think of all other strangers that smiled at us, frowned at us, played with us, scared us, rocked us, or abused us? What did our home and surroundings mean to us?

We don't have a complete grasp of all these experiences. Most of these data are unavailable to us. Similar things can be asked of things that happened in the later stages of our lives. How many of us can remember all that happened while we were in school? Some of those experiences were good; some of them were bad. How many of us can remember all that happened every minute and every day of our life? Everything that happened had an impact on us, but we don't remember all of it.

We don't know how many thousands of experiences we had or how we absorbed all of them. Everything that happened was significant, but most of it remains a mystery to us. We will never know fully how we felt our experiences or what they did to us. Some of us who have super memories may remember a few things that happened when we were two or three years old, but they are still small fragments of a much larger experience. It is a fact that there is very little or almost a total absence of memory prior to age four or five. And yet those years are the most formative of all years in our lives. How many traumas or experiences are remembered and how many "needed to be forgotten?" Even those experiences that we remember do not tell us completely how we felt and how they impacted us at that time. In many ways, it is to our own advantage that we don't remember most of those experiences. Imagine how it would be if we were to remember everything that happened at every moment of life. The capacity to forget is a great blessing.

However, we know that many things that happen in our lives have an impact on us. Theorists and researchers who have studied early life experiences have provided us with some information about how things impact our lives. Unfortunately, much of this information is based on limited observations and tests of the subjects they studied. Many of the theories and conclusions are based on speculations and generalizations. There is no firsthand information on many of these things. It is like someone telling a story about me without directly hearing it from me or without asking me what it is like "to be myself." Some of it may be true, but it is still incomplete without hearing from me how I experience my life and being. Unfortunately, that is the only way available to us to study most of the psychological and emotional processes of our early lives.

Our technological developments and sophisticated equipment, tests, and observations today may give us rich data about the physical processes taking place in an infant in the womb or a child who is one or two years old. But to capture the psychological and emotional processes taking place in the infant in the womb or a one-year-old child, we don't have too many tools available to us. The infant in the womb or a one-year-old child cannot share with us what it is like to be himself or herself in that particular moment or stage of life. That infant or child does not have the language and the ability to verbalize or communicate comprehensively how it experiences what it experiences. So the only tools available to us are limited interactive processes, testing, and observation of behaviors, brain functions, and body movements of the infant or child. The data may be accurate in many ways, but it is still incomplete.

We cannot get into the mind or psyche of the child and see what is going on there. Even in a psychotherapeutic process, a person may not be able to bring to his or her awareness all that happened in his or her early life. The therapist can help the patient with the process of becoming aware of certain experiences and memories, but neither the therapist nor the patient has a magic wand that can lay them all open just like that. So when we think of returning home, the first thing we must do is be aware that we don't have access to everything that happened in our past, and that some of those experiences are ammunition for negative survival and thriving and problems in our lives.

Even though we don't have access to all of our experiences, we can assume that we are all eligible candidates for picking up or developing negative DTS and DTT, and wrong accents, either in our early life or at a later stage. None of us comes out totally unscathed from the pricks and prods of life. None of us can claim that we were totally happy with leaving our mothers' wombs. We cannot claim that we would have been happy to stay in the womb forever either. None of us can claim to have had totally infallible parents, grandparents, or generations that went before them. They all had their own flaws, and more likely than not, they left an indelible mark of their flaws on our lives and personalities. None of us can claim to have had a perfect childhood or family (if there is any such). All these life experiences, both positive and negative, have had tremendous impact on how we live our lives today. Some of us were more exposed to negative experiences than positive ones. Some of us might have absorbed the negatives more than the positives even though we have had both experiences more or less in the same measure. We all fall into the large spectrum of people who have mismatched accents;

some of us are well on the negative side, while others are more toward the healthy side of the spectrum.

If there are ways to get to some of our past experiences and memories that have a negative impact on our growth and development, or relationships, those opportunities should not be ignored. Even if not completely cured of all the negativity and mismatch in accents, a person who learns to give less power to those negative memories and experiences will be a much better resource to the building up of God's kingdom than someone who continues to be heavily influenced by such negative and traumatic experiences.

If a person has a consistent difficulty in healthy development and healthy relationship with others, that person may need to go back home and examine past experiences in life as much as possible to understand why he or she is unhealthy. These experiences could be from one's early stages of development or even from the recent past. A psychological and psychodynamic evaluation might help one to understand the problems better. The evaluation might include a detailed understanding of the person's behavioral patterns; problem areas; character structure; childhood history; prenatal history; history of the parents and preceding generations; cultural background; religious beliefs; perception of self and others; physiological health issues; traumatic experiences; addictive behaviors; level of emotional intelligence and psychological mindedness; availability of support in the family and community; family history of depression, suicide, alcoholism, drug abuse or any other mental health issues; capacity for impulse control; capacity for frustration tolerance; and so on and so forth.

It is important to ask what his or her early life experiences were. What kind of thriving avenues and chances of survival did and does the person have? What is the person's culture and society like? How does he or she perceive himself or herself? What is his or her sense of identity, purpose in life, and ultimate destiny? A detailed evaluation of the person's past and present might offer a better understanding of where and how the person developed negative DTS and DTT and unhealthy characteristics.

It should be noted that not all children who develop negativity about self, others, and the world come from bad or dysfunctional families.

Even when they grow up in reasonably good and healthy families, some children develop negative characters and personalities. It may not be clear to anyone where it all originated. Families most people would consider as reasonably healthy sometimes have one or two children who are totally negatively oriented and destructive. We hear those parents asking the self-blaming question "Where did we go wrong?" They cannot understand how it happened. In all honesty, they did their best to care for and raise their children in a healthy way. But what happened? How did those children get it wrong? Did they take in certain negative experiences in their early lives so deeply that it blurred all positive experiences before and after? For the most part, it might remain a mystery forever. However, it is important to explore into the past experiences and memories of such people.

Our past may not have been very pretty, and our present may be suffering from its consequences. Many things might have caused our negative survival and thriving. But it doesn't have to continue that way for the present and the future. The damage has already been done, and we need to seek ways to rectify and reroute our life. We cannot change our past, but to a great extent, we can stop giving power to our past experiences to determine our present and future. We don't need to reenact and perpetuate the sins of the past generations.

What is important is that we return home to those elements and experiences that cause our negative DTS and DTT, and mismatches in accents. It may be too idealistic to expect a complete return or a total transformation. We may not get to everything that happened in our past that made a negative impact on our present life, and the mismatch in our accents may not disappear completely either. But if we return home, we might be able to do better in our personal growth and interpersonal relationships. It might also help our families and friends to deal with the situation better.

34

Beginning with the End

We saw that for everyone, the beginning years are very significant for later development and experiences. The home environment, to a great extent, will determine how a person's DTS and DTT are going to be channeled and manifested later in life. The future is in the present. The father is in the son, or today's son becomes tomorrow's father. The mother is in the daughter, or today's daughter becomes tomorrow's mother. Tomorrow's actors on the world stage are the infants in the wombs today. The course of tomorrow, to a great extent, will be determined by the history of these infants. History can take any direction—good or bad, constructive or destructive. Everyone participates in the larger history of the world, bringing in his or her own history. In other words, world history is a collation and interaction of individual histories. Each individual's personal history is significant in determining world history.

Having said that, we know that no one can begin on a clean slate, as no one is independent of the influence of the preceding generations. As obvious as it is, our world carries its own baggage of issues. Limitations of the world are part of being human and being born in this world. However, before the infants in the wombs receive the baton of history, their parents and others have a privileged and sacred role to hand over to these infants a near-clean platform for survival and thriving. The brief exploration of the working of DTS and DTT through the developmental stages has shown us how the subsequent stages of development and thriving are built on the preceding stages. The discussion particularly pointed to the indispensable role played by parents or parent substitutes.

When we search for a solution to our negative survival and thriving, and our debilitating accents, parents have an immensely important role to play. To a great extent, they determine the course of our world in the future. They form men and women who will carry forward the mantle of our aspirations and longings, stories and legends, and ideals and dreams.

Every child, Alice Miller said, has a legitimate narcissistic need to be noticed, understood, taken seriously, and respected by its mother. The healthy narcissistic development of a child requires an environment in which the mother or parents are confident and willing to allow the child to "use" them. The term "Use" does not mean anything negative. Erna Furman gives a few hints about what this "using" would mean in a parent–child relationship. It would mean that the child does not need to feel scared or guilty for growing up. The parents will help the neutralization of the aggressive impulses of the child without being upset. The parents will not see the child's need for autonomy as an attack on them. The child will not feel the need or pressure to please anybody. In short, it means creating an environment where the child can grow and develop without being afraid and uncertain about his or her environment.

Mothers and fathers who steer their DTS and DTT and modulate their accents in such a way that it helps the fruition of their mothering and fathering roles and assists the healthy development of the child are a true blessing and gift to their children. They make a gift of themselves. They do what they do, not after knowing everything about parenting or after knowing what it entails to raise children. Most parents choose not to allow their DTS and DTT to manifest itself in a negative and destructive way. Most parents don't decide to become parents by saying, "I am going to mess this up." They begin with good motivations. By choosing to be parents, they are not scuttling their survival and thriving either. They are not stopping their personal growth and development. They are steering their DTS and DTT in such a way that it brings into fruition their drives to be parents, and that simultaneously benefits the fragile, not-so-conscious, and dependent baby that has taken form from and in them. Their accent is different from the accent of the baby. They tune their ears and hearts to understand the language of the baby. Instead of insulating their territory with self-focused endeavors, they accommodate the needs of the fragile and dependent child.

For parents, their parenting role is a gift from their child. If they had no child, they would never have been parents, in the normal sense of the term. So the parents give birth to the child, and the child gives birth to the parents. Or the parents make the baby, and the baby makes the parents. Parents make a gift of themselves to their child. It does not diminish their importance, but rather increases it. For such parents, their positive survival and thriving do not stop with the birth of the baby but continue for years and years to come. They don't stop being fathers and mothers, and they don't stop desiring the best for their children either.

Thus, in one sense, a baby is an advancement in a couple's survival and thriving, because the baby helps them to achieve another milestone in their development— becoming a father or mother and parent. But in another sense, a baby is an interruption in their survival and thriving. The decision to have children presupposes certain limits to the otherwise open-ended drive to survive and thrive. Caring and nurturing have to continue for years and years after birth. There are financial concerns; restrictions on movement, career choices, and job performance; and many other considerations that come into play when caring for children. The conception and birth of a child brings about a significant change in a couple's life and daily routine. With the arrival of a child, it is no longer two people, but three. Particularly with the first child, it is often more than they had anticipated. The interruption is real.

If a couple views having a baby as a real interruption in their survival and thriving, all the other developmental needs of the baby in the subsequent years will add to their fears and frustrations. Men and women who have not had supportive and nurturing parents themselves will have great difficulty in providing a healthy environment for their children. They often cannot provide something they themselves have not experienced. If they experienced negativity and encountered a debilitating mismatch of accents from their own parents and caregivers it will be no surprise if they do the same to their children. They become another link in the long chain of people communicating with mismatched accents.

A decision to have and nurture a baby is a choice for selfless survival and thriving. It is not a complete sacrifice of one's self, but rather an act of giving priority to the child, whose life and growth will be hard without that generosity. In fact, many of us are beneficiaries of such generosity from our parents. If parents, for whatever reason, put their pleasure needs before their children's need to live and grow, many infants would not be alive. Every child born and raised in a reasonably healthy way in this world is a sign of the generosity of their parents, who make their DTS and DTT a source of support for that child. Children who have been deprived of this generosity of parents often end up with great difficulties needing long-term care and treatment. The experiences that children are exposed to at the beginning of their lives—both while inside the womb and outside of it—have enormous implications and repercussions for their later life. If it is begun well, we can be pretty much sure that the end product will be reasonably good. Hence, there is a great responsibility for parents to "begin with the end in mind" when they take on the mantle of being parents.

35

You Are Unique

I discussed nature placing us at a fork with prongs of independence and incompleteness. This two-pronged aspect makes us recognize two things about ourselves. First, we are all unique. Second, we are all united. Our sense of independence and individuality comes from our uniqueness. Our sense of incompleteness and disconnectedness comes from our unity. This knowledge of us being unique and united is essential for transcending our accents. Let me first talk about our uniqueness.

Every now and then, I come across people in the United States who ask me all kinds of questions about India. They ask me about Indian food, Indian music, Indian language, Indian religion, and so on and so forth. Many of them think that there is one food, one music, and one language for all of India. And often it takes some time to explain to them what is universal and what is unique for Indians. To an outsider India might look like a single cultural unit, whereas for an Indian, it is one of the most diverse societies in the world. Every state and region has its own cuisine, music, dress, climate, ethnicity, race, customs, and traditions. We have varieties of all of these.

There is no doubt that there is a great sense of unity among cultures and communities in India. But we are immensely different. For an outsider, this may not be too obvious. The great sense of unity is a result of the respectful acceptance of the diversity that is undeniable.

Similar things can be said of other cultures and countries. Some time back, I visited the two countries of Bolivia and Chile in South

America. The few weeks of my stay there took me to a world that was very different from what I had been used to. In Bolivia, in particular, I noticed how the different shades of life from different eras and cultures were interwoven into the present-day culture and life of the Bolivians. In general, I was told that there were three groups of people in Bolivia, the "indigenas/indigenous," or the original inhabitants of the land, the "mestizos/mixed," or the mixed race of the Spanish or others and the indigenous people, and the "blancos/white," or the descendants of the Spanish and other Europeans who colonized or migrated to the land. But within these groups, there are several other subgroups. There is a great mix of the indigenous people, Europeans, Africans, and Asians. All of them are very different regarding history, culture, language, beliefs, practices, customs, and traditions. To an outsider, many of them might look alike, but an *Aymara* knows how he or she is different from a *Quechua, Uru, Chiquitano,* or *Chulupi.*

This fact of being unique and different applies not only to communities and groups but also to each individual person. We differ in who we are and what we experience. Whether we are Christian or Hindu; Jewish or Muslim; Malayali or Marathi; American or Indian; Aymara or Quechua; or black, white, or brown, life is different for all of us, and the experience of life is unique to each individual.

Many of the Indian languages contain the word "*anubhava*" or "*anubhavam*," which more or less translates as "experience." It is a very valued concept in Indian culture. And when it comes to anubhava, or experience, it is unique to each individual. Anubhava is not explainable in its totality. It is to be experienced, to know what it is. God, for example, is often understood as a being or reality to be experienced. Explanation of God does not give us a true experience of God. One of the evangelists and disciples of Jesus who knew the value of anubhava is Saint John. He had experienced God very personally in Jesus. He says, "We declare to you what was from the beginning, what we have heard, what we have seen with our eyes, what we have looked at and touched with our hands, concerning the word of life" (1Jn 1:1). He experienced God personally, and he found no better term to call that experience than "love." So he says, "God is love" (1Jn 4:8). To know what love is, we know we have to experience it. If someone tries to explain it to us, it doesn't give us a true sense of what love is. Similarly, God is to be experienced. Explaining him doesn't give us a true sense of who he is. And when it comes to that experience, or anubhava, it is unique to each individual.

The same principle applies to life in general. We all have our own unique anubhavas, or experiences of life, and that makes us all unique and different. There is no other human being in the whole world that has the same anubhava as I have. We all are uniquely different from each other. The Psalmist says, "For it was you who formed my inward parts; you knit me together in my mother's womb. I praise you, for I am fearfully and wonderfully made" (Ps 139:13–14). Each one of us is special to God. We all belong to different turfs and territories. Even in one family, each individual occupies a different turf of uniqueness. We may come from the same parents, but we are not all the same. We may come out of the same cast, but we don't have the same constitution. Each one of us has a unique experience of life, with no equivalent in the world whatsoever.

We get to know the details of this uniqueness only when we get to know a person. It is like recognizing the difference between an aerial view of the forest and a ground inspection of it. The aerial view might present a panorama of greenery, while a ground inspection would reveal the strength and sturdiness, as well as the decay and the darkness, that envelops each tree. As I mentioned about learning a language, when it comes to really getting to know other people, most of us are mere beginners. Sometimes some of us may look alike, but in reality, we are vastly different from each other. But with our limited experience, we might tend to put others in a box and conclude that they are one thing or another. But that is too dangerous and unkind to do that. By putting someone in a box or within certain categories that we have created, we are denying ourselves the opportunity to see the wonder and mystery of God's creation in that person.

People often tried to put Jesus in a box, but he proved to them that he was more than what they thought. To some, he was an ordinary carpenter (Mt 13:54–58). He was a man from Nazareth, and the people of his town knew his family. But he was more than a carpenter. For some, he was a teacher (Mk 1:21–22). He taught them with authority and power, not like their scribes and Pharisees. But he was more than a teacher. For some, he was a healer (Mt 8:14–17). He healed numerous people. They came to him in huge numbers. But he was more than a healer. For some, he was a wonder worker (Mk 8:1–13). He performed numerous miracles, and some people were amazed at all that he did. But he was more than a wonder worker. For some, he was an exorcist, driving our demons (Mk 1:23–27). Demons and evil spirits trembled before him, and he drove them out from people. But he was more than an exorcist. For some, he was a liberator and savior (Mt 8; Mk 2). He liberated them from their sins and sicknesses. He forgave them and cured them. He liberated them from their misery, shame, and pain. He touched the lepers, outcasts, and tax collectors. But he was more than a liberator and savior. For some, he was the master and Lord (Mt 8:23–27; 17:1–8). The winds and seas obeyed him. He appeared as the Lord of the universe in all his glory at the transfiguration. But he was not just a master and Lord. He was also a servant (Jn 13:1–20). He washed the feet of his disciples, which only the slaves did in those days.

Jesus was all of these things, but he was more than that. From the first-century Christians to people today, no one has been able to put Jesus in a box. Jesus keeps encountering us in many ways, and we keep encountering him in many ways. He is a God bigger than we think. But he is also a God who is very close to us. If we ever think that we know Jesus fully, that we know God fully, then we stop growing spiritually. Every day, we have to remain open to God's revelations. Every day, we have to grow in our knowledge and love of Jesus.

We have to take the same approach when we deal with each other. If we ever think that we know somebody fully, we stop growing. We already talked about the number of ways in which we differ from each other. But we don't know everything about everybody. Only God has that perfect picture. We have to acknowledge and accept this truth about each other. Uniform furniture can be stacked up without the danger of one piece damaging another. Unique items, however, need to be packed separately because they may have corners and curves that don't match. Human beings are like unique items that need to be packed separately. Every single individual needs to be understood as though there is only that one person in the whole world. We perceive and experience the world differently.

Unique as we are, the life that we live brings its own uniqueness every day. Although we may have tried to give it a definition, most likely all of us would reach the conclusion that life is pretty much open-ended. It cannot be categorized as a definite thing or material, made up of certain definite components. But many of us, if not all, have an urge to have it all together. The more we try to have it all together, the more flabbergasted we are by life's unpredictable twists and turns. Definitions and words are very limited. They cannot capture the experience fully. And our experience of life is not a finished product. It is dynamic; it is ongoing.

The moment we define life, we make the mistake of putting it in a box. Life is not something that can be boxed in. Life unfolds itself in multiple ways to everyone in his or her own unique way. These experiences are ever evolving. And these experiences are not accidental happenings. Life does not exist independent of us. It is what it is because of us. I am what I am because of these experiences. My life and I are not two separate entities but one reality. I can speak of my life and my "I-ness" as distinct entities, but I cannot speak of one without the other. I can talk about my experiences, but I cannot separate them from me. That is the beauty of my being. I can be the subject and object of my experiences, thoughts, and conversations.

Life is also a continuum of experiences. And because it is a continuum of experiences, I cannot separate the past, the present, and the future phases of my life. I can, however, speak of them as distinctive phases of my life. Even before I complete this sentence, a part of it has already become something of the past. And even before I realize I have done so, I have moved into the future part of this sentence. That is what happens with my thought processes. That is what happens with the story of my life. What I call my past was my present and my future at one time. What I call my present and my future now will become my past even before I realize it. Because these phases of our life are so closely intertwined, they are not fully comprehensible. However, they are distinct. What I experienced yesterday is not what I am experiencing now. What I experience today may not be what I experience tomorrow. They are distinct but interconnected.

Life being unique to each moment and each person, I have to admit that what I experience may not be what my colleague, roommate, partner, family member, or community member experiences. Persons of the same age, culture, language, and religion experience life differently. Members of same family experience life differently. Life means different things to people on two different continents. Between the little hut of a poor family in a remote village in an underdeveloped country and the mighty skyscrapers in a city like New York, there is a wide range of lives and lifestyles that have too little in common.

The majority of the people in Kannur, my hometown in Kerala, have little idea about what life is like in St. Louis, the town that has been my home for the past few years. There is way too much difference between the details of a nomad or hunter-gatherer's life in an unknown African, Asian, or South American region and a busy executive's life in a metropolitan city in Europe or the US. The things depicted in the newspapers or in other media are only glimpses of the different shades of life out there. What often gets to the front pages of newspapers are the details of the executive's life and not those of an unknown person in an unknown land. Only once in a while do some explorers, reporters, or researchers peek into the lives of such unknown people and write a story. But the scarcity of their stories in "civilized society" does not in any way invalidate or negate the lives and experiences of those unknown people. Their lives, too, are lives in their own unique way.

Even if somebody has attempted to describe life in some way, it is to be taken as his or her personal opinion based on his or her personal experience, context, and thinking. I may see someone with a smiling face, but how do I know that there is no pain behind that smile? What do I know about that person's conflicts, complications, and complexities in life? I don't know even one hundredth of what is going on in his or her life. My knowledge and experience of the other is always incomplete, however much I may know him or her.

Sometimes we hear people making generalized comments about certain things, applying them to the whole world. They say things like "All over the world, it is like that," "All over the world, people do this," "The majority of the people in the world think this way." Such comments are often not true. Nothing can be the same all over the world. What we often refer to as "the whole world" is a small world. There are cultures and peoples that do not fall on our radar. The people in those cultures and communities may have little in common with what we are talking about. Even in the cultures and among the people we are familiar with, things may not be exactly as we describe. In this time of international franchising and around-the-world tours offered by cruise lines and airlines, it is possible for us to fall into the false belief that we know the whole world. Companies trying to promote their products or groups trying to inundate the world with their values or ideologies might try to convince others that everyone in the world acts or thinks as they do. But that is a very narrow and far-from-the truth perspective about the world. They try to present a picture-perfect, uniform view of the world. Our world is so complex and diverse that no one person can ever experience it in its totality.

We cannot pretend or live with the false belief that we all experience life in the same way. We all come with different accents, and life opens itself to us in its own unique way. When I cannot claim that I know everything about even my own life, how could I claim to know much about your life? We are two worlds apart in many ways. We experience life's novelty in manifold ways every day in our own unique ways. We each carry an incomprehensibly complex collection of experiences of our own.

The path to ridding ourselves of our negative DTS and DTT and transcending our accents begins with a willingness to accept that we are all unique. The uniqueness, the individuality, and the independence of each person are to be acknowledged and accepted before we can talk about our commonality.

36

The Invisible Web

Each one of us is unique, but we are not absolutely unique so as to be disconnected from the rest of the world. The forked position that our nature places us at makes us unique and yet inseparable. As I conceive of myself as a unique person with my own unique constructs and experiences, I also realize that my uniqueness is always in the making. It is a dynamic uniqueness and not a static uniqueness. And that dynamism is not only due to my internal workings but also because of my constant interaction with the external realities. I am part of an invisible web of relationships. I am who I am because of that dynamic web of relationships. It may seem like I am all by myself, but there is a large network of relationships and connections that I am part of. I call that network the "life web."

The life web includes everything and everyone that directly or indirectly affects my life. It refers not only to the immediate context of my life but also everything beyond. This life web includes my immediate family, extended family, friends, neighbors, school, Church or faith community, profession, colleagues, and clients. It includes my ethnic community, race, and country. It includes my values, beliefs, ideas, ideologies, and thoughts. It consists of my house, car, computer, and all such things. It includes nature, the birds, the animals, the stars, and the planets. It includes heaven and hell, saints and sinners. And above all these stands God. God is the source and center of this life web that I am part of. Isaiah says, "The Lord is the everlasting God, the Creator of the ends of the earth" (Isa 40:28). I am who I am because of my constant interaction with God and all the other components that make up my life web.

We say that we are a tiny speck in the large universe. "Universe" is a big term, and even while referring to it, I am aware that I am talking about something that is incomprehensible. People often talk about the universe expanding always. I assume that it is not only the universe that is expanding (if it is expanding) but also our comprehension of the universe. I know only an iota of the universe, and hence I don't claim that I have knowledge of the universe expanding. When we think of the universe we think of stars, planets, solar systems, galaxies, and intergalactic space.

One of the latest discoveries about the universe is the discovery of a large formation of seventy-three quasars, which is the largest structure discovered in the universe so far. It is believed that in the center of most galaxies there exist supermassive black holes (regions that absorb anything, with a point of no return). Think of something like a big hole in the middle of a city that absorbs anything that comes into its vicinity. A quasar, which stands for "quasi-stellar radio source" or "quasi-stellar object," could be considered as a super supermassive black hole in the center of a massive galaxy. Quasars are extremely luminous, energetic, and powerful. They emit extremely powerful light, radio, and x-ray waves. The light emanating from these quasars is so bright and powerful that we can see it from the other end of the universe. If a quasar is a super supermassive black hole, we can imagine how big the newly discovered formation of seventy-three quasars is.

The newfound quasar group is understood to be so large that it would take four billion years to cross it at the speed of light. Light travels at the speed of approximately 186,282 miles per second. If light travels so many miles in a second, how many miles could it travel in a year? Approximately 5.9 trillion miles. And how many miles could it travel in four billion years? I am not even going to attempt to calculate it.

If this new group of seventy-three quasars is so large that it takes light four billion years to travel across, how big might be the galaxy that surrounds this massive formation? If our universe consists of thousands and thousands of such massive galaxies and intergalactic spaces, how big must be our universe? As per the current understanding, our universe is so big that it would take ninety-three billion light years to travel across it. The latest discovery might even bring into question the current understanding of the vastness of the universe. It might be much larger than it is currently thought to be. Then there are some who think of even larger concepts, such as a multiverse that consists of many universes. We can talk about these things, but we ourselves are aware that we know very little about what we are talking about. It is in fact overwhelming to think about even one planet, let alone the whole universe or universes. Considering such vastness and incomprehensibility of our universe or multiverse, we also know how tiny we are. We are next to nothing. We are not even a speck. We might wonder whether we mean anything much in this universe.

I don't dismiss the insignificance that we feel in the face of such enormity and vastness that we see around us. However, we should not dismiss our significance either. Even if we are a speck, we are a significant speck. We have a significant place in this vast universe. Our significance comes not from our size but from who we are. We are of the same material as the creator of the universe. We are created in the image and likeness of our creator, God (Ge 1:26–27). That is where our significance comes from. There is nothing else in this creation or vast universe that can claim that unique position.

Thus, in the life web that consists of the universe and everything else, we have a significant place. We cannot separate ourselves from this life web. If we separate, the life web will no more be the same. It is like talking about my family. For the sake of talking about my family, I can step out of it and talk about it, but at the same time I know that the family that I am talking about is not a family without me. I am an integral part of that family. I cannot really step out of it. That family is what it is because of me, and I am what I am because of that family. My family minus me will not be the same family anymore. I minus my family will not be the same me anymore. The same principle applies to our life web. The life web minus us will not be the same life web anymore. We minus the life web will not be the same us anymore. We cannot really separate ourselves from our life web. We are one with it. Everything in our life web, or everything that is out there, may not have a direct impact on us in our everyday lives, but we are still part of all that is. We cannot separate ourselves from it. Each one of us is unique, but we are inseparable from everything and everyone around us.

Take what I am doing now, for example. These very thoughts that are going on in me are being put into the words of a language that is comprehensible to others, and then they are typed on a computer. It is amazing to note how many connecting links are involved in this process of having these thoughts and ideas and transferring them to this computer. I have these thoughts arising in me. Those thoughts are "languaged" and put into words. Even before I complete that process, it is already transferred to this computer. And from this computer, those words will be transferred to a book or other devices and disseminated to many people.

Where do these thoughts arise from? Are they wired or acquired, or both? Where did I get these words or the language from? Where and when did I learn to connect certain words with certain feelings, thoughts, or actions? Did they come as feeling words, action words, and thought words, or did I first have the feelings, then connect those feelings with those words, and then do the same with thoughts and actions? Who gave me those feelings, thoughts, and actions? Were they inborn, or were they learned? Who gave me those words and language? How do you read and understand what I am writing? How do you feel what I am feeling? Did I put those feelings in you? Did your parents put those feelings in you? Do these words bring those feelings to you? How do you connect with me on the emotional and intellectual level? Our families, communities, schools, cultures, societal structures, ideas, thoughts, emotions, feelings, customs and traditions, values and beliefs, and all other things that I mentioned in the list of items that make up our life web have played a part in making these processes something of our own. So when you connect yourself with these thoughts and feelings in my mind or book, you are connecting yourself with thousands of people, things, and non-objects.

How about this computer onto which I am transferring these thoughts and ideas? Isn't this a replica of the large and complex life web that I am connected to? Even when I transfer these thoughts and words into a digital or electronic format, I am aware that I am connected to this machine to make it possible. Where did this computer come from? All its parts were made somewhere, all the parts were assembled somewhere else, the assembled unit was transported to some other place, from there it was distributed to some company somewhere, and finally it came to a place where I could go and purchase it. In this age of outsourcing and globalization, the various parts of this computer may have come from various countries. Think of the materials, people, and processes involved in getting this machine into my hands. This computer is just a tiny thing that influences my life a great deal. How about everything else that I can think of?

Of course, even before I think of all these thoughts and ideas, computers and materials, I should know that I would not be here in the first place if I had not been born. My birth would not have been possible if my parents had not been around. My parents wouldn't have been around if it were not for my grandparents. Going back through generations and generations of my ancestors, I could conclude that my being here today would not be possible if it were not for those countless persons in my genealogy and in the human race. I am unique, but I cannot claim an absolute separation from my parents, my family, or the rest of the world. The whole human race would not have been around if it were not for a conducive world and environment. I cannot claim an absolute separation from the world and the environment. The human race and the conducive world would not be around if not for God, who created all of it. Since God is the source of everything, including my life, I cannot claim an absolute separation from God.

God and human beings, the world of objects and non-objects, communities and cultures, earth and sky—the life web includes all of these. Our words, thoughts, feelings, imaginations, ideas, and all such things are intimately connected to many persons, things, and realities. Some of it is visible to us, but most of it remains invisible. It is a large network or web of connections and relationships. It is an invisible web. I can speak of all these components of my life web as separate entities, but even when I speak about them I know that I am part of all of them. I cannot separate myself from them. They are integral parts of my life. If I cannot separate myself from my life web, then I cannot separate myself from you, because you are part of my life web. In the same way, you cannot separate me from you, because I am part of your life web. Hence, you are part of me and I am part of you. We can desire and try to be independent, but we are incomplete without each other.

Maia Szalavitz and Bruce Perry suggested that life, from its beginning to its end, is a dance of connections. We cannot be totally independent. We are and we have to be interdependent to be healthy and happy. Relationships are necessary for healthy living. Isolation or disconnection from others can be destructive. It can create many health issues, such as high blood pressure, suppressed immune system function, memory loss, irritability, anger, depression, hopelessness, suicidal thoughts, anxiety, panic attacks, and many other mental and physical dysfunctions. It can also make a person violent and aggressive toward others. We are not meant to be isolated beings. We are meant to live in communion with others.

In Indian culture and spirituality, there is a very valued concept called "*Vasudeva Kutumbam*," which means "universal family" or "one family under God." According to this concept, you and I, along with God, make up a family. This family includes everything in creation, both animate and inanimate beings, humans, and the divine. This is the kingdom of God that Jesus talked about (Lk 17:21). We are one family, united with God and one another. We cannot separate ourselves from this family. You and I are united because it is God who is uniting us. He is the source of life for both of us. We are created in his image and likeness (Ge 1:26–27). We have to deal with each other with an awareness of this sacred union. All of us have a responsibility to keep this union and relationship strong and steady. We have to live with an awareness that we are part of a large family, and we have to be watchful about things that might cause any damage to this relationship. This means living with an awareness that it is not just about us; that it is not just about me. It is much more than that.

When we acknowledge and respect the sacredness of others, we are, in fact, respecting our own uniqueness and sacredness. To disrespect and disregard the sacredness of others is to disrespect ourselves, because others are our own family.

Being different doesn't necessarily mean that we have to be difficult for each other. Life involves enough roadblocks and hurdles even without our volition. We don't need to create more of those for each other. The problem is not with the differences, but rather our failure to find a balance between our uniqueness and universality. When we miss one or the other—that is, when we fail to recognize each other's uniqueness or our connectedness in the life web, we might end up having problems. We are unique, but we are not isolated individuals surviving and thriving on our own. Our survival and thriving are undeniably connected with the larger life web, which includes all of us. Whatever we do has an impact on the life web, just as whatever happens in the life web has an impact on us.

Our universality is not a threat to our uniqueness or vice versa. These are two dimensions of our human life. We are unique and independent, but we are universal as well. However, an absolutization or denial of either of these dimensions can cause problems in our personal growth and relationships. My life and experiences are unique to me. What others experience is not what I experience. But at the same time, I don't have the last word on everything about life. The experiences of others around me are as valid as my own experiences. I should have the humility to listen to their experiences as well.

We see how cultures and societies that deny or ignore one of these aspects over the other end up having problems. An absolutization of the uniqueness and individuality of persons leads to the dangers of extreme individualism, relativism, and denial of objective truths. An asbolutization of our universality leads to the dangers of extreme absolutism, inflated collectivism, and denial of individual rights. We need a balance of both uniqueness and universality.

The way to find this balance between our uniqueness and universality is to live with the awareness that we are part of the vasudeva kutumbam, or the kingdom of God. To God, each one of us is unique and special, and yet we are all one in him. Given our context of negative survival and thriving and mismatched accents, vasudeva kutumbam is a work in progress. God is often like a father and mother who wait for all their children to come for the family reunion. The father and mother notice that one or two of their children are staying away because they dislike or have issues with their siblings. However, the father and mother do not give up or stop loving them. They hope that one day they will all be together as one family. Our mismatches in accents may keep us away from each other. But God is patient. He waits for our renewal and return. And we all have a responsibility to work toward making this kingdom of God a reality as much as possible. We need to live with an awareness that each one of us is unique but we are inseparable. We are independent, but we are incomplete without the other. You and I are not one, but you and I are not two either. We are a vasudeva kutumbam. The kingdom of God is within us and among us (Lk 17:20–21).

37

Correction and Connection, not Condemnation

Another important requirement for transcending our accents and containing our negative survival and thriving is to have the willingness and opportunity to correct and connect. If we wish to see the world changing, it has to first begin with us. We need to first repair and heal those areas in our lives that are unhealthy and debilitating. We need to recognize the negativity in our own survival and thriving, and make an effort to change it. When we change, it will have an impact on our family and community. When more and more people do that, it will have a greater impact on the larger world.

Those who have their accents mismatched with those of others or those who are surviving and thriving negatively need to recognize it, deconstruct it, and reconstruct it in the right way. We cannot shy away from taking the responsibility for our present and future. Blaming others for all our ills is not going to take us anywhere. Some people might find it convenient to blame others for all their ills so that they don't have to take any responsibility for any change. Many things and many people from their past might have caused damage to their positive survival and thriving. But the past cannot be undone. Those responsible for the damage could be made accountable, but they have to find ways to break the negative courses of their lives so that they can grow and develop and bring the best out of themselves. Blaming or passing the buck doesn't help them or anybody else. The process of rectification and change might involve educating oneself more on all the things that lead to negative survival and thriving, reading books on spiritual and mental health problems and their contributing factors, revisiting one's sense of self and vision of life, and seeking personal growth services, therapeutic assistance, or other healing remedies.

Some people may not be even aware that they are negatively surviving and thriving. But their families, friends, and acquaintances can come to the aid of such individuals by helping them realize the negativity and destructiveness they are immersed in and encouraging them to seek help from people who can help them. Of course, when it comes to family, friends, or acquaintances, pointing out something negative or unhealthy in someone is not a pleasant job, because not many people like to feel judged or corrected. If you say ten good things about me, I will feel great and on top of the world. But if you say one bad thing about me, my whole world might collapse. I might feel offended, misunderstood, misjudged, and greatly hurt. Giving or receiving corrections or negative feedback is a very difficult and unpleasant experience for the giver and the receiver.

These days we see businesses and service providers using "best practices" and "customer care" as benchmarks for evaluating the quality of their service. As part of upping the ante, they ask customers for their feedback or evaluation of their service. Based on customers' feedback, they are willing to make changes if need be. This might work out well in business relationships. But when it comes to personal relationships, giving feedback or pointing out something in another is not a pleasant task. Even those who appear to be open and welcoming about receiving feedback may not show the same enthusiasm when they really hear what we have to say. And some cultures are such that no one wants to hurt the feelings of others. So those who dare to do that unpleasant task of extricating their family members, friends, and colleagues from their negativity and destructiveness need to be prepared for pushback. But the fear of being rejected or pushed back against shouldn't stop them from doing what they should do. Taking that risk is better than colluding with them to continue the path of negativity and destruction. And sometimes it has to be taken as a duty and responsibility.

God said to Prophet Ezekiel that he had to be like a watchman for his people, warning them to turn away from their sins and iniquities:

"Mortal, I have made you a sentinel for the house of Israel; whenever you hear a word from my mouth, you shall give them warning from me. If I say to the wicked, 'You shall surely die,' and you give them no warning, or speak to warn the wicked from their wicked way, in order to save their life, those wicked persons shall die for their iniquity; but their blood I will require at your hand" (Eze 3:17–18). If the wicked people died in their iniquities because they were not warned, God said, the blame would be on Ezekiel. Ezekiel had to take it as his responsibility to warn and correct his people. Jesus also spoke of the importance of correcting one another: "If another disciple sins, you must rebuke the offender, and if there is repentance, you must forgive" (Lk 17:3). Fraternal correction is important for a person and the community to grow.

But correction is not judgment and condemnation. Jesus is very clear about that. Those who correct or point out someone's negativity in survival and thriving have to find appropriate ways to help the person gain greater awareness of what is going on with his or her life without stepping into the realm of judgment or condemnation. Jesus offered a healthy model of fraternal correction (Mt 18:15–17). According to that model, if a person lives in sin or survives and thrives negatively, first it has to be brought to his or her attention, and it has to be done in private, one-on-one. It is not for the whole world to know. It has to be done with respect, love, and compassion. If the person does not listen or change, one should seek the assistance of one or two others and do it all over again. If that too does not bring any positive results, the matter should be brought to the community, and the community should find ways to correct the person. So there is a gradual way of leading someone through the process of change. But despite all that, some still don't change. They live as if they are determined to go to hell or stay away from God and the community. In such cases, Jesus says, we have to simply consider them as a gentile or tax collector (Mt 18:17).

But even with such people who refuse to listen or change, Jesus does not ask us to be judgmental, condemning, or cruel. Considering them as a gentile or tax collector would mean thinking of them as those "that do not know what they are doing" (Lk 23:34). They are blinded by their sin, and their hearts are closed to God and others. It may be beyond our ability to make them understand the negativity and sin that they are living in. It is not God or us that condemn them. They condemn themselves because they love darkness and sin rather than light and love (Jn 3:17–21). They choose hell rather than heaven.

Despite all our effort, we may not be able to bring any change in them. Hence, we leave them to the mercy of God and continue to pray for them. To keep the community or society free from their threat, we may have to restrain them, but we continue to show them love and mercy as well. In all that we are able to do, we should try our best to help them. And in all that we do, the foundational principles, according to Jesus, should be love, respect, and concern for the other. The focus is not judgment and condemnation, but rather bringing the individual back to God and the community. It is correction and connection that we seek, not condemnation.

In all of these, it is to be noted that for Jesus, the ultimate goal is to bring all of us together as one family. For that, every community and group has to help their members to stay away from negative survival and thriving. It is not about one particular community or sect turning against others to make everyone rally behind their ideals or ideologies. It is about all individuals and communities turning away from negative survival and thriving. The only ideal is to become a loving human community, united with God and one another. Fraternal correction is not about a homogenizing mob mentality against those who are different from us. It is rather about love being the guiding principle of life across human cultures and communities. In every community we find people deviating from the path of healthy survival and thriving. All communities need to make effort to bring back such individuals to the right living. And when every community takes upon themselves that responsibility we will have a better world community and kingdom of God as envisioned by Jesus.

We see Jesus relentlessly trying to correct and purify the ways of his disciples. When they started following him, his disciples had their own negativity and drawbacks. Their accents were not matched with that of their master, Jesus. We see two of the disciples, James and John, lobbying for power and position in Jesus' kingdom: "'Teacher, we want you to do for us whatever we ask of you.' And he said to them, 'What is it you want me to do for you?' And they said to him, 'Grant us to sit, one at your right hand and one at your left, in your glory'" (Mk 10:35–40). Jesus had to make them understand that following him did not mean being vested with power and position. The same disciples were filled with rage and wanted to call down fire from heaven to destroy a village that rejected Jesus and his message: "Lord, do you want us to command fire to come down from heaven and consume them?" (Lk 9:54). Jesus rebuked them for their anger and told them that forgiveness, mercy, and love were the ways to win hearts and build God's kingdom.

The disciples fought among themselves to see who was the greatest (Lk 9:46–48). Jesus reminded them that being his disciples meant self-renunciation and humility rather than self-inflation: "If any want to become my followers, let them deny themselves and take up their cross daily and follow me" (Lk 9:23).

Jesus gathered his disciples from different walks of life, and they all came with their own ideas about what it meant to live in this world. A few of them were fishermen, one was a tax collector, another one was a lover of money, and yet another one was a zealot, or fanatic. Their primary focus was not building up the kingdom of God or giving their best to God and others. Jesus had to gradually transform them and help them to purify their intentions. Sometimes gentle, sometimes harsh, he transformed them gradually. To begin with, they were self-focused and worldly, but with the guidance of Jesus, they were on the road to a new purpose and vision of life. They were transformed into men who would become great pillars of the church, bringing the good news of God's love to the ends of the earth. Jesus corrected them but never condemned them.

But the hearts and minds of some people are so closed to God and his ways that nothing sinks into them. They continue on the path of negative survival and thriving progressively. Their accents never match with those of others. They break their relationship with God, others, and even their own selves. We see this progression of negative survival and thriving in Judas Iscariot, the disciple who betrayed Jesus. We read that Judas was a lover of money (Jn 12:4–6). His heart was not changed much even after being with Jesus for a few years. As the chief priests and elders of the people were plotting to kill Jesus, Judas went to them and asked how much they would pay him if he betrayed his master to them.

"Then one of the twelve, who was called Judas Iscariot, went to the chief priests and said, 'What will you give me if I betray him to you?' They paid him thirty pieces of silver. And from that moment he began to look for an opportunity to betray him" (Mt 26:14–16).

Jesus warned Judas about the path of destruction that he was taking: "When it was evening, he took his place with the twelve; and while they were eating, he said, 'Truly I tell you, one of you will betray me' ... 'The Son of Man goes as it is written of him, but woe to that one by whom the Son of Man is betrayed! It would have been better for that one not to have been born.' Judas, who betrayed him, said, 'Surely not I, Rabbi?' He replied, 'You have said so'" (Mt 26:20–25).

Even after this warning, Judas went ahead with his plan. His heart was taken over so much by his sin that the warning of Jesus did not really sink in. We read, "While he [Jesus] was still speaking, Judas, one of the twelve, arrived; with him was a large crowd with swords and clubs, from the chief priests and the elders of the people. Now the betrayer had given them a sign, saying, 'The one I will kiss is the man; arrest him.' At once he came up to Jesus and said, 'Greetings, Rabbi!' and kissed him. Jesus said to him, 'Friend, do what you are here to do.' Then they came and laid hands on Jesus and arrested him" (Mt 26:47–50).

But it did not stop with that. His sin led to his own self-destruction: "When Judas, his betrayer, saw that Jesus was condemned, he repented and brought back the thirty pieces of silver to the chief priests and the elders. He said, 'I have sinned by betraying innocent blood.' But they said, 'What is that to us? See to it yourself.' Throwing down the pieces of silver in the temple, he departed; and he went and hanged himself" (Mt 27:3–5).

In all these developments, we don't find Jesus condemning Judas. He made every effort to purify the intentions of Judas as he did with his other disciples. He corrected him and warned him, but Judas was closed to all of that. However, Saint Matthew reports that after he saw what had happened, Judas's eyes were opened, and he acknowledge his sin and repented. But it was too late to undo what he had done. He could not live with that guilt, and so he went and hanged himself.

Judas's sin led him to his own death, but the gospel does not say God condemned him. God does not give up on anyone. Referring to the purpose of his incarnation, Jesus said, "Indeed, God did not send the Son into the world to condemn the world, but in order that the world might be saved through him" (Jn 3:17). Jesus came as a savior for all, including those who live and behave like Judas. But the sad truth is that sometimes we do colossal damage to ourselves and others before we repent and change. Hence, the earlier we realize and make efforts to change our negative survival and thriving, the better it is for us and for others. All efforts have to be made to restore the broken relationships, and we have to help people to return to healthy living.

When Jesus talks of correcting and helping the negatively oriented and sinful people, it includes all possible avenues—professional, familial, or personal interventions. Taking one or two others with us or taking the person to the community means that we have to utilize all possible methods to help people change their negative and sinful ways. Whatever may be the means and paths taken, the focus is to restore the broken relationships and help the person to bring the best out of himself or herself. Our goal is to build the kingdom of God in our hearts and in our world.

Personal or fraternal correction should automatically lead to or go hand in hand with finding the connections. When our accents are mismatched with those of others, or when we survive and thrive negatively, our union with God and others is splintered and fractured. The connections are lost. But with corrections and transformations, those lost and broken connections could be restored. We have to find ways to correct and connect.

As we have seen, connecting with others even in normal circumstances is not easy, because we all differ in our accents. We may be used to only our world. Our eyes, ears, and minds are not very quick to adjust to things that are different. Take a name, for example. When we hear a name that is not common in our culture or society, we tend to ask the person to repeat the name. My last name, Edathumparambil, for example, is a tongue twister for many in the United States. When they hear it, they just blink their eyes and go on with other conversations.

When we hear a new and unfamiliar name, our brain does not find any data that matches with that new name or sound, and our ears are not attuned to that name or sound, so our first reaction may be to disconnect. The person will have to make another attempt to bring the ears and mind back to listening mode. It may succeed or fail. If it fails a second or third time, the brain might give a signal of being tired of trying, and the person might move into another conversation. Like names, when accents are different, it is difficult to understand and connect. When personalities, interests, and backgrounds are different, it is difficult to connect.

Sometimes connections become difficult also because words don't mean the same thing for all people. When we talk about something, what we mean is not what others mean. It is not that either of us has gotten it terribly wrong; we just happened to learn and understand things differently. But that difference in our understanding can create some disconnect, because although we know what we are talking about, we are unaware that it means something else for others.

So one of the requirements to connect with people is to come down to their level and enter into their world. We have to simply acknowledge and accept that there is a world or many worlds out there that are different from what we have known and experienced, and we must be willing to enter into those worlds to see and know what they are like.

A few years back I was traveling by train from Munich, Germany, to Annecy, France. When I switched trains at a station in France, there was only one other gentleman in the whole coach. We sat across from each other as our tickets indicated. To begin with, we sat there in that gorgeous and yet lifeless compartment, occasionally glancing at each other. After a few minutes of awkward silence, we made some attempts to acknowledge each other's presence and enter into a conversation.

He spoke French and I spoke English; we didn't know any other language that would connect us. The travel time was going to be six hours. We could have avoided any interaction with each other by reading or sleeping, but totally ignoring each other didn't appear to be the best option. I knew it was going to be a lot of work if we were to stay engaged. But we did. We began with a smile. We tried to say something to each other but soon realized that it was futile. We didn't understand each other. So we started employing all our faculties and abilities to communicate. I would say one word in English, and he would try a French word to match it. If I felt that it made some sense, I would move to the next word; if not, he would try another word. And I would do the same when he said something. Gestures and movements of hands were great tools that became handy. I felt we were not too different from our ancestors who communicated without a written or spoken language! Since there was no one else around, there was no worry about disturbing someone with our loud articulations and pronounced gestures. At the end of the journey, I was exhausted, but we had communicated and connected. It was hard work, but it was not impossible.

Coming down to another person's level and entering into his or her world is not easy. We have our own realms and turfs from which we operate. To step out of that realm or invite someone else into that realm is not easy. We can assume that leaving Ur, the land of his fathers, was not easy for Abraham. We are used to certain ways of doing things, and any change from that learned pattern is difficult and threatening. Sometimes the only world that we have known and in which we have been operating is our world. Some of us are totally unfamiliar with anything else. It is always a challenge to step out of that comfort zone and embrace something that we are unfamiliar with.

We are also used to certain types of persons. Relating to an unfamiliar person is a totally different ball game. We don't know what kind of person the other one is. We may have our apprehensions and uncertainties. We may have our prejudices. We have our own likes and dislikes about look, color, gender, age, height, weight, and all such things when it comes to dealing with a person. We can listen to, read about, and talk about accommodation and unconditional love, but we are often comfortable with what we are used to. It is very challenging to step out of our familiar world and embrace something or someone just like that. There is a lot of internal debate that takes place before we can take a baby step toward accepting or accommodating another person. Things can become even more challenging if we have our own ghosts and skeletons in the cupboard, meaning our own unresolved issues. They may come alive when confronted with a challenging situation. These are all part of the package that comes with our lives as unique individuals.

We may teach and listen to lectures about the importance of examining our own beliefs, values, biases, and other cultural constructs that we carry with us so that these elements don't blur our views of other people and their experiences. But when it comes to our daily lives, we might struggle to translate some of those good lessons into practice. Even while teaching about going beyond our blurred glasses, our glasses may be blurred. My guess is that we all struggle with entering the worlds of others or meeting them at their level. Experiences in my own limited clinical practice and pastoral work have shown me how difficult it is to enter the world of another person. Because of our own individual characteristics, our vision of the world and others may be blurred more often than we realize. Even as I pen these thoughts, I know that my vision about other people and things may be blurred. Even these thoughts are results of viewing things with my own glasses in my own particular way.

All of us need to make an effort to tune our minds and ears to understand what others are saying. We need to make an effort to meet others where they are. This was the amazing ability that Jesus had. He was able to come down to the level of other people. His incarnation itself is a testimony to that. He comes down to our level. Saint Paul describes this beautifully in his letter to the Philippians: "… though he [Jesus] was in the form of God, [he] did not regard equality with God as something to be exploited, but emptied himself, taking the form of a slave, being born in human likeness. And being found in human form, he humbled himself and became obedient to the point of death-even death on a cross" (Php 2:6–8).

This amazing ability of Jesus to come down to the level of others is seen throughout his public ministry. Jesus went to Galilee and called Simon, Andrew, James, and John, who were all fishermen. (See Mt 4:18–22.) He called them to follow him. No other rabbi had done that before. The fishermen did not matter much to the higher-ups in the society or religious circles. But Jesus came down to their level. He spoke to them in a language they could understand. But he also gave them a higher goal to follow. He gave them a new purpose and vision in life. He said, "Follow me, and I will make you fish for people" (Mt 4:19). They knew what fishing meant. He used the same language but gave them a higher purpose.

In normal circumstances, their fishing was focused on taking care of themselves and their families. But Jesus wanted them to expand that mission to the larger world. He wanted them to become partners with him to build up God's kingdom. One of the things that probably touched them was that he spoke in their language. They found something special about him that they could not find in others.

Jesus did the same with many others. He went down to the level of tax collectors and sinners and spoke to them in a language that they could understand, and he gave them a new purpose in life. (See Mt 9:9–13.) He went down to the level of little children and spoke to them in a language that they could understand. (See Mt 19:13–15.) He went down to the level of people who were sick, suffering, sinful, and dying (See, for example, Mt 4:23–25; Lk 7:1–17; 36–50).

If we really want people to correct and connect, we have to come down to their level. We have to speak to them in a language they can understand. We have to come down to their level so we can lift them up and give them a higher purpose in life. Being frustrated about how some people don't understand us, we may have complained saying, "They don't get it" or "You don't get it." They may not be getting it because we are staying on our level without coming down to their level and they are not able to understand our language. We hear parents expressing their frustrations about their children and children doing the same about their parents. Spouses and friends sometimes do the same thing about each other. Such frustrations and complaints could be heard about people in many other relationship settings as well. Coming down to the level of another person and speaking in a language that is understandable for him or her is one of the essential things in getting him or her to correct and connect. But often we don't realize that we are operating from our level that may be too difficult for others to comprehend and catch up with.

People who have very serious flaws and defective DTS and DTT need special attention to rectify their issues. Given their circumstances, they may be doing the best they can. And they may not even know that they are operating with defective DTS and DTT. If they could have done better, they would have done so. But those who have attained a greater self-awareness and are better at understanding others' accents can help such individuals to realize their negative survival and thriving or help them to seek help. Our effort and energy need to be spent not on blaming or condemning but rather on seeking help and helping those who need help. "There is therefore now no condemnation for those who are in Christ Jesus" (Ro 8:1). Our goal is to restore the broken relationships and build up the kingdom of God. For that, all of us need to feel the need to correct and connect.

38

The Hard Truth

As individuals and communities, we have achieved much. We have made great discoveries and amazing advancements in different fields. However, sooner or later we have to come to terms with the hard truth that we are limited. We may not like it, but that is how it is. We want to survive and thrive, but we don't have it all together.

We come in touch with our limitedness when we are faced with certain difficult and painful situations. Sufferings caused by illnesses, natural calamities, accidents, and death are everyday occurrences that we have become used to. Fortunes give way to misfortune, good health to ill health, prosperity to poverty, and calmness to calamities. Listen to the news on radio or television, or read the newspapers; it's all about sufferings and pain humanity is subjected to. Thousands die as a result of natural disasters and mishaps. Millions succumb to diseases and maladies. The tragedies and sufferings that we see and hear about sicken us. They have become so common that sometimes they are just news to us. We become a helpless observer or uninvolved listener. Constantly faced with it, we fall into a certain kind of numbness and amnesia. The only time we wake up from this numbness and shake ourselves up is if and when we personally encounter these experiences.

Sufferings caused by diseases are indescribable. Every now and then we wake up hearing about a new illness, flu, or bacterial infection in some parts of the world. Swine flu, bird flu, dengue fever, Ebola— these have been some of the latest of those scary outbreaks. Sometimes sicknesses come from out of nowhere. We who seem to be hale and hearty end up on the bed or in the hospital unexpectedly. The long waits for diagnoses and treatments are stressful moments, and our physical illnesses give rise to emotional and mental upheaval. Anxiety comes along with death if an illness turns out to be terminal. No one has an answer. The consolation and comfort we can offer to those who suffer are limited. Apparently illnesses come all of a sudden for many. And illness sometimes strikes the apparently healthiest persons.

Nowadays we speak often of organ-specific illnesses: heart-related illness, brain-related ailments, kidney-related malfunctions. The lungs, liver, spleen, gall bladder, intestine, and whatever we can think of, they all are prone to disease and death. Some ailments begin as organ-specific and then metastasize, and when one organ is taken care of, another falls apart. They are all interrelated so much so that some people become "frequent fliers" between hospitals, nursing homes, and rehabilitation facilities.

Newborn babies are sometimes struck with maladies that are incurable or irreversible. We hate to see them suffering. Sometimes the best and the holiest of all people are struck by terminal illnesses and untold sufferings. They go through inexplicable agony and pain. There are many who live in distress due to mental and psychological ailments. They not only dread their illness but also carry the stigma and shame that go with it.

Diseases and death are lurking at our door all the time. We get scared and frustrated. A good understanding of the human body might be helpful in reducing our frustrations and accepting ourselves better. The human body, like any other living organism in the universe, is corruptible. We are prone to diseases and decay, degeneration and death. Old cells die, and new cells are born. And since this constant process of change happens in millions of ways, it is possible that the equilibrium is lost. Even a scientist who studies the functioning of a cell in another person does not know how stealthily and fast the cells in his own body keep changing. Just because one is a doctor who treats patients or a scientist who discovers medicines for various illnesses, he or she is not exempt from this degeneration and death. Even a near-perfect body is in a constant process of degeneration and death. When certain organs of the body maintain equilibrium, others may not do the same. If all the organs of the body work in unison, the body remains healthy. But in reality, that is not what we often experience.

As we recognize the corruptible nature of our bodies, it is also important to realize that the things we do and the way we live affect others. The intergenerational transmission of certain characteristics—physical and psychological, emotional and spiritual—is something we should be constantly reminded of. It is important to take note of our contributions in making others' lives what they are.

The realities of nature make us feel very small. Nature presents its beauty and unpredictability to us as one package. Be it the sun or rain, everything has its own beauty and unpredictability. The same force can be a blessing for some and a curse for some others.

Rain is good. It is a blessing for animals, plants, and human beings. It brings life and freshness to everything. It quenches everyone's thirst. It cools down the temperature and keeps people and animals hydrated. It helps seeds to sprout, grass to grow, and plants and trees to flower and bear fruit. But the same rain can be a curse for many people. Heavy rains and clogged waterways create floods. Rivers overflow, crops are destroyed, homes are washed away, and people die.

A gentle breeze cools and refreshes everyone, but a thunderstorm or tornado kills people. Wind power produces energy and helps sailboats, but the same wind can be disastrous and terrifying. It overturns buildings, trees, and vehicles. Hurricane Sandy, which hit New York, and the killer typhoon Haiyan, which hit the Philippines in the recent past, have not faded from our memories.

The sea is good. Fish and other resources bring life to us and help our sustenance. The sea helps with travel and transportation. But the same sea can grow rough and furious. It can swallow anyone and anything into its belly. Deadly waves in their monstrous dance take one step forward and swallow people and animals alive, and in their next step they return with their dead bodies. The people who stand and watch its beauty at one moment can become victims of its fury in the next. For example, the monster tsunami that developed in the Indian Ocean in 2004 claimed over 230,000 lives.

The sun gives us light and heat. It keeps us warm. It dispels the darkness and produces energy. It helps the sustenance of our flora and fauna. But the same sun can be life-threatening. It causes drought. It causes sunstroke. People, animals, and plants die from excessive heat.

Snow is good to watch and play with. But the same snow can have devastating effect on human beings, animals, and plants. It brings the temperature down, holds up vehicles on the roads, and causes fatal accidents. Just as people die as a result of sunstroke, heat waves, and floods, they also die as a result of extremely cold weather.

Our earth is rich and beautiful with all its resources. But the same earth can open its mouth and swallow people into its belly. Earthquakes, volcanoes, and landslides are things that people are often unprepared for. When a natural or cosmic disaster breaks out, everyone, without any distinction, becomes a victim of the occurrence.

Sufferings and death caused by natural calamities are beyond description. They don't kill just one or two but annihilate thousands and thousands in one stroke. Many lives are lost, people are left homeless, and properties are destroyed. Despite all the forewarnings and safety measures, our preparedness is still inadequate.

There are still many other things in nature that threaten our survival. Animals and birds add beauty to our lives. Our lives would be colorless without the beautiful flora and fauna around us. But despite all their beauty, some of these creatures can be dangerous and deadly. They are fierce and venomous. Human beings can fall prey to them.

From the point of view of the victim or others, these are all calamities. But for nature, it is just normal and natural. Nature or the cosmos is not going to change its course of action and functioning just because we are hurt or feel resent. We have learned to face these challenges to a large extent. Centuries back, people could not imagine the weather forecasts that we have today. We have made progress in leaps and bounds, but we are not completely insulated either. Maybe a few decades from now the effect of a tornado or an earthquake on human lives will be much less than at present because we will learn better ways to equip ourselves and be prepared to face these challenges.

Sometimes some of our sufferings are of our own making. We know that the food that we eat is not always the best and the healthiest, yet still we eat it. The air that we breathe and the water that we drink are not always clean. We pollute our rivers and imbalance our ecosystem. We smoke, consume alcohol, and use other drugs, endangering our lives. Some people deprive themselves of adequate sleep, rest, and relaxation. They know that it ultimately affects their health, but still they do it. There may be many reasons why people do all these things, but recognizing the negative effects of such habits and the ability to change them will help minimize the damage they do to people's lives and the sufferings that arise from them.

The hardest of all sufferings seems to be those inflicted by human beings on their fellow human beings. The type and nature of these damages differ according to their context. Sometimes it involves one person, and at other times it involves a whole group. Sometimes it is within the group, and at other times it is intercultural. Sometimes it is regional, and at other times it is international. Gender, race, religion, denomination, class, and caste have all been causes for human beings to inflict pain on each other. Nations, communities, and groups are at war with each other. People are mercilessly killed or hurt every day. People engage in abuses, violence, aggression, and threats. Mental torture and harassment characterize many people's everyday lives. In multiple ways human beings are different, and in multiple ways they inflict pain on each other. There seems to be no letting up in such senseless attacks on each other.

We face our limitations not only in our environment and physiology, but also in our psychology, emotions, and spirituality. We don't have it all together when it comes to the working of our mind. Sometimes we are overwhelmed by our emotions and feelings. Often we don't have much control over where our mind takes us. We lose count of the number of thoughts, imaginings, and fantasies that we have every day. Our mind takes us through certain thoughts and imaginations, and the same mind makes us ask why we think and imagine such things. We develop attitudes and ideas that sometimes leave us clueless about how and where they originated. We make choices and decisions that we sometimes think we had no part in. We experience emotions and feelings that we sometimes don't want to be part of. Sometimes we feel lonely and lost. We feel all alone in the crowd. We feel that even God is far away from us. We experience our finiteness in all sorts of ways.

Whatever may be the type of suffering, and whoever may be the initiator of the suffering, it is very personal and painful for the sufferer. It affects the normal rhythm of life and turns everything upside down. The sufferer alone knows the intensity of the suffering. Howsoever I try to describe it, I still find words inadequate to let another know what I am going through.

When faced with these realities of suffering, death, and decay, we are often taken aback. Why? Why me? Why is life unfair? Does anyone care? How much longer? These are questions that many sufferers ask. When it happens, we don't philosophize on the meaning of suffering. We look for some relief.

Although we experience all these limitations, our culture, which prides itself on all its latest technological developments, discoveries, and medical advancements, may be giving us an illusory idea that we are going to be here forever. Although we are grateful for all the advancements and facilities, the possibilities for prolongation of life and other advancements in our world may have made us less tolerant of pain and frustration and more fearful of death.

We have many capabilities and strengths. We have come a long way in taking care of ourselves. We have a better grasp of the working of our body and mind than in the past. But still we are not omnipotent. We are fragile and limited. It may be hard to admit and accept that we are fragile. We may want to be in control of our lives, but we have very little control over many things. We want to survive and thrive, but there are many threats to our survival and thriving. Degeneration, death, pain, and frustration are parts of our lives. No one knows how or how soon he or she is going to die. We can seek all the help available to reduce our pain and improve the quality of our life. We wish and hope that no untoward incidents, fatal emergencies, or untimely deaths occur for ourselves or others. However, reminding ourselves of our mortal nature and limitations helps us to be more accepting of our life changes and less fearful of death.

Benjamin J. Sadock and Virginia A. Sadock offer a very valuable counsel to physicians. They suggest that although physicians might wish to have complete control over their patients' illness and cure, they have to accept the fact that a full realization of this wish is impossible. They may be very caring, competent, and conscientious, but they have to accept the fact that in some situations, certain diseases are incurable and death is inevitable or unpreventable. Physicians are not omnipotent. This awareness is necessary not only for physicians but for all people. We are amazing in what we can do, but we have our limitations too.

39

We Are Not God but Human

Another important requirement for transcending our accents and moving toward a healthy life is to recognize and accept that we are not God, but human. Although certain developments in certain societies might make us float on a false belief that we are unlimited and unconquerable, the simple realities of everyday life bring us back to the ground level. Our body cannot fly as fast as our mind does. We are not omnipotent. Our world does not operate the way we would like it to operate. There are some who are frustrated with the world because it is not moving fast enough, and there are others who are mad at the world because it is moving too fast. In any case, there is bad news for slow movers as well as perfectionists and control freaks. We may be frustrated about the state of affairs that we find ourselves in, but that's how it is. We are not God; we are human.

As mentioned, we have a privileged position in creation because of our creation in the image and likeness of God (see Ge 1:26–27). We have the perfection of God in us. But that doesn't make us God. We are not omnipotent and omniscient. We are not the center of the universe. The universe does not revolve around us. We might like to think that way, but that is not how it is. Having a privileged position in creation doesn't mean that we are able to have or do everything that we might like to have or want to do. We may be the most sophisticated inhabitants of this universe, but we don't have control over everything, especially the physical realities. We talked about our helplessness before the forces of nature, diseases, and death. We have many limitations. We are not God, but human.

But we are not like other animals and beings in the creation either. We have many capabilities that they don't posses. We are extraordinary beings. There is nothing in this creation (to the extent we know it) that can claim a unique identity as we do. We possess something more than our physical beauty and traits. We possess something more than our faculties of intelligence and will. We are something more than our thinking, feeling, and imagination. We seek beauty and fulfillment not only in this limited physical reality of the world but also in the nonphysical, spiritual, and eternal realm. We ourselves cannot fathom the wonder of our being.

If we get this wrong, we are going to be in a lot of trouble. We might begin to act like God, which we are not, and we might begin to act like animals and other beings in creation, which also is not true to our nature. Sharing in divine nature doesn't make us God. Sharing in animal nature doesn't make us like other animals. We are human beings, and our perfection consists in being that perfectly well.

Saint Francis de Sales very well expresses this idea of being perfectly human in his famous saying, "Be who you are and be that well" (De Sales & De Chantal, 1988). The source of this maxim is one of the letters that he wrote to Madame Brulart, the wife of Nocolas Brulart, president of the Burgundian Parliament, who sought spiritual guidance from him. Besides his episcopal responsibilities, Francis was a greatly sought after spiritual director. In his letter to Madame Brulart, he wrote, "It seems to me that white is not the color proper to roses, for red roses are more beautiful and more fragrant; however, white is the distinctive characteristic of lilies. *Let us be what we are and be that well*, in order to bring honor to the Master Craftsman whose handiwork we are" (De Sales & De Chantal, 1988). So what is actually needed is to be who we are and be that perfectly well.

But what does that mean? How do we live perfectly as human beings? I believe the answer lies in what Saint Francis de Sales says in his book, *Treatise on the Love of God*, which I mentioned previously, "God in creating man in his image and likeness wills that just as in Himself so too in the human person everything must be regulated by love and for love" (De Sales, 2005). Our perfection consists in being true to our nature, that is, to be the images of God in this world. And being the images of God would mean living and manifesting love because God is love (1Jn 4:8). This is exactly what Jesus commanded us to be, "Be perfect, therefore, as your heavenly Father is perfect" (Mt 5:48). Many might interpret this as a command to be God. I don't think that is what Jesus meant. I read this command of Jesus as a call to be directed by love and for love. We don't become God, but living in him and deriving our perfection from him, we become his visible presence in this world. In other words, our survival and thriving will be regulated by love and for love.

According to St. Francis de Sales, the one person who lived fully this ideal of being regulated by love and for love is Jesus. Jesus is the perfect embodiment of love. Jesus showed us what it means to live and love as human beings. In him we see the perfection of humanity and the perfection of love. And the love that Jesus lived and manifested had two main characteristics. It was both self-emptying and God-driven. His incarnation itself was the greatest self-emptying act (see Php 2:6–8). And that self-emptying continued throughout his life until he gave himself up on the cross. For the sake of love, Jesus gave himself totally. He asked the same of his followers, "If any want to become my followers, let them deny themselves and take up their cross and follow me. For those who want to save their life will lose it, and those who lose their life for my sake will find it" (Mt 16:24–25). If anyone wants to live and manifest love as Jesus did, they have to empty themselves.

The love that Jesus lived and manifested was also always God-driven. Jesus said, "I have come down from heaven, not to do my own will, but the will of him who sent me" (Jn 6:38). Again in the same gospel he said, "My food is to do the will of him who sent me and to complete his work" (Jn 4:34). In everything that Jesus did, the focus was not on him, but on his heavenly father. Jesus always gave glory to his heavenly father for all that has been done through him (see Mt 11: 25–26). True love is God-driven rather than self-driven.

This self-emptying and God-driven love of Jesus was seen both in his active ministry as well as in his silent suffering during the last few hours of his life. Jesus had only one focus, that is, to love. Jesus shows us what it means to be truly human.

Seeing this perfection of love in Jesus, Saint Francis de Sales tells us that if we really want to be true to who we are, we have to "Live Jesus." Out thoughts, affections, actions, decisions, work, devotion, and everything has to be animated by Jesus. Both through active ministry as well as silent sufferings we have to love and live Jesus.

This ideal of seeking perfection by living and manifesting love or living Jesus is an ever evolving and dynamic process. Since we are constantly in a process of change and becoming, we cannot even say when we will actually reach the point of perfection. Every day, we perfect ourselves. Every day we try to live Jesus. But that is a process that goes on with us, human beings, because we have the ability to perfect ourselves every day. We can make conscious choices to move in that direction. When we think of the rest of the world as an entity separate from human beings, we don't associate it with the same kind of consciousness or intelligence as that possessed by humans. It is what it is.

In many ways, the world may be in the process of change, but that change occurs according to its inherent nature, and not because of a conscious decision to change, as often occurs in humans. If we want to transcend our accents and make progress in our lives, we have to reexamine our perceptions about our world and ourselves. There may be some of us who think of this world—specifically the physical realities of this world—as limited and imperfect. We may think that all our ills are caused by the imperfectness of this world. But that may be because we look at the rest of the world through the glasses that we use to look at ourselves. This could be because we are frustrated with ourselves, frustrated with our inability to be perfect, or frustrated with our inability to find a balance between our perfections and imperfections. It could also be because we see ourselves as an entity separate from the world, distancing ourselves from it and looking at it as imperfect and limited. We may be projecting our imperfections onto the world.

When it comes to the rest of the world, the truth is that this world cannot help but be like this. How do we define perfection? I believe perfection consists of staying true to one's nature and reaching the highest potential. In our case, as human beings, our perfection consists in staying true to our nature, which God has bestowed on us. And that would involve living and manifesting love or living Jesus. But in the case of the rest of the world, this is how the world can be and how it is meant to be. I may want the sun to shine twenty-four hours a day in my part of the world, or the rain to fall only in certain places at certain times. But it is not going to happen that way, except maybe in movies. I may want to call it the imperfectness of the world, but as far as the world is concerned, it is as perfect as it can be. This is what makes the world what it is, and we simply have to accept it as it is. And if at all the world should become better, it is our duty to make it better. If the world and nature have become unhealthier, a large part of the responsibility for it falls on us. We have made it that way by our exploitations and manipulations.

Being part of this "limited" world, we might take it as an excuse for our own imperfections. We may say that since we cannot separate ourselves from the world, we cannot help but be like it. That may be true to a great extent. But we have to be cautious as well, because we are not just like everything else in the universe. We are not talking about similar things. We have abilities that other beings don't possess. We have the ability to make conscious changes in our life, but other beings do not have that ability. If we say we are imperfect and we cannot be any different, it could lead to a state of indifference, laziness, and justifications of our behaviors. For example, one can engage in destructive behaviors and justify it by saying that he or she cannot be any different. That may be true for that specific moment; he or she probably could not have been any different. There may be reasons why he or she engaged in destructive behaviors, and we have already looked at some of those reasons. But the person can be different in the next moment if he or she chooses to be or if he or she is helped to be different. The person doesn't have to continue to be destructive. God has given us intelligence and power to change our ways.

Similarly, one can be lazy and justify it by saying that it is the way he or she is and he or she cannot be any different. It may be true for that moment. If the person were able to be different, he or she would have been different. But it doesn't have to be that way for the rest of his or her life. In the next moment, he or she can choose or be helped to be hardworking and be different.

Because we are not able to have things as we desire, we may be unhappy and frustrated. But we simply need to accept that being unhappy and frustrated is also part of being human. We may be able to reduce our unhappiness and frustration by making certain prudent and intelligent decisions. However, we may not be able to rule out unhappiness or frustration entirely from our lives. We may be able to make some cosmetic changes here and there, but even then we will not have everything that we would like to have.

Thus, in many ways we are like the rest of the world, but in many other ways we are not like the rest of the world. We can stop or change our negative survival and thriving, but the rest of the world does not even come under its purview, because negative survival and thriving are specific to human beings. Everything else in this world functions according to its nature without deciding or intending to do otherwise. The operation of the rest of the world is sometimes unfriendly to our life and existence, but they are not results of some well calculated and consciously thought-out decisions. The earth is not going to command itself to stop its quakes and volcanic eruptions just because they threaten our lives. That is how nature works, and it is not because it has some grudge against us. But that is not how human beings work. We can hold grudges against people and do things consciously to harm them. That is what amounts to negative survival and thriving.

For us, perfection consists of recognizing our inherent good qualities and impeding elements, and making decisions to nurture and develop the good qualities for the betterment of self and others. The real, positive, and constructive orientation of our DTS and DTT consists of this. We have to be regulated by love and for love. We have to live Jesus. We may have different elements of our past and our culture influencing us, but we have to still make effort or be helped to make effort in orienting our DTS and DTT in positive and constructive ways. We have to recognize that we have an accent, refine and correct whatever needs to be refined and corrected, and make efforts to go beyond all that and help others to do the same. Only then we will survive and thrive in the true sense. And it is an ongoing and dynamic process.

40

Progress with a Price Tag

In one sense we of the present day can say we are the most fortunate people who might have ever lived on this earth. We have made great progress in scientific and technological developments. We have increased food production and varieties of products that cater to our needs. We have advanced medicines and treatment opportunities. We have better ways and means to protect ourselves from all life-threatening situations. We have better equipment and facilities to make our lives convenient and comfortable. Education and research are not restricted to a select few in society. Almost everywhere, except maybe in a few countries, people can pursue studies in any field they are interested in. We have come a long way in our political involvement. In many countries, power lies with the people rather than a king or a dictator. As consumers, we have several choices for things that we want to buy and use. As a global community, we have connected with almost every region and community in the world. We have roads, railways, sea routes, and airlines that take us to almost every part of the world. It is possible that at no other point in human history have people connected with each other so much.

However, this progress is not without a price. Every inch of growth that we make takes us a step closer to degeneration and death. Take anything that we have developed for our comfort and convenience, for example. Many of them are quick satisfiers but silent killers. Progress goes along with regress. There is an illness in the cure. Every medicine that we have developed has some side effect. Every vehicle that transports goods or people has a negative impact on our ecosystem. Every new communication device that we come up with makes us more mechanical and impersonal. It is a progress with a price tag.

The fact of progress coming with a price tag is true of everything in our lives, from a tiny product like a thumb pin to a huge machine used to produce hydroelectric power. Take, for example, the computer that I am using. It is an amazing tool that helps my work and activities. But this product has not come without a price. I don't mean its monetary value, but the negative consequences that arise from its production and usage. With regard to its production, each of its hardware parts was probably manufactured in a different unit or factory in a different country. The factories that produce these parts and thousands and millions of other computer hardware parts leave behind hazardous materials that are not so healthy to our environment, especially to those living in the vicinity of those factories. With regard to its usage, although it helps my work and activities tremendously, it takes away much of my time from other people. The more we are glued to our machines, the more mechanical and disconnected we become.

Day by day we are discovering and developing new things to make our lives better and more convenient. Every new leap we make is either to develop a new device to guard ourselves from a threat or to make our lives more comfortable and easy. On the one hand, I become the beneficiary of these products, but on the other hand I become a helpless victim of the dangerous system that these developments have brought about. Some of them may not directly or immediately affect us, but they affect many other human beings like us. When I have the pleasure of using this computer, some others experience the pain of the aftereffects of its production. Although previous generations could be blamed for such actions, those of us who belong to the contemporary era have a greater blame to shoulder, as we appear to be the most sophisticated and development-frenzied folks of all time.

Medical advancements have helped us tremendously to fight illnesses and epidemics. We now have cures for many illnesses. We have advanced equipment and brainy doctors to fix our health problems. But there is an illness in that cure. Our broken legs or collapsed lungs may be fixed, but the postsurgical medications that we take cause other health problems in the long run. Some people take fifteen to twenty pills every day. But do they stop taking those pills because of the side effects or potential threats? No. We take care of what is immediate, and we are happy that we have the means to do so. What comes about in the long run is of less importance then. That is the price we pay for the progress that we have made. We have to also wonder whether these diseases and health issues that we face today are results of what we have done to us and our environment. We can assume that many of these diseases we are fighting today did not exist some ten thousand years ago.

Fast-food places with the drive-through option are a common sight in many economically developed countries. We can drive up to one window, place our order there, and collect our food at the next window. While traveling or when hard pressed to find time for cooking, fast food places are a blessing to many people. Some, of course, like to eat junk food every day. But in general, those places serving fast food have made it convenient for people to grab a quick sandwich or meal. Getting out of the car, of course, would burn a few calories, but sometimes convenience takes the priority.

Anyhow, such places and fast food help people in many ways. They are forms of progress we have made. However, the progress comes with a price tag. For every juicy burger, every greasy stack of bacon, and every buttery sandwich that we consume, our bodies pay a price. If we eat such foods regularly, we are going to be unhealthy. Such habits affect our relationships as well. They simply become additions to our busy lives and lack of time for each other. Home-cooked meals provide not only a healthy diet but also opportunities for family time. Because of our busy lives and the availability of fast foods, families are hardly together. They grab some food from somewhere, and then they are on the run.

The problem of progress coming with a price tag is enormous in the relational aspects of our lives. As mentioned before, many societies have moved into a lifestyle of busyness and endless choices. Freedom of choice is an important concept in certain societies today. Some people will not trade their freedom for anything. It is a highly valued concept. It has helped people to break free from the shackles of undue control and domination exerted upon them by others who had power. It has helped the establishment of a more egalitarian society. In certain societies, in which such freedom and individual choices are assured, people decide what they want to do with their lives. They can decide what they want to study, where they want to work, whom they want to associate with, which faith community they want to belong to, whom they want to marry (or whether they want to marry at all), how many children they should have (or whether they should have children at all), and so on and so forth. No one can force them into something, and they are not compelled to decide on something either. They have a lot of freedom and a lot of choices.

In many ways, we can consider this as progress, in contrast to societies that suppress their members' freedom. However, this progress in personal freedom and choices is not without its price. It has made people more individualistic, narcissistic, and dissatisfied. It has become very difficult for some people to be satisfied with what they choose. They keep switching their choices. Take marriage, for example. In many societies, families or communities do not force their members into marriage against their will. Individuals don't have to marry to please somebody or to fulfill obligations. Men and women have the freedom to choose when they want to marry and whom they want to marry.

However, in many such marriages, individual satisfaction doesn't seem to be balanced with the satisfaction of the couple. Married people seem to be finding it hard to meet each other's expectations. John Gottman, one of the leading researchers in the field of marriage and family, reported on the state of marriages in the United States in the 1990s. The chances of first marriages ending in divorce ranged between 50 percent and 67 percent, and the breakup of second marriages remained at the same level or 10 percent higher. Rudolf Richter and Sandra Kytir reported that in Austria, the divorce rate in 2005 was 46 percent or more. In Belgium, according to Wilfried Dumon, the figures on divorce were more or less the same, about 45.1 percent. Some of the negative consequences of the dissolution of marriages, according to Gottman, are increased risk of psychopathology, increased rates of automobile accidents, increased incidence of physical illness, suicide, violence, and homicide, and decreased longevity. Divorces and separation lead to a rise in single-parent households and step- and blended families.

In one sense, individual freedom and satisfaction and multiple choices with regard to marriage and marital partners have helped people to make decisions that are reasonably healthy for their future. But in another sense, this development has created more stress than health in their lives. Individual satisfaction is often not matched with couple satisfaction. People often find it difficult to find a balance between the good of the individual and the good of the family or community. Finding a balance between flexibility and stability and between freedom and restrictions is often a daunting task.

Mobile phones, instant-messaging applications, Facebook, Twitter, Instagram, and all such media of communication speak of the tremendous progress we have made in the area of social connections and communication. Millions of people are in a network of relationship. A century back, we couldn't imagine people on two ends of the world communicating with each other live while looking at each other. We couldn't conceive of someone having 1,500 "friends." We couldn't imagine writing a full-page letter to somebody and the other person getting it instantly. We have come a long way in our connections and communications. It is a tremendous progress that we have made. But it comes with a price.

We have become more mechanical and impersonal in our communications. If we go to a restaurant, we see people sitting around the table, each one glued to his or her phone or communication device. There is barely any conversation taking place between them. They put their phones on hold just to place their orders, and then they are back at it. When the food arrives, they still check their phones every now and then. Some families are no different. They are glued to their computers, phones, iPads, iPods, and whatever device they can find. They have connections with everyone except those inside. A lot of people assess their worth, lovability, self-esteem, and likability based on how many "likes" they receive. Have these developments affected our lives and relationships? I believe they have. We have developed great devices and methods for communication, but we have become very disconnected, mechanical, and impersonal with each other. Superficial connections and relationships have replaced more sustaining and personal connections.

We may not like it, but progress comes with a price tag. If we are thrilled about and want to enjoy the benefits of the progress that we have made, we also have to be prepared to accommodate the price that comes with it. It comes as a package. We can try to minimize the price we have to pay and the pain we have to endure, but we may not be able to completely rule them out. And all the progress that we make may not be in our best interests either. Finding a solution to our negative DTS and DTT and moving toward a rejuvenating life also means we must promote what is most healthy and helpful for us individually and collectively. The more sophisticated we become, the more sorry we might be about our lives and relationships.

41

The Swing

Every society keeps changing. To determine whether such changes are progress or regress, we have to evaluate how they impact our lives. If the change helps us to bring the best out of ourselves and help others to do the same, we can say we are making progress. But if it makes us deviate from that goal, then we are in the process of regress, and the change is ultimately going to destroy us. We may assume that we are limitless and uncontrollable, but it is not so. Death and decay are part of our being.

There is a limit to which we can stretch our lives. A rubber band cannot stretch more than its elasticity allows. If it is stretched more than its elastic capacity, it breaks. Sometimes we stretch our lives too much. Sometimes we dig our own graves. As I mentioned, a person who eats a stack of bacon and burgers every day may not be too far from landing in the hospital with a bloated belly and blocked arteries. A person who does not reverse the course of his or her negative survival and thriving will soon find himself or herself at the brink of a total self-destruction or premature end. A family that does not contain its negative relationship patterns will soon find itself breaking up into pieces. A people who forget the real meaning of their privileged position in the universe will take themselves and others toward destruction and death. A world that is overly adamant about building its stockpiles of arms and ammunition may not be far away from a total blowup and annihilation.

Whether it is regarding an ideology or a lifestyle, moving to any extreme position is going to be too much of a stretch. A time will come when the person, community, or society in question cannot take it anymore. They will either swing back or disintegrate and die. If they swing back, the inherent danger in that return swing is that they will go to the other extreme. In the case of a community or society, it may take a few hundred years for this return swing to reach the other extreme. Many generations might pass by before the community or society moves from one end to the other.

For example, a community or society may be moving in the direction of extreme conservatism and control. Individual freedom may be excessively curtailed, blind obedience and complete allegiance to the authority and the ideals of the community or society may be demanded, and dissenting voices may be suppressed and punished. As the community or society moves in this direction, there may be some noises and protests made by a few who are leaning more toward a liberal approach. But those few voices are either inundated by the larger voice of conservatism that is growing or suppressed by the larger group.

Conservatism and control will continue to grow and will reach a point where they become suffocating for the advocates and supporters themselves. The majority will begin to smell death and decay. Realizing the mistake, and as an antidote for the impending death and decay, they may begin to swing in the opposite direction. A few might want to still hold on to the conservative ideals and controls, but the majority will begin to rally behind the new movement. They will swing back, loosening their muscles.

It may take a while before they can get to a breathing point, but once they get to that breathing point, they begin to swing toward the other extreme. They keep loosening their muscles and move toward extreme liberalism, where there are no more controls. Their reverse movement becomes a protest and repudiation of the extreme conservatism that they were subjected to. But their protest makes them move toward the other extreme. Again, the same drama continues. Liberalism will keep growing. There will be a few noises and voices protesting against it, but the majority will be moving toward extreme liberalism, and their voices will inundate the voices of those who dissent. It will come to a point where the society cannot take it anymore. They will begin to smell death and decay. The society will start to disintegrate and die. Again a new movement will start taking shape, and it will swing back to a more conservative stand. When societies swing to extreme positions, people experience enormous amount of mismatch in their accents.

We see this swing between the extremes with many things in almost every society and community. There was a time when in some societies, no one could question anything. Now it is just the opposite; people question everything. In some communities, deference to authority was dogmatic and unquestionable. Now respect for authority in those communities is a rare virtue. There was a time when certain systems, organizations, and communities followed a top-down approach to the decision-making process and the executions of things. And then we saw just the opposite—a bottom-up approach. We see societies that follow a sterile philosophy of life, moving to extreme secularism and obsession with the pleasures of this world, and we see societies that follow a removed spirituality, having no regard for this world. Some societies are extremely collectivistic, and some societies are extremely individualistic.

Does a society ever reach a point of balance between the extremes? Yes, it does. But it does so in passing.

Society is often like a ship that goes from one port to the other. It doesn't dock in the middle of the sea. The ship doesn't dock in a port permanently unless it is decommissioned. If it docks somewhere permanently, it gets rusted and worn out. Communities and societies do not remain the same all the time. They keep changing. If they get stagnant, we will begin to see signs of rust and ruin. But in that change and transition, they also pass through moments of extreme positions, disintegration, and death. The swing from one extreme to the other is studded with rust and ruin, death and decay.

Often ships or boats run into the danger of thousands of barnacles adhering to their hulls. They can weigh the ship or boat down and slow down its forward movement. One of the ways to get rid of these barnacles is to bring the ship or the boat to fresh water. Barnacles grow in saltwater and cannot survive in fresh water. Individuals, communities, and societies that swing to extreme positions and get stuck there are akin to a ship or boat being weighed down by the barnacles. They engage in negative survival and thriving. Our negative DTS and DTT and our mismatched accents slow us down. To experience a new life, we have to go into some fresh waters—that is, fresh ideas, new outlooks, and movement toward a healthy middle ground. We have to keep renewing and refreshing ourselves constantly.

I am reminded of the story of Noah and the flood (Ge 6–8). It is said that the whole earth had become corrupt and wicked to the point of no return. God regretted creating human beings because they had turned so wicked. God decided to destroy the whole human race except one man—Noah—and his family. According to the story, Noah was six hundred years old, and God found him upright and righteous. Except him and his family, God decided to destroy every creature on earth. God was to send a flood by making it rain on earth for forty days and forty nights. God asked Noah to make an ark to protect himself and those with him.

At this point we see that the story differs depending on the source or tradition. God told Noah to take into the ark pairs of creatures of every kind on earth. One account says that God asked him to take two of each kind, both male and female, and the other account says that God asked Noah to take seven pairs of every clean animal, a male and its female, and one pair of every unclean animal, a male and its female. Whatever may be the number, that ark must have been enormous to contain representative couples of all the animals and birds on the earth, particularly if there were animals like dinosaurs and elephants. God asked Noah to take them in so that their species would be preserved.

Noah followed God's instructions and made the ark. He and his family, and all the animals, birds, and other creatures as stipulated entered the ark, and it started raining. It rained for forty days and forty nights. The waters rose and covered the whole earth, and it is said that even the highest mountains submerged under the waters. All living things on the earth, except the ones in the ark, were wiped out. When the flood subsided and the grounds became dry, Noah, his family, and all the living creatures in the ark disembarked. God blessed them, and they once again spread all over the earth and multiplied.

The story of Noah and the flood is not a fairy tale. As I said of the story of Mahābali and Abraham and his descendants, we have to look at this story on two levels: the physical and the spiritual, the manifest and the latent, the surface and the deeper, and the actual and the symbolic. On the physical, surface, manifest, and actual level, it may be hard to say when and how this might have happened. But what is more important is to focus on its spiritual, latent, deeper, and symbolic meaning. This story tells us volumes about what might have been happening in human history over and over again. Noah represents a new life that emerges from death and destruction.

We don't know for sure how old our earth is. Maybe it is millions and billions of years old. And we don't know for sure how long human beings have been around. May be we have been roaming this earth for millions and billions of years. But one thing seems to be sure: we are capable of digging our own graves. We have the capacity to take the whole world and ourselves to the brink of total annihilation. We are capable of moving to extreme positions that lead to degeneration and death. Instead of taking care of our earth, we are capable of destroying it. We have our death instinct fighting to overtake our life instinct. We become self-destructive and destructive toward others. As individuals, groups, and nations, we allow our aggression to have the upper hand. World wars and other conflicts do not fall out of the sky; they are of our own making. We sometimes actively pursue our own death and destruction. In all of these matters, of course, it may be a specific group of individuals, groups, or nations that leads everyone to death and destruction. However, we don't disappear totally. When we reach the point of near total annihilation, we wake up from our sleep, and from the ashes and debris a new life arises. Life builds up once again, and we continue our drama.

Noah's story may be a story of a super-sophisticated world that existed once upon a time. Maybe there were human beings who were scientifically and technologically more advanced than our present generation. This is mere speculation, but we cannot rule out that possibility.

God asking Noah to build an ark and take in creatures of every kind, male and female, clean and unclean, could be indicative of a new beginning, where everyone and everything in this universe once again began to live in harmony and communion with each other. It is a fact that as individuals and communities we differ in our accents. We have the world around us that may look imperfect and limited. And we have creatures and forces in nature that are unfriendly to us. But with all these, God wills that we learn to live in harmony with each other and the creation. He wills that we care for the creation and care for each other. And he wills that we remain cognizant of the dangers of the swing to extreme positions. When we fail to transcend our accents and become intolerant and fearful of each other, or become exploitative and manipulative toward the rest of the creation, we could end up in extreme positions of unhealthy survival and thriving. We might do that as individuals and communities. The people of Noah's time were doomed because they took to the extreme position of sinful survival and thriving, moving away from what God intended for them.

There is another little story in the Bible that follows immediately after the story of Noah and the flood. It is the story of the Tower of Babel (Ge 11). After the flood and restoration, the earth was once again teeming with life. Human beings had become very skillful and sophisticated. They had become so sophisticated and technologically advanced that they began to build a mighty city and a tower with a top reaching heaven. The story says that when God saw this, he scattered them, because he knew that if human beings decided to do something, they would do it. Because God scattered them, they stopped building the city. Although God is depicted as a tyrant who scuttles the plans of human beings, the story makes me speculate that human beings had begun to dig their own graves again. Maybe they had achieved many things, but at the same time they might have become arrogant and proud. Maybe they had become corrupt and wicked like the people of Noah's time. Maybe they were capable of building cities like New York, Dubai, or London.

Our skyscrapers, such as Burj Khalifa in Dubai, One World Trade Center in New York City, and Shanghai Tower in Shanghai, do not reach heaven, as the Tower of Babel did, but they are sure signs of our ingenuity and intelligence. The Tower of Babel may not have looked pristine and sophisticated, as some of these present-day skyscrapers do, but it must have been a breathtaking structure for the people of the time. If it was built a few billion years ago, we may not have much of its remains left. We may not see any remnants of those cities and towers they built if the whole earth was wiped out by a flood like that of Noah's time or some other calamity. Maybe a killer asteroid hit the earth and turned it into an inferno. Maybe human beings set the earth on fire in nuclear warfare. We don't have proof for any of these scenarios. But even if we are not hit and destroyed by an asteroid or killed by some other cosmic disaster, given our history and pattern of behavior, we are capable of taking ourselves to the edge of total destruction and death.

We tend to swing from one extreme to the other. We experiment with something new, and then we get fed up with it. Our human history is full of examples of this constant change and swinging from one extreme to the other. We do it in small and big ways. It has happened with religious communities, political systems, and social institutions. What happened to those emperors and kings who once terrorized and ruled lands and territories? They ruled and reigned for a while, and then society had to move to something else. The demagogues and dictators also had to bow out and make space for something new. Theocracies and oligarchies had a stint in the history, but people were fed up with them. Revolutions and uprisings have had their appeal, and in some places they still continue to do. Democratic systems have been doing the rounds in many countries for some decades now, and who knows for how long such arrangements are going to last?

Look at the geopolitical arrangements and constellations that have formed in our history. Did anybody foresee some fifty years back that the whole of Europe would move into an empire-like system with countries coming under it like individual princely states? Is the European Union the beginning of a series of similar arrangements all across the world? Will we see an Asian Union, American Union, and African Union along similar lines? Or is it going to be the other way around? Maybe the large countries of the present times will be broken up into small independent nations some day. It wasn't too long back that the Soviet Union was split into several independent nations.

Look at marital and family systems and how they have changed over the years. Arranged marriages have given way to romantic marriages or marriages of choice in many societies. Large joint families have given way to small nuclear families. Marriage used to be between a man and a woman. Now it can be between members of the same sex in many societies. Family used to be defined as a unit consisting of the father, mother, and children. Now the definition is open-ended. Marriage used to be a norm for family life. Now cohabitation and other living arrangements without marriage are becoming more common.

Who knows what the world will look like after two hundred or three hundred years? What we had a hundred years back is not what we have now. New players will replace the old ones. Pieces on the chessboard will be moved around. However, the game will remain pretty much the same. We will continue the swing from one end to the other. In the meantime, several generations may pass by.

We might want to think that we are the most sophisticated people who ever lived on this earth. We might want to think that we are making a never-ending forward movement in our progress and development. But our history tells us something different. Our progress is not without a price. We sometimes regress faster than we progress. If we grow wicked and corrupt to the point of no return, we are setting ourselves up for our own destruction. If we deplete our earth of all its rich resources and pollute the environment, we are digging our own graves. If we consistently put unhealthy materials and junk into our bodies and minds, we cannot expect too much of a good outcome in terms of physical and mental health. If we disrespect our uniqueness and disavow our unity, we are going to be at each other's throats. We are making explorations to the moon, Mars, and other planets and stars. I am afraid that we are going to extend to those planets and stars the negative things we have fostered here on earth: aggression, domination, death, and destruction.

We need to be aware of the swing that we are caught up in. If we leave the healthy middle ground and move toward either of the extreme positions in our ideas and ideologies, political leanings and religious beliefs, social structures, and personal preferences, we are setting in motion a wheel of negative survival and thriving. We need to keep the ship of our lives sailing without letting it rust and rot at any of the extremes. If we are already weighed down by the barnacles of negative and unhealthy elements that may have adhered themselves to the hull of our lives, we need to take our ship—our life, our society, our community, and our world—into fresh waters. If and when we are ridden of all the burdensome and unhealthy elements, we can sail on smoothly without the danger of becoming rusted and rotten.

42

Bridging the Gap

I explained about all of us being part of the life web and how we need each other to make progress and bring the best out of ourselves. I also discussed the enormous inequality that is prevalent in our world with regard to survival possibilities and thriving avenues. And I explained that this inequality has a potential to create negative DTS and DTT, and mismatches in accents in relationships. To find a solution to our problems in life and relationships, we need to find ways to bridge the gap that exists in our communities and societies.

It is not uncommon to see and hear about people who want to rectify historical errors. But it is difficult to define what a historical error is. It is in fact an ongoing phenomenon that appears and reappears in different forms and colors in human history. Every generation has its own dark phase but doesn't realize it or doesn't care about it as much as it cares about the wrongdoings of past generations. Can we say that our current generation is the best, with respect to all such inequalities and issues? We might, but we need to wait for the future generations to see whether they will rate us with the same compliment when they look back on our era and generation. And, fortunately or unfortunately, we won't be around to hear it.

Every society tries to deal with this problem of inequality in its own way. Some societies maintain the status quo, while others try to do something about it. Societies that try to do something to bridge the gap or remove the wide difference, especially in the thriving avenues, primarily focus on social and economic realms. However, it is not just in economics, politics, or religion, but in almost every aspect of our lives, that we see enormous inequality in the thriving avenues and survival possibilities.

An absolute equality, we have to accept, is more a fantasy than a possibility. A perfect order of things where everyone has equal chances of surviving and thriving is a near impossibility. Even this book that I am writing, I am aware, is not going to make it into the hands of everyone in the world. It is going to be read only by the "privileged" class. There are millions for whom this book would be a luxury. They don't have the money to buy it, the time to read it, or the ability to read or understand it.

In certain societies, some people might say that everyone has equal opportunities and chances. This may be more of an ideal than a reality. In reality, we don't have equal opportunities and chances. Even the word "equality" does not mean the same for people belonging to different levels of the social, economic, political, religious, and intellectual realms. Our opportunities and chances are dependent on multiple factors. The way we perceive equality may not be what others mean by equality. We live in the midst of enormous inequality; this is a fact we must live with. Inherently we all have the same worth and dignity as human beings and children of God, but unfortunately, when it comes to living our lives, we have to face this stark reality of inequality. There will always be some individuals from the lowest ranks of the society who will surprise everyone with their resilience, resoluteness, and indomitable spirit. They beat all the odds and challenges of life and survive and thrive well. But they are to be seen as exceptions rather than the norm.

An absolute equality in everything is not what we want to focus on. Our effort should rather be on creating an environment of respect for each other's dignity and ensuring an availability of things for everyone according to his or her need. Now there is too much gap in both these respects. Not everyone's dignity is acknowledged and respected, and not everyone has things available according to his or her needs. In the early Christian community, we hear about everyone being valued and respected; they were provided according to their needs. (See Acts 4:34.) But we also hear about a couple, Ananias and Sapphira, whose fraud and dishonesty led to their own death and destruction (Acts 5:1–11). Fraud and dishonesty lead to our own death and destruction and division in our community and world. Our world today is no stranger to fraud and dishonesty.

To keep our world on the path of growth and development, prosperity and peace, we have to find ways to bridge the gap as much as possible. We have to find ways to make the vision and mission of Jesus come true: "… to bring good news to the poor. He has sent me to proclaim release to the captives and recovery of sight to the blind, to let the oppressed go free, to proclaim the year of the Lord's favor" (Lk 4:18–19). One or two generations may not be enough to bridge the gap and undo what has been done unjustly in the past. However, that should not stop us from doing what we are able to do.

Bridging the gap becomes possible when the more independent, able-bodied, and privileged individuals, groups, communities, and nations steer their DTS and DTT in such a way that they survive and thrive and bring the best out of themselves and simultaneously become a support system for the less independent, less powerful, and unprivileged individuals, groups, communities, and nations to do the same. Their thriving and bringing the best out of themselves are important for the progress of the world. At the same time, their support for the lesser folks is necessary to make the kingdom of God a reality. The poor and the less fortunate need to be lifted up and helped to survive and thrive well.

To bridge the gap, first and foremost, there is a need for everyone to value and respect life. This means valuing and respecting one's own life and the lives of others. It means avoiding any intention or action of causing harm or damage to one's own life or to others' lives. To make it happen, there is an immediate and urgent need to cease or contain all kinds of crimes and aggression in our personal and communal lives. Wars and violence between nations and communities need to be contained. The shedding of the blood of innocent people has to stop. Children should be raised in safety and peace. Nations and groups have to learn to invest in the health and well-being of their people rather than in arms and ammunition.

To bridge the gap, extremist ideas and ideologies need to give way to dialogues and reconciliation. Borders and barriers have to be broken down, and people need to learn to coexist peacefully. Making children grow up in an environment of hatred and revenge has to give way to teaching them about the dignity of every person. Whether they are political, religious, or social in nature, groups and communities have to stop planting the seeds of hatred and extremist views in young minds. Those who live with a sterile philosophy of life and removed spirituality have to make way for a new vision of life where there is a place for God, others, and themselves.

To bridge the gap, those of us who claim to be superior with respect to our caste, class, race, gender, or religion have to shed our superiority and reconnect with the members of the so-called inferior caste, class, race, gender, or religion. We have to simply accept the fact that our superiority is not a divinely ordained right but rather a human design arising out of our master syndrome and defective DTS and DTT. We simply cannot assign to ourselves a right to dictate and dominate. Roles and responsibilities given to us are not for subjugation and exploitation of others, but rather to serve and make this world a better place. We can and need to survive and thrive well, but we do not do so by trampling others under our feet.

To bridge the gap, everyone needs to work hard. Everyone is not equally gifted or talented, but all of us are gifted and useful in some way to make this world a better place. Saint Paul has some good instructions for those who are lazy and taking advantage of others. He says, "For even when we were with you, we gave you this command: Anyone unwilling to work should not eat. For we hear that some of you are living in idleness, mere busybodies, not doing any work. Now such persons we command and exhort in the Lord Jesus Christ to do their work quietly and to earn their own living" (2Th 3:10–12).

The importance of working hard is very emphatically highlighted in the parable of talents that Jesus shared with his followers (Mt 25:14–30). It is the parable of a man about to go abroad who called his servants and entrusted his property to them. Distributing the property in terms of talents, he gave each of them talents in proportion to their ability. To one, he gave five; to another, two; and to another, one. Then he went on his journey. The man who received five talents went and traded with them and made five more. Likewise, the man who received two talents went and traded with them and made two more. Each of them worked hard and multiplied his talents. When the master returned from the journey, they both brought to him what they had made, and the master appreciated and rewarded them for their hard work. But the one who received one talent was a lazy, fearful, and critical servant who doubted and scrutinized his master's intentions. He dug a hole in the ground and buried his master's money. When the master returned, he returned the money as he had received it. The master chastised him for his laziness and dubious character. His one talent was taken away from him, and he was punished.

Looking at this story in terms of God's plan for us, it first of all tells us that none of us is left out of God's plan. Each one of us is given talents, graces, gifts, abilities, and power. There is no one who is useless in God's sight. In God's sight, all of us are useful in one way or another. All of us are equal as God's children; we all have the same dignity. But we all are not same in what we have and what we are given in terms of talents and abilities. We are all given things according to our needs and ability. We are all different. And God wants us to do the best we can, based on what we have and what our abilities are. He wants us to bring the best out of ourselves.

Some can do better than others in some areas. People who are old and sick cannot engage in physical activities and help others as those who are healthy and strong. People who are mentally and intellectually healthy and strong can do better in certain areas than those who are weaker in those respects. People who are richer and more resourceful can do more for the betterment of the society than those who are poor. But all of us have to do our best, each according to his or her ability, and bring the best out of ourselves. Notice what the ones with five talents and two talents did after they multiplied their wealth. They brought it to the master. They didn't keep it to themselves. We bring the best out of ourselves not to keep it to ourselves, but to bring it to the master, our Lord and God, who is the giver of all good gifts. We offer them as our contributions to make this world a better place. We receive, and then we give. We don't keep it to ourselves. And when we do that, our lives become better and this world becomes better. There is no question that we all are given some talents. But what we do with them determines how our lives and our world are going to be. Hard work is the key to that transformation of our lives and our world. God wants all of us to do the best we can, and he does not expect from us more than what we are capable of.

To bridge the gap, the rich have to come to the aid of the poor. There is too much disparity between the rich and the poor in our world. Individuals and communities have to find ways to reduce that disparity and bridge the gap. People who are starving or burdened by poverty need urgent help. The language they will understand is that which comes in the form of food and financial help, respect and love. They need to be lifted up from their poverty and misery. We cannot be blind to such realities and claim that everyone has equal opportunities to survive and thrive. Everyone needs to pitch in as best as he or she can to help those in poverty.

An aggressor and a victim, a political leader and an ordinary citizen, a religious leader and a member of the community, a community leader and a disadvantaged person, a doctor and a patient, a high class and a low class, a high caste and a low caste, an advantaged race and a disadvantaged race, a privileged class and an unprivileged class, a rich person and a poor person, a man and a woman, a parent and a child, a teacher and a student, a young person and an old person, a saint and a sinner—in all of these pairings, there is one privileged person or group and one unprivileged person or group, one powerful person or group and one less powerful person or group. To bridge the gap in the survival and thriving avenues, everyone, each according to his or her position and power, needs to steer his or her DTS and DTT in such a way that he or she excels in what he or she is and becomes a source of support for the less advantaged individuals or groups.

The privileged and the powerful must make a generous gift of themselves to the less advantaged ones. We need saints who embrace sinners. Even saints are in a privileged state because they are in a state of grace, whereas a sinner is in a less privileged state because he or she is in need of grace. If we find ourselves in a privileged and advantaged position, it is because of the generosity of many people and the availability of better survival and thriving avenues. Now it is our turn to extend that generosity to others who need our support and strength.

One danger with such engagements with disadvantaged and less privileged people is the possibility of turning the goodwill gestures into tools for scoring political mileage or establishing strategic partnerships for one's own advantage. Such hidden agendas, taking advantage of the weaker ones for one's own thriving, are yet another manifestation of negative survival and thriving rather than being a support system for the less privileged. That is not what the world needs. The world needs generous people without a hidden agenda in their magnanimity.

By becoming a support system for the less privileged, the more privileged and advantaged persons, communities, or nations are not losing their importance or honor but rather gaining a greater dignity and honor. They accomplish another milestone in their survival and thriving. Their call is to excel in who they are and bring the best out of themselves. When they do that and become a support system for others, they achieve that milestone.

In this act of steering one's DTS and DTT to bring the best out of oneself and to be a support system for the less privileged, everyone has a role to play. We all have something to give. Even the less privileged will find still more disadvantaged people among the members of their groups and communities. They need to steer their DTS and DTT to help such people, just as others do for them. Everyone needs to take the responsibility of doing the best he or she can to further his or her own growth and development and be a support system for those who are less privileged. All need to contribute to the betterment of their own lives as well as that of those around them, according to their ability.

That is the antidote for the negative survival (DTS) and thriving (DTT) and mismatch of accents that exist everywhere. We may not get it perfect, but we can bridge the gap to a great extent. Such an action is going to redefine relationships and the direction that the world is going to take.

The people who are able to steer their DTS and DTT in such a healthy and positive way may not be very numerous in our world today, but they are inevitable for every family, group, community, and nation. They keep the world from going insane. They are like the hidden steel in the pillar. They keep the negative DTS and DTT from blowing out of proportion. They are able to transcend their accents and understand what the other is saying. They keep the ship of our world sailing, saving it from rust and rot, and death and decay. Their commitment is necessary to save the world from getting weighed down by the barnacles of negativity and sin. How wonderful would it be if everyone could do that! To build up the kingdom of God, where we walk hand in hand with God and each other, where we prosper and flourish, and where we live in righteousness and peace—we all need to do that. But it all begins with one thing: recognizing and transcending our accents.

Conclusion

Certain rivers that end in the ocean spill and spew into it mud and dirt. But that doesn't turn the whole ocean muddy and dirty. The ocean is much larger than the rivers. It has tremendous capacity to absorb the dirt and mud and still remain clean and blue. Our world experiences troubles and struggles of life in many ways. It sees both the good and bad sides of our humanity. Some spill and spew dirt and filth into it. Others give their best. Those who spill and spew dirt and filth engage in negative survival and thriving. They speak with wrong accents. And they become a problem for themselves and others. But those who live and act sane and steady outnumber them.

We experience the same in our personal lives. Our lives may be burdened by problems and evils in many ways. But the power and presence of God in our lives are much stronger. Our perfections outweigh our imperfections. Our capacity to rise above the evils and sins is much greater than what we realize. We have tremendous capacity to absorb and bear sufferings and evils and still remain sane and steady. We don't condemn and reject ourselves or the perpetrators of evils and sins. We condemn and reject the evil and sinful attitudes and behaviors in others and us. The rivers themselves can turn clean and blue when the storms cease, when the grounds beneath them are not raked up, and when their banks remain sturdy. Change and transformation are possible even for the most dreaded criminal. There is a saint in every sinner. The storms in their lives need to cease; the grounds beneath them need to remain strong; and the banks of their lives need to be stable. For that, they need help.

But big or small, all of us are in need of that change and transformation. We need to bury the sinner and bring out the saint in us. We need to transcend our accents and develop a language that everyone can understand. For that we make personal efforts, and we seek God's grace and strength. In the letter to the Hebrews, we read, "Because he [Jesus] himself was tested by what he suffered, he is able to help those who are being tested" (Heb 2:18). Jesus knows our troubles and struggles, and he will be our strength when we call on him.

I remember someone talking about what it takes to master something—Practice. For a minimum of ten thousand hours. Be it mastering a musical instrument, becoming a competent medical doctor or psychotherapist, or learning to be a parent, it takes time and effort. It takes time and effort to make something part of our being and feel that we know what we are doing or talking about. We have to practice it over and over again. Even after ten thousand hours, we may realize that we have still more attempts to make to get to a satisfactory level of the ideal. The repeated attempts and efforts may be hard, exhausting, and even boring, but there seems to be no other easy way.

The same rule applies to life as well. Life is not easy, and life is not very predictable either. Not many of us feel that we have it all together. Lessons of life have been presented and re-presented to us over and over again. Books, lectures, talks, seminars, and conferences disseminate wisdom in different shapes and forms. There are millions of books that have been written about how to live a good life. The motivational speeches and lectures on bettering oneself that have been given are too numerous to count. Each of us can attest to the million pieces of advice and counsel people have given us about how to lead a good life. There is no lack in the number of theories and therapies offered to help people handle their lives better. Despite all these lessons we have learned; books we have read; lectures, sermons, and spiritual talks we have listened to; and people we have tried to emulate, life is still something that is hard to get a handle on.

We know how babies learn and grow. They do so in baby steps. The mother may have to say something ten thousand times before the baby can really take it in. It may be boring, tiring, and hard, but does the mother stop? No. She keeps repeating it in different forms, sometimes harshly, sometimes gently, and sometimes playfully. Her hope is that one day the baby will get it. Does that mean that the baby will get it all together? No. The baby will get one piece at a time. Does the mother give all the lessons together? No. She gives them in baby measures, one piece at a time. The process of learning and perfecting continues. Similar things happen with the baby's consumption of food. The baby starts with breast-feeding. Then the mother introduces the baby to light and liquid food. Gradually the baby is introduced to solid food in small quantities and metabolized forms. It takes a while before the baby can chew and digest more solid food. As far as the baby is concerned, everything happens in baby steps.

We live and learn about our lives in baby steps. And we need to receive our lessons in different forms. This book is another attempt to metabolize the lessons of life. It is my hope that this book helps you to make another baby step toward healthy and happy living. God said, "… do not fear, for I am with you, do not be afraid, for I am your God; I will strengthen you, I will help you, I will uphold you with my victorious right hand" (Isa 41:10). With God on our side, and love, compassion, and courage in our hearts, we will be able to bring the best out of ourselves and become a blessing for others.

Bibliography

Baquet, D., ed. The *New York Times*, November 26, 2014. Columbia, Missouri, edition. A1–A19.

Cambridge Advanced Learner's Dictionary. 2nd ed. S.v., "accent."

Ainsworth, M. "Infant-Mother Attachment." *American Psychologist* 34 (1979), 932–37.

Akhtar, S. *The Damaged Core: Origins, Dynamics, Manifestations, and Treatment.* New York: Jason Aaronson, 2009.

Akhtar, S. "A Third Individuation: Immigration, Identity, and the Psychoanalytic Process." *Journal of American Psychoanalytic Association* 43 (1995), 1051–84.

Akhtar, S. "Object Constancy and Adult Psychopathology." *International Journal of Psycho-Analysis* 75 (1994), 441–55.

Augustine, S. *The Confessions of Saint Augustine.* H. M. Helms (Ed.). Brewster, Massachusetts: Paraclete Press, 2010.

Bach, S. "Sadomasochism in Clinical Practice and Everyday Life." *Journal of Clinical Psychoanalysis* 11 (2002), 225–35.

Bal, H. S. "Indian Craft is Lofted Toward Mars, Trailed by Pride and Questions." The *New York Times*, November 5, 2013. http://www.nytimes.com.

Baradon, T. "'What Is Genuine Maternal Love?': Clinical Considerations and Technique in Psychoanalytic Parent-Infant Psychotherapy.'" *Psychoanalytic Study of the Child* 60 (2005), 47–73.

Beebe, B. "Coconstructing Mother—Infant Distress: The Microsynchrony of Maternal Impingement and Infant Avoidance in the Face-to-Face Encounter." *Psychoanalytic Inquiry* 20 (2000), 421–40.

Bion, W.R. *Learning from Experience.* London: Tavistock, 1962.

Block, R. W. & Krebs, N. F. "Failure to Thrive as a Manifestation of Child Neglect." *Pediatrics* 116 (2005),1234–1237. doi: 10.1542/peds.2005-2032.

Bollas, C. *The Shadow of the Object*. New York: Columbia University Press, 1987.

Bollas, C. "Loving Hate." *Annual of Psychoanalysis* 12 (1984), 221–37.

Bowen, M. *Family Therapy in Clinical Practice*. New York: Jason Aronson, 1978.

Bowlby, J. *A Secure Base: Clinical Applications of Attachment Theory*. New York: Routledge, 2005.

Bowlby, J. *A Secure Base: Parent-Child Attachment and Healthy Human Development*. New York: Basic Books, 1988.

Bradsher, K. "Struggle for Survival in Philippine City Shattered by Typhoon." The *New York Times*, November 11, 2013. http://www.nytimes.com

Brenner, C. "A Psychoanalytic Perspective on Depression." *Journal of the American Psychoanalytic Association* 39 (1991), 25–43.

Bronfenbrenner, U. *The Ecology of Human Development: Experiments by Nature and Design*. Cambridge, England: Harvard University Press, 1979.

Buckley, C. & Wong, A. "Clashes Erupt in Hong Kong as Police Try to Clear Part of a Protest Group." The *New York Times*, A6, November 26, 2014.

Cathie, S. "What Does It Mean to Be A Man?" *Free Association* 1 (1987), 7–33.

Chang, K. "Curiosity Rover Lands Safely on Mars." The *New York Times*, August 6, 2012. http://www.nytimes.com

Chess, S. & Thomas, A. *Temperament: Theory and Practice*. New York: Brunner/Mazel, 1996.

Davey, M. & Fernandez, M. "Governor to Triple Guard Presence in Ferguson." The *New York Times*, A1, A16–19, November 26, 2014.

De Sales, F. *Treatise on the Love of God* (Vol. 1). A. Mookenthottam, A. Nazareth, & H. J. Kodikuthiyil (Trans.). Bangalore: SFS Publications, 2009.

De Sales, F. *Introduction to the Devout Life*. A. Mookenthottam, A. Nazareth, & A. Kolencherry (Trans.). Bangalore: SFS Publications, 2005.

De Sales, F. & De Chantal, J. *Letters of Spiritual Direction*. P. M. Thibert (Trans.). New York: Paulist Press, 1988.

Dewald, P. A. *Psychotherapy: A Dynamic Approach*. New York: Holt Rinehart and Winston, 1971.

Dumon, W. "Belgium's Families." In B. N. Adams & J. Trost (Eds.). *Handbook of World Families* (215–34). Thousand Oaks, California: Sage Publications, 2005.

Erdbrink, T. "Breaking Silence, Top Leader Says Iran Is Standing Up to West in Nuclear Talks." The *New York Times*, A4, November 26, 2014.

Erikson, E. H. *Childhood and Society*. New York: W. W. Norton & Company, 1963.

Fairbairn, W. R. D. "Synopsis of an Object-Relations Theory of the Personality." *International Journal of Psycho-Analysis* 44 (1963), 224–25.

Fairbairn, W. R. D. "Object-Relationships and Dynamic Structure." *International Journal of Psycho-Analysis* 27 (1946), 30–37.

Francis, P. *Evangelii Gaudium*. Vatican Press, 2013.

Freud, S. "The Ego and the Id." In J. Strachey (Ed. & Trans.), *The Standard Edition of the Complete Psychological Works of Sigmund Freud* (Vol. 19, 1–66), 1923. http://www.pep-web.org.

Freud, S. "Beyond the Pleasure Principle." In J. Strachey (Ed. & Trans.), *The Standard Edition of the Complete Psychological Works of Sigmund Freud* (Vol. 18, 1–64), 1920. http://www.pep-web.org.

Freud, S. "Formulations on the Two Principles of Mental Functioning." In J. Strachey (Ed. & Trans.), *The Standard Edition of the Complete Psychological Works of Sigmund Freud* (Vol. 12, 213–26), 1911. http://www.pep-web.org.

Freud, S. "Three Essays on the Theory of Sexuality." In J. Strachey (Ed. & Trans.), *The Standard Edition of the Complete Psychological Works of Sigmund Freud* (Vol. 7, 123–246), 1905. http://www.pep-web.org.

Furman, E. "Mothers Have to Be There to Be Left." *Psychoanalytic Study of the Child* 37 (1982), 15–28.

Gabbard, G. O. & Wilkinson, S. M. *Management of Countertransference with Borderline Patients*. Washington D.C.: American Psychiatric Press, 1994.

Gorski, E. F. *Theology of Religions*. New York: Paulist Press, 2008.

Gottman, J. M. *The marriage Clinic: A Scientifically Based Marital Therapy*. New York: W. W. Norton & Company, 1999.

Guntrip, H. *Schizoid Phenomena, Object Relations and the Self*. New York: International Universities Press, 1969.

Hermans et al. "Stress-Related Noradrenergic Activity Prompts Large-Scale Neural Network Reconfiguration." *Science* 334 (2011), 1151. doi: 10.1126/science.1209603.

Higgins, A. "At European Parliament, Pope Bluntly Critiques a Continent's Malaise." The *New York Times*, A4, A10, November 26, 2014.

Hughes, D. A. *Attachment-Focused Parenting: Effective Strategies to Care for Children*. New York: W. W. Norton & Company, 2009.

Hughes, D. A. *Attachment-Focused Family Therapy*. New York: W. W. Norton & Company, 2007.

Idris, H. & Gladstone, R. "Two Suicide Bombers Kill Dozens in Nigeria." The *New York Times*, A9, November 26, 2014.

Jacobson, J.G. "The Advantages of Multiple Approaches to Understanding Addictive Behavior." In S. Dowling (Ed.), *The Psychology and Treatment of Addictive Behavior* (175–190). Madison Connecticut: International Universities Press, 1995.

Keirsey, D. *Please Understand Me II: Temperament, Character, Intelligence*. Del Mar, CA: Prometheus Nemesis Book Company, 1998.

Kernberg, O. F. "Factors in the Psychoanalytic Treatment of Narcissistic Personalities." *Journal of the American Psychoanalytic Association* 18 (1970), 51–85.

Klein, M. *Envy and Gratitude and Other Works, 1946-1963*. New York: The Free Press, 1975.

Koplow, L. *Creating Schools That Heal*. New York: Teachers College Press, 2002.

Kohut, H. *The Analysis of the Self: A Systematic Approach to the Psychoanalytic Treatment of Narcissistic Personality Disorders*. Chicago: University of Chicago Press, 2009.

LaFarge, L. "Interpretation and Containment." *International Journal of Psycho-Analysis* 81 (2000), 67–84.

Lally, J. R., Mangione, P. L., & Signer, S. *Flexible, Fearful, or Feisty: The Different Temperaments of Infants and Toddlers*. http://www.pitc.org/cs/pitclib/view/pitc_res/814.

Mahler, M. "On the First Three Subphases of the Separation-Individuation Process." *International Journal of Psycho-Analysis* 53 (1972), 333–8.

Mahler, M. S., Pine, F., & Bergman, A. *The Psychological Birth of the Human Infant*. New York: Basic Books, 1975.

Mathew, K. "The Onam Festival." *Skipping Stones* 21 (2009), 29.

McDonnell, E. *God Desires You: St. Francis de Sales on Living the Gospel*. Stella Niagara, NY: DeSales Resource Center, 2008.

McWilliams, N. *Psychoanalytic Diagnosis: Understanding Personality Structure in the Clinical Process*. New York: The Guilford Press, 2011.

McWilliams, N. *Psychoanalytic Psychotherapy: A Practitioner's Guide*. New York: The Guilford Press, 2004.

Medora, N. P. "Strengths and Challenges in the Indian Family." *Marriage & Family Review* 41 (2007), 165–93.

Miller, A. Depression and Grandiosity as Related Forms of Narcissistic Disturbances. *International Review of Psychoanalysis* 6 (1979), 61–76.

Mohamed, N. "The Abiding Lore and Spirit of Onam." The *Hindu*, August 20, 2010. http://www.thehindu.com.

Morgan, D. *Essential Islam: A Comprehensive Guide to Belief and Practice*, 2010. http://web.b.ebscohost.com.ezp.slu.edu

Navarro, M. "Relying on Hotel Rooms for Thousands Uprooted by Hurricane Sandy." The *New York Times*, March 29, 2013. http://www.nytimes.com.

Noelle-Neumann, E. "The Theory of Public Opinion: The Concept of the Spiral of Silence." In J. A. Anderson (Ed.), *Communication Yearbook 14* (256–87), New York: Routledge, 2012.

Odede, K. "Terrorism's Fertile Ground." The *New York Times*, A21, January 9, 2014.

Peters, J. W. "After Obama's Immigration Action, a Blast of Energy for the Tea Party." The *New York Times*, A15, November 26, 2014.

Piaget, J. "The Affective Unconscious and the Cognitive Unconscious." *Journal of the American Psychoanalytic Association* 21 (1973), 249–61.

Richter, R. & Kytir, S. "Families in Austria." In B. N. Adams & J. Trost (Eds.). *Handbook of World Families* (201–14). Thousand Oaks, California: Sage Publications, 2005.

Rowland, T. L. *Everything You Need to Know About Jean Piaget's Theory of Cognitive Development*, 2012. http://web.b.ebscohost.com.ezp. slu.edu.

Sadock, B. J. & Sadock, V. A. *Kaplan and Sadock's Synopsis of Psychiatry: Behavioral Sciences/Clinical Psychiatry*. Philadelphia: Lippincott Williams & Wilkins, 2003.

Schmitt, E. "U.S.-Led Raid Rescues Eight Held in Yemen." The *New York Times*, A1, November 26, 2014.

Schwartz, B. *The Paradox of Choice: Why More is Less*. New York: Harper Perennial, 2004.

Shattuck, C. *Hinduism*. London: Callman & King, 1999.

Simanowitz, V. & Pearce, P. *Personality Development*, 2003. http:// web.b.ebscohost.com.ezp.slu.edu.

Smeets, T., Otgaar, H., Raymaekers, L., Peters, M. J. V., & Merckelback, H. "Survival Processing in Times of Stress." *Psychonomic Bulletin & Review* 19 (2012), 113–18.

Spitz, R. A. "Hospitalism-An Inquiry Into the Genesis of Psychiatric Conditions in Early Childhood." *Psychoanalytic Study of the Child* 1 (1945), 53–74.

Spitz, R. A. & Wolf, K. M. "Anaclitic Depression-An Inquiry Into the Genesis of Psychiatric Conditions in Early Childhood, li." *Psychoanalytic Study of the Child* 2 (1946), 313–42.

Stern, D.N. *The Interpersonal World of the Infant*. New York: Basic Books, 1985.

Sturm, L. "Temperament in Early Childhood: A Primer for the Perplexed." *Zero to Three* 24 (2004), 4–11.

Szalavitz, M. & Perry, B. D. *Born for Love: Why Empathy is Essential – and Endangered*. New York: Harper Collins Publishers, 2010.

Thompson, J. M. & Cotlove, C. *The Therapeutic Process: A Clinical Introduction to Psychodynamic Psychotherapy*. Lanham, Maryland: Jason Aronson, 2005.

Trevarthen, C. "Intrinsic Motives for Companionship in Understanding: Their Origin, Development, and Significance for Infant Mental Health." *Infant Mental Health Journal* 22 (2001), 95–131.

Tronick, E. Z. "Emotions and Emotional Communication in Infants." *American Psychologist* 4 (1989), 112–9.

Tronick, E., Als, H., Adamson, L., Wise, S., & Brazelton, T. B. "The Infant's Response to Entrapment Between Contradictory Messages in Face-to-Face Interaction." *Journal of the American Academy of Child and Adolescent Psychiatry* 17 (1978), 1–13.

Tyson, P. and Tyson, R. L. *Psychoanalytic Theories of Development: An Integration*. New Haven: Yale University Press, 1990.

Wall, M. *Largest Structure in Universe Discovered*, January 11, 2013. http://www.space.com.

Winnicott, D.W. *Playing and Reality*. London: Tavistock Publications, 1971.

Winnicott, D. W. "The Maturational Processes and the Facilitating Environment: Studies in the Theory of Emotional Development." *The International Psycho-Analytical Library* 64 (1965), 1–276.

Winnicott, D. W. "The Theory of the Parent-Infant Relationship." *International Journal of Psycho-Analysis* 41 (1960), 585–95.

Winnicott, D. W. "Transitional Objects and Transitional Phenomena-A Study of the First Not-Me Possession." *International Journal of Psycho-Analysis* 34 (1953), 89–97.

Printed in the United States
By Bookmasters